Springwatch

GREAT BRITISH WALKS

100 Wildlife Walks Through Our Beautiful Countryside

LUKE WATERSON

BBC
BOOKS

BBC Books, an imprint of Ebury Publishing
20 Vauxhall Bridge Road
London SW1V 2SA

BBC Books is part of the Penguin Random House group of companies
whose addresses can be found at global.penguinrandomhouse.com

Penguin
Random House
UK

This book is published to accompany the television series Springwatch
broadcast on BBC Two. Springwatch is a BBC Studios production.

Executive Producer: Rosemary Edwards
Series Editor: Joanna Brame
Series Producer : Laura Whitley

With thanks to Céline Nyssens

First published by BBC Books in 2023

www.penguin.co.uk

A CIP catalogue record for this book is available from the British Library

ISBN 9781785948183

Commissioning Editor: Albert DePetrillo
Project Editor: Phoebe Lindsley
Design: seagulls.net
Production: Antony Heller

Printed and bound in Great Britain by Clays Ltd, Elcograf S.p.A.

The authorised representative in the EEA is Penguin Random House Ireland,
Morrison Chambers, 32 Nassau Street, Dublin D02 YH68.

Contents

LONDON & SOUTHEAST ENGLAND

EASTERN ENGLAND

MIDLANDS & THE PEAK DISTRICT

SOUTH WALES

MID & NORTH WALES

Foreword

Rhythm of body, rhythm of mind, rhythm of time. Balance, purpose, pace, step, tread, trace. We wander, we traipse and we sometimes trip, stumble, slip or slide. Sometimes we steal in secrecy, sometimes we mark the ground with our footprints. Sometimes we walk this way once, sometimes we step through the ghosts of many of our journeys and tattoo those ways with our memories. We walk alone, we walk in love, we walk in pain. We walk in joy, for joy, and if we walk in sadness, then inevitably we can walk back to happiness. And how far we have walked! As a species, across the world, and as individuals all the miles as we criss-cross the maps of our lives. We walk from A to B, along uncertain paths, in directions unknown, into our distance. As we live we walk, and we walk to live, and if we ever stop to think about those commonplace human things we take for granted, then just as we breathe or beat our hearts, we recognise that walking is simply wonderful.

Size 4, 5 or 10½, it was not Nancy's boots that were made for walking, it was her feet. Humans are walking apes, walking machines. We are very good at walking, made for it

step by step over the last 4.4 million years. I'll prove it … Find a wide-open empty space with level ground, flat and stable substrate, perhaps a beach at low tide, and choose a far-off spot and begin to walk towards it. There's no rush, so just tread as your body says, go with your own flow and find that sweet spot that feels right. Swing your arms, relax into a gait, a pattern of perfect movement, just do your locomotion. And now be brave and close your eyes, shut down your dominant sense and focus on your body. Begin at your feet, feel your soles on the ground, lowering and lifting, and then move on up – legs, hips, chest, shoulders – until you sense your head balanced on top of all those swaying bones and muscles, constantly falling forward under complete control. Meet your walking self and revel in the simple satisfaction of moving with efficiency, rhythm and maybe even grace!

Some of us go for a walk just to walk. Some of us have to walk, some choose to walk rather than ride or drive and some of us will only walk for a necessary purpose. Why do you walk? I walk to either get where I need to be or to see what I want to see. If it's the former, I walk fast, I'm focused and I don't think much about walking, just getting there. If it's the latter, I might stroll, amble even, perhaps stop walking to look. And for me, walking provides both a pace and perspective, which maximises my connection with the world that I want to experience. My senses seem optimised with my walking speed as I can scan, squint and swivel to peer wherever I wish. I thus see more when I'm walking and I invariably want to see it all. Imagine a drive-thru art gallery – that wouldn't work would it! No. So, how do we imagine that driving through the world allows us to properly connect with that world? It doesn't – we must walk.

This book is for walkers and would-be, wannabe walkers. It has got all we need: plans, paths, maps and hints and tips about what you might or might not find en route. If they are monuments, then they will be there, which is cosy and satisfying. If they are living things, then they might not, which is challenging and exciting. Best of all, you will find new things. Some good – like secret spots to stop and smile. Some bad – like litter (pick it up even if it isn't yours, it's your planet isn't it!). The book offers you the security of forward planning, timings and, even better, maps through the best our beautiful, spectacular and stunning UK landscape has to offer, come sunshine, rain, wind or snow. Be sensible, though walking in unruly climes is so good. There is no such thing as 'bad weather', only being badly dressed for it. Stamping up a hill in a hailstorm instils defiance! Struggling across the shore in a gale makes us all storm-tossed souls!

Most of all, I like walking alone at night along familiar paths in the woods. I sneak reverently through my spaces, my sense of time decays and I feel necessarily insignificant. My head clears, my life clears and I get a better perspective. I am grounded one step at a time. So good.

Chris Packham, New Forest 2023

Introduction

My Grandad always maintained that you could do a walk eight times: there and back again in every season. Researching this book, I came to truly understand what he meant: walking a walk eight times over, indeed, may not be nearly enough.

The walks in this book are a little different to those that normally populate walk books. The walks featured here look at the countryside of England, Wales, Scotland and Northern Ireland – city parks to mountain peaks, beaches to moors, woods to waterways and glen bottoms to wold tops – primarily through the prism of wildlife. And wildlife is ever-changing and all-transforming. The woodland enchantingly tinged by April's bluebells can seem far more solemn when November has snatched its last leaf; the seashore turned radiant pink by June thrift has become a more elemental thing by the time February's gannets come back to breed on the cliffs. And then there are the infinitesimal subdivisions within the seasons – the fleeting winter weeks when snowdrops flourish, the mere month that swallowtail butterflies have to live their lives – that can give a single location umpteen utterly different appearances.

So, while this book details 100 of the finest countryside walks for getting close to the UK's showstopping flora and fauna, in reality you have many, many more ideas for days out here if wildlife-watching is your passion. Hiking Tomintoul to Cairn Gorm via Glen Avon (Walk 84), snow might still be lingering in May as Great Britain's only free-roaming reindeer give birth. Yet September's russet mountainside backdrop here, as the beasts rut, seems like another world entirely, while in summer the colours kaleidoscopically change on an almost daily basis as the high-altitude flowers in the UK's only true Arctic-Alpine climate work their magic.

And the walks – like the plants and creatures they spotlight – pass through incredibly diverse terrain. This, of course, is one of the compliments often bestowed upon the landscapes of the British Isles: the abundance of variation in relatively short succession. Take on the montage of wetlands, seaside, heath, woodland and farmland around Suffolk's Minsmere (Walk 33). Or try the yomp along Northern Ireland's Causeway Coast (Walk 100), with its startlingly multifaceted shoreline of sandy bays, dunes, broken cliffs, serrated skerries and chunky basalt columns resembling a mad maritime metropolis of rocky hexagonal high-rises.

Wonderfully, choosing the walks for this book took the 'I' more or less right out of the equation. The selection was chosen according to where wildlife likes to go best, not where humans do. This is another respect in which this book differs from many other walk books. Muddy estuaries sometimes replace the pretty beaches you may have been expecting; iconic beauty spots are often swapped out for moors, marshes and scrub – because these are the places much of our most mesmerising wildlife inhabits. Some truly exquisite landscapes and landmarks are visited, but Dorset's badgers, Wales' sessile oaks, Scotland's beavers and Northern Ireland's harbour porpoises are the stars of the shows.

The UK has some unique nature. You may have whetted your appetite for it on your screens, watching BBC's *Springwatch*, *Autumnwatch* and *Winterwatch* over the years.

Now it's time to get out walking right into the heart of it.

Luke Waterson, Mid Wales 2023

The walks in this book are arranged into chapters of geographical location and then by level of difficulty within these chapters. Each walk includes a map, the key for which can be found below. Each walk also highlights key species to look out for; when setting out please always try not to disturb wildlife and leave any space as you found it.

Map Key

START **1**	Direction Points
Red squirrel hide ●	Place of interest
————	Walking route line
- - - - - -	Detour route line
A123	Major Road
————	Minor Road
————	Access Road
——— - - -	Railway/tunnel
0 500 m	Map scales (different for each map)

Before you embark on any walk, please check:

- Any restrictions, fees and opening hours that may apply to your chosen walk and/or sights and wildlife along its route.

- You have appropriate shoes, clothing and enough food and water for the walk.

Please see the back of the book for further things to consider before setting out on these walks.

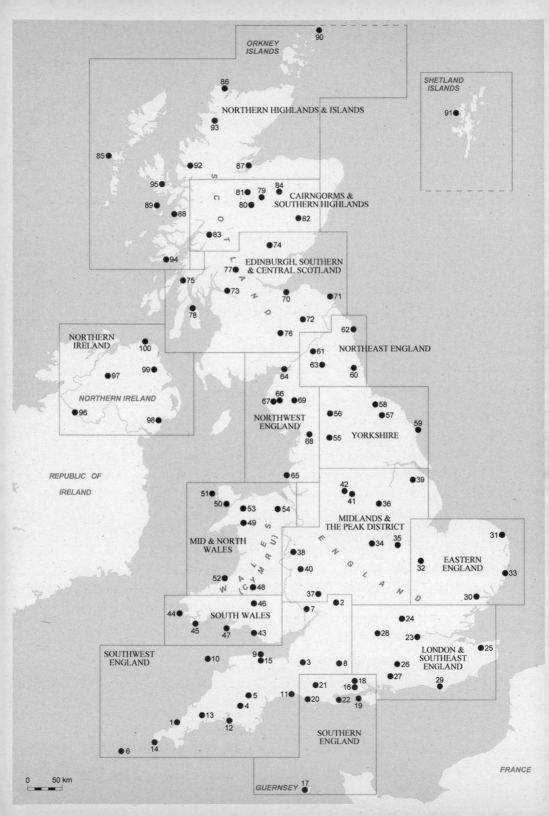

SOUTHWEST ENGLAND

1. St Agnes Head, Wheal Coates & St Agnes Beacon

Discover how Cornwall's industrial heritage and a host of birdlife survive in harmony along this stunning coastal heath

NEED TO KNOW

START/FINISH: St Agnes Head car park, TR5 0NU, off Beacon Drive – 2.75km (1¾ miles) northwest of St Agnes (parking free)

DISTANCE: 6.5km (4 miles) (circular)

TIME: 1½–2 hours

KEY SPECIES: Red-billed chough, kittiwake, basking shark

MAP: OS Explorer 104

TRANSPORT: St Agnes Institute bus shelter (buses to Redruth) – 3.75km (2¼ miles) southeast

WALK ACCESSIBILITY: Partly accessible to wheelchair/ pushchair users; dogs allowed

DIFFICULTY: Easy

MORE INFORMATION: nationaltrust.org.uk

Kittiwake

Could there be a more iconic Cornish scene than that of the gaunt Wheal Coates tin mine ruins standing out of radiant coastal heath, bounded by a fiercely blue Atlantic? This walk offers valuable insights into Cornwall's industrial past, yet where miners once toiled, wildlife now thrives. Seabirds provide the action on the cliffs these days – the headlands are among Cornwall's best for sighting basking sharks and if you keep vigil around St Agnes Head,

you may glimpse the red-billed chough, which became extinct in England and then naturally re-colonised from 2001 onwards. Stay for the night show: this is a dark sky reserve too.

Come in early summer, when heaths are blanketed in wildflowers, seabirds are established in their clifftop roosts (before their July departure) and basking sharks are out and about (until early autumn). The walk sports the usual Cornish coast ups and downs but the most significant ascent, St Agnes Beacon, is still simple. Paths are easy to follow and surrounding quiet lanes and tracks mean wheelchairs/pushchairs can cover some ground hereabouts too.

ROUTE DESCRIPTION

1) This walk's car park choice gives you a good indication of the area's appeal. The start is the road-end car park at St Agnes Head itself, though there is another just beforehand and another still closer to Wheal Coates on the walk serving equally well. Yet **St Agnes Head** is a special viewpoint to kick things off, with vistas stretching all the way to St Ives 22km away in good weather and high chances of spying a red-billed chough. Also scour the ocean for basking sharks and dolphins between here and Wheal Coates. From the headland, you head south (keep the sea on your right), watching for summertime's blazes of pink sea thrift, following the coast path. In 550m, reach the out-and-back right-hand path to **Tubby's Head**, site of a promontory fort. Continue south along the coast path again afterwards, arriving 500m later at the striking collection of buildings that is **Wheal Coates tin mine**.

2) The path lands you first at **Towanroath shaft and pump engine house**. Take a look, then bear left (inland) before the building

> **KITTIWAKE**
> This gull's name is derived from its call – kitte-wa-aaake. It is the friendliest-looking of the birds in Britain's seabird metropolises, with a yellow bill and dark eyes. Despite the country boasting over 200,000 breeding pairs, this is a red-listed species due to the decline of sand eels, their favourite food.

to climb steps up to the **main engine house** building complex. If you think the climb is tough today, imagine walking such paths after a 16-hour shift underground. Information boards within the engine house detail the area's mining history; the derelict yet photogenic buildings are now the domain of ravens and jackdaws. After exploring, continue on the main path inland for 250m, crossing heath that is a sea of purple heather in summer, to the edge of the NT car park. A path skirts left around the car park, hitting the road at Beacon Drive.

3) Turn left for 100m, then right at the entrance to Beacon Cottage Farm, a caravan park. The drive curves left behind buildings, where you turn right, straight afterwards ignoring caravan pitches on the right and the left turn into the farmyard. At a lay-by on the left immediately after this, pass through a gateway. Keep straight ahead (east) across the field, picking up the edge of the heath surrounding St Agnes Beacon

3

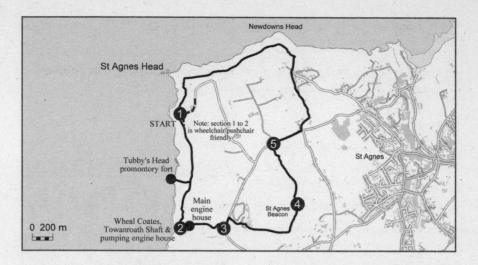

on the left. Continue along the field edge and ahead onto the heath after a gate. Within 100m, you come upon two left-hand paths ascending towards St Agnes Beacon: take the second, reaching the beacon 275m later.

4) St Agnes Beacon, at 192masl (metres above sea level), could be Cornwall's best viewpoint. You can see northeast to untamed Bodmin Moor and southwest down to St Ives across the flower-rich heath from here: no wonder it was one of the beacons lit to warn of the approaching Spanish Armada in 1588. Two paths descend from here to the northwest: take the right-most of these. This bears initially north-northwest, crossing straight over a wider path after 175m. The path then swings northwest again, divides in two, rejoins, comes alongside a field edge

on the right and descends to Beacon Road 675m after leaving the beacon.

5) Turn right for 300m. Where the road branches right to Mingoose, turn left on a track that immediately bends right, then left around a farm, then heads north-northwest to a second farm approach track in 275m. Turn left on this, then immediately right on a path. This crosses another farm approach track in 200m before making its way on to join the coast path. Turn left for just over 1.5km to return to St Agnes Head and the car park, looping around St Agnes Head NCI along the way. Just after rejoining the coast path you pass **Newdowns Head**. This is the spot for end-of-walk seabird-spotting: kittiwakes, razorbills, guillemots, fulmars, shags, cormorants and black-headed gulls nest along the cliffs.

2. Cleeve Hill & Cleeve Common

Be breathtaken by butterflies and rare flowers on the picturesque chalk grassland of this classic Cotswolds leg-stretch

NEED TO KNOW

START/FINISH: Cleeve Hill and Cleeve Common car park (800m/½ mile north of GL54 4EU, the closest postcode for sat-nav purposes) – 8km (5 miles) northeast of Cheltenham (parking free)

DISTANCE: 10km (6¼ miles) (circular)

TIME: 3–3½ hours

KEY SPECIES: Duke of Burgundy butterfly, adder, red hemp-nettle

MAP: OS Explorer 179/OL45

TRANSPORT: Noverton Park Desert Orchid Road bus stop (buses to Cheltenham) – 3.25km (2 miles) southwest

Adder

WALK ACCESSIBILITY: Mostly accessible to wheelchair/pushchair users; dogs allowed but on leads in Prestbury Hill Butterfly Reserve Mar–Jul

DIFFICULTY: Easy–Moderate

MORE INFORMATION: cleevecommon.org.uk

The Cotswolds AONB is the enchanting epitome of Englishness – of teashops and pubs full of oak beams and open fires, of honey-hued stone villages and seemingly endless settlements with duck ponds and delicious-looking delis. Such things are close on this walk, but this is all about exploring the terrain defining these low, lovely hills: chalk grassland. Few could dispute Cleeve Hill and Cleeve Common being called the ideal introduction to Cotswolds walking: the highest point and biggest common of the AONB are here, and the wildflowers and butterflies put on a very pretty show.

Lepidoptera order members loving these conditions include the Duke of Burgundy, chalkhill blue and brown argus butterflies, and June is the month to see them and the area's rare flowers, like red hemp-nettle. Summer is also good for spotting the reptilian quartet of adder, grass snake, common lizard and slowworm.

You might detect scrub-loving birds like yellowhammers, plus skylarks and buzzards, year round. Fieldfares, here for berry-bingeing, are wintertime avian visitors.

This is a straightforward hilltop walk, with one notable steady climb. Mostly on national trails, the paths followed are well defined. With no stiles or severe gradients, wheelchair/pushchair users could likely manage all of this one, and certainly the first stage on open common.

ROUTE DESCRIPTION

1) Cleeve Hill and Cleeve Common car park, surrounded by radio masts, is by far the walk's most unsightly point, but it's conveniently high up, thus saving much climbing. Head back down the road 100m to a lay-by and gate on the right and pass into **Prestbury Hill Butterfly Reserve**. This has been critical in conserving the common's species diversity, with all aforementioned butterflies present. Adders and gorse-loving yellowhammers are also seen. Proceed with wooded scrub off right, swinging slightly right upon joining another path, then left on a grassy path 300m later. After another 375m, you meet the Cotswold Way coming up from the left at a gate and information board.

2) Watch out for skylarks and buzzards above as you continue

DUKE OF BURGUNDY BUTTERFLY
This small orange-and-brown fritillary-like butterfly adores scrubby grassland. Its only established populations are in Central-Southern England and isolated pockets of Northern England.

northwest along the escarpment edge, wooded slopes on your left. You presently reach **The Twins**, two wind-bent beech trees, at a bench. Cross the semi-circular earthworks of the **Iron Age hill fort** ahead, cutting above the Cotswold Way then rejoining it afterwards. Then the **Memorial Tree**, a lone beech and the Cotswolds' highest tree, is glimpsed off right. As the path then swings north, there is denser woodland below left and at a tall wooden signpost by a v-junction of grassy paths, you bear right to clamber up to **Cleeve Hill**. This, at 317masl, is not the hill high point (you pass that later) but is the best viewpoint. Some of Southern England's loveliest countryside vistas fan out below.

3) This area is also partly Cleeve Hill Golf Course, muddling the paths somewhat. However, look for a bench and a signpost close to the summit and from here descend off the top northwest to the next signpost where you turn right. Then immediately take the lower path fork, contouring through scrub to hit a well-defined earth-and-grass path. Turn right here for 700m to reach the golf club on the left. A sign on a grassy triangle then indicates the Cotswold Way leading past a car park off right.

4) After 975m, pass through a 7-bar gate onto a track junction. Yours is the wide well-worn path descending straight ahead with woodland just left. At a marker 125m later, branch left into these woods. You soon come alongside a stone wall, pass through a gate and swing left through two more gates to reach Postlip Hall's entranceway. Continue straight, through a kissing gate and on along the stone wall for 225m, then turn right on a drive. Postlip Farm is off left: after the farm outbuildings, where the farm track swings right,

pass left through a gate and with the fence on your immediate right, descend the field edge into Breakheart Plantation. You may surprise a roe or muntjac deer on these woodsy common fringes.

5) After 300m curve up to a gate, pass through a tree-dotted field and turn right on the track afterwards. The path through the woods soon branches left: do the same and follow its meanderings almost 1km up to emerge into fields. Continue straight ahead onto a track, turn right, leave the Cotswold Way and at deserted Wontley Farm turn right. This track gently rises back onto the common. With the masts marking your start point ahead, now take the right-hand path fork. This loops around the trig point marking Cleeve Hill's actual top and then on down to the masts.

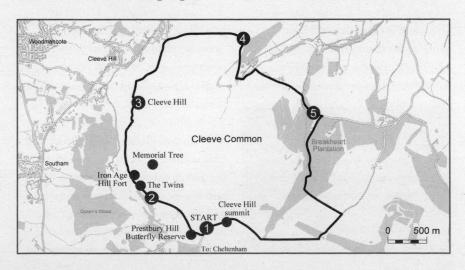

3. Glastonbury Tor & the Bittern Trail to Avalon Marshes

Climb a legendary Somerset summit then wander bird-rich wetlands

NEED TO KNOW

START/FINISH: Draper & Co car park, Glastonbury, BA6 8DP/Avalon Marshes Centre, BA6 9TT (parking and entry charges may apply)

DISTANCE: 12km (7½ miles) (one way)

TIME: 3–3½ hours

KEY SPECIES: Bittern, starling (murmurations), swallow

MAP: OS Explorer 141

TRANSPORT: Glastonbury town hall bus stop (buses to Bristol) – 1km (¾ mile) west

WALK ACCESSIBILITY: Accessible to wheelchair/pushchair users, except Glastonbury Tor section; no dogs (Shapwick Heath NNR), dogs on leads (Ham Wall NNR)

DIFFICULTY: Easy–Moderate

MORE INFORMATION: nationaltrust.org.uk and avalonmarshes.org

The final resting place of King Arthur; the haven to which Joseph of Arimathea brought the Holy Grail after the Crucifixion; a portal into the Welsh fairy kingdom of Annwn – and all that purportedly taking place at this walk's beginning alone: Glastonbury. Such compelling associations with myth and legend are Glastonbury's big draws but the tor, a distinctive 158masl church-topped hill, is also encircled by the natural beauty of the Somerset Levels. This is a 700-odd km² wetland-dotted plain of international wildlife importance, with Avalon Marshes at its heart. The tor was once an island, its surrounding

BITTERNS

A species of heron, bitterns depend upon marshy reed beds. As such habitats dwindled, bitterns almost became extinct in the 1950s (and again in the '90s). The elusive birds are easiest to spot in spring, thanks to the males' booming mating calls.

flatlands underwater. Much of the patchwork-quilt farmland you see today has been drained in the last thousand years, but a multitude of mires remain.

These wetlands entice many waterbirds, notably the bittern. The Shapwick Heath and Ham Wall nature reserves' extensive reed beds, through which this walk passes, attract one of Britain's biggest bittern populations. The official Bittern Trail runs from Glastonbury's Market Cross to Avalon Marshes Centre, where you can learn more about the wealth of wildlife. This walk also offers a breathtaking clamber up Glastonbury Tor beforehand.

On the tor, summer brings butterflies like the marbled white; rabbits, foxes and badgers are seen year round. In 2020, *Springwatch* filmed three species of egret that live side by side on the marshes – little egret, great white egret and cattle egret. In the marshes, bitterns are also permanent residents; swallows visit in spring and the wintertime headlines are the starling murmurations – flocks many thousands strong wheeling overhead.

The route is all well-surfaced and well-marked. There is one short, sharp climb up the tor, otherwise it's level throughout the walk.

ROUTE DESCRIPTION

1) Turn right out of the car park along Chilkwell Street. Pass **Chalice Well and Gardens**, an ancient holy well in which Joseph of Arimathea is said to have placed the Holy Grail and given the water rejuvenating properties. Turn left onto Wellhouse Lane, then immediately right on a well-surfaced path soon climbing to the NT land surrounding Glastonbury Tor at a gate.

2) Cross the meadow beyond on a distinct path to another gate. A stepped path then twists up to the ruined tower of 14th-century **St Michael's Church** atop **Glastonbury Tor**. An earlier medieval church and a 5th-century fort previously occupied this spot, likely a site of significance for millennia. This is one of Somerset's best viewpoints, with spectacular 360-degree panoramas across the Somerset Levels.

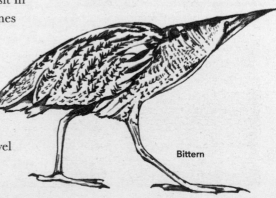

Bittern

9

3) Descend from the church's southeast side (the only other clear path down besides your approach path). The route curves around the hillside to exit NT land at a hedge gate on the tor's northeast corner. Then take a path through a long, thin meadow to a gate onto Stone Down Lane.

4) Turn left, soon bearing left onto Wellhouse Lane, to reach the junction with Lypatt Lane. Turn right, following Lypatt Lane up to where it kinks sharp right. Now, take the track left (west) across the field, keeping the hedge on your left and passing through a copse, to reach a gate. Continue along a metalled lane onto Dod Lane ahead.

5) Turn left on Dod Lane. Turn right onto Chilkwell Street, following the stone walls of **Glastonbury Abbey** grounds to turn left onto Silver Street. Turn right before a car park, cutting alongside Victoria Buildings onto High Street.

6) Turn left here, through Glastonbury town centre and down to Market Cross. After the High Street bends sharp left, turn right onto café-flanked Benedict Street.

7) Follow Benedict Street 650m west to its end, passing St Benedict's Church and a recreation ground. At a red-brick wall straight ahead, pass through the non-vehicular access onto the A39 road. Straight across the A39, Park Farm Road continues on behind a line of metal railings. Blue cycle route signs now demarcate your route to Avalon Marshes Centre.

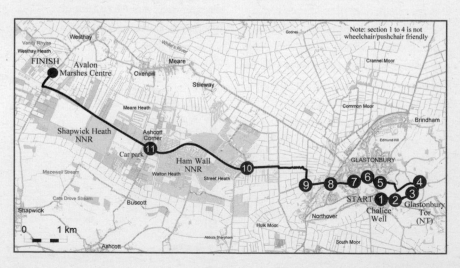

8) Head along Park Farm Road between industrial estates to a roundabout after 150m, from which Porchestall Drove continues in a similar direction west, initially with Sydenhams Timber Centre on the left. Keep on this lane for just over 1km, as it leaves the industrial buildings behind and becomes bounded by fields, until it reaches the right-hand turn onto Middle Drove.

9) Turn right here and, after 300m, turn left on the blue-signed cycle path alongside the waterway of South Drain. There is a pleasant picnic area here. After 700m the cycle path crosses the River Brue. Turn right on the lane beyond then almost immediately left on another lane alongside a stand of conifers.

10) After 600m, at Sharpham Cross, this lane meets a junction by a post box. Bear left, then turn almost immediately right on a track signposted 'Peat Moor Centre'. Proceed through a metal gate on a metalled track traversing a glorious expanse of protected wetlands. Continue through **RSPB Ham Wall NNR** for 2.5km to the nature reserve car park at Ashcott Corner. Almost 2km along this stretch, a left-hand path across the drain leads to **Tor View Bird Hide,** a place frequented by bitterns and other waterbirds.

11) The track continues straight across a lane and the car park to traverse the **Shapwick Heath NNR** wetlands, following the line of South Drain for another 2.9km. Upon reaching Station Road at some lay-by parking, turn right for 300m to reach **Avalon Marshes Centre**.

RETURNING TO START: Car or bike

4. Wistman's Wood from Two Bridges

Encounter epiphyte-rich Celtic rainforest, adders and legends on Dartmoor's rolling moors

NEED TO KNOW

START/FINISH: Car park opposite Two Bridges Hotel, PL20 6SW – 2.5km (1½ miles) northeast of Princetown (parking free)

DISTANCE: 6.5km (4 miles) (circular)

TIME: 1½–2 hours

KEY SPECIES: Atlantic oak, adder, Dartmoor pony

MAP: OS Explorer OL28

TRANSPORT: Hotel bus stop (buses to Exeter/Tavistock) at start

WALK ACCESSIBILITY: Not wheelchair/pushchair accessible; dogs allowed

DIFFICULTY: Easy–Moderate

SPECIFIC EQUIPMENT: Compass

MORE INFORMATION: visitdartmoor.co.uk

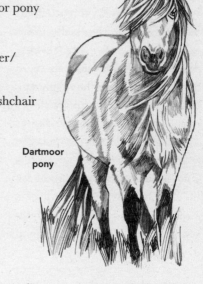

Dartmoor pony

This is a moorland march of two halves. On the first, the focus is Wistman's Wood, a surreal tract of gnarled high-altitude oak trees draped in rare mosses and lichens and billed as one of Britain's last and finest fragments of rainforest. The preponderance of scattered boulders also makes this a refuge for adders. For the second half, return along a quintessential Dartmoor ridge via three broken granite tors, bizarrely shaped spectres in themselves, where Dartmoor ponies graze. This scenery, which *Springwatch* captured in 2020, has captivated many over the years: writer John Fowles, meditating lengthily on Wistman's Wood, called it 'Fairy-like, self-involved, rich in secrets …' while these moors also secrete the legend of the Dartmoor spirit, Old Crockern.

The walk is moodily magnificent year round, although doing it free of cloud simplifies navigation and improves views. Paths are muddy.

ROUTE DESCRIPTION

1) The start's free car park has limited spaces; if full, park in **Two Bridges Hotel** car park opposite (pay to park or buy something at the hotel). Go through the gate and along the track, a wall and the West Dart River beyond on your left, to a farmhouse. A broad well-surfaced path skirts right of the farmhouse. Just after this path veers right, away from the river, take the rougher grassy left-hand path. This runs to the right of a bush and straight ahead to scale a tumbledown dry-stone wall.

2) The path, distinct but rock-strewn, now rambles for 900m with the river off left and Wistman's Wood visible ahead. Cross a stile in another dry-stone wall.

3) You now reach **Wistman's Wood**, teased along the valley bottom. Looming out of bare moorland, these mythical, contorted old oaks huddle close to the ground, their low-lying branches enticing blankets of moss, lichen and other epiphytes to grow upon them to an extent remarkable within Britain. Look on the boulder-scattered woodland floor for adders,

HORSEHAIR LICHEN

A lichen is not one thing but a symbiotic relationship between a fungus and its photosynthetic partner, algae or cyanobacteria. Wistman's Wood's trees harbour many lichens including one of the country's most elusive epiphytes, horsehair lichen, which is fine, brown and hangs off branches in threads.

supposedly once so prevalent here they became the stuff of legend. A sign diverts you away from the SSSI- and NNR-designated wood itself so that this vulnerable environment remains well-preserved.

4) After the wood's far end, the muddy but distinct path curves right (northeast), another woodland fragment to the left, ascending to Longaford Tor.

5) Longaford Tor is actually two separate stony mounds: turn right (south) through the rocks of the smaller tor. Your return path now follows the ridge top. With a dry-stone wall below left, proceed along the ridge to Littaford Tors, after which the left-hand dry-stone wall meets another at an acute angle below and straight ahead. Descend to the wall meeting point, crossing the walls via a ladder stile, and pick up a grassy path on the other side.

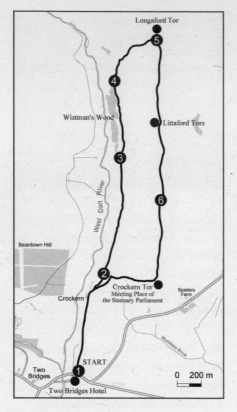

6) Ascend over the moor, keeping right of some wind-stunted thickets, to **Crockern Tor** ahead. When tin mining was at its height here in the 15th to 18th centuries, this assemblage of rocks was where Dartmoor's Stannary Parliament met to set much local law, effectively rendering the region a mini-state within a state. At the tor, with the B3212 road ahead, swing right on a faint path descending west to a pillar-flanked gap in a dry-stone wall. Pass through and bear slightly left onto a continuation of the broad well-surfaced path of your outward route. This delivers you down to the farmhouse and start.

5. Castle Drogo & the Teign Gorge

Linger in this lovely tree-carpeted Dartmoor gorge to sight butterflies, riverside birds and leaping salmon

NEED TO KNOW

START/FINISH: Castle Drogo NT car park, EX6 6PB – 2km (1¼ miles) southwest of Drewsteignton (parking and entry charges may apply)

DISTANCE: 7.25km (4½ miles) (circular)

TIME: 2–2½ hours

KEY SPECIES: Pearl-bordered fritillary, kingfisher, leaping salmon

MAP: OS Explorer OL28

TRANSPORT: Castle Drogo Drive bus stop – 800m (½ mile) north

Salmon

WALK ACCESSIBILITY: Not wheelchair/pushchair accessible; dogs allowed but on leads in Castle Drogo grounds

DIFFICULTY: Easy–Moderate

MORE INFORMATION: nationaltrust.org.uk

Some walks wow wildlife-watchers, some appeal to aesthetes, some to history enthusiasts and some to those fancying a ramble before or after a tearoom or pub. Few enthral all comers like this special circuit beginning at Britain's youngest fortress, Castle Drogo, before plunging through the wooded Teign Gorge along to an idyllic tucked-away inn, then returning along a ravishing section of wood-flecked moor. This is Dartmoor giving you its very best.

The gorge has superb butterfly-spotting, with gems like the pearl-bordered fritillary basking on the commons in summer. Common lizards might also be caught sunbathing at this time. The woodsy riverside could treat you to a kingfisher or heron year-round, while the fallow deer rut and the salmon vaulting the Teign to their spawning grounds are autumn highlights. Then, of course, there are those trees. Splendid examples of centuries-old oak and beech beckon, while one of Britain's biggest woodland restoration projects is helping return more broadleaf to the gorge.

There is only one real climb through the woods on the return, but these paths do get mighty muddy.

ROUTE DESCRIPTION

1) Castle Drogo (charges may apply) is not strictly a castle, but a castle-style country house designed in granite by Sir Edwin Lutyens and built between 1910 and 1930 for grocery tycoon Julius Drewe. The man knew how to pick a view for his pad and you can look inside certain rooms and visit the **gardens**, which contain enviable collections of rhododendrons and roses. From the car park, walk back along the entrance drive, following signs for 'Teign Valley Walks'. After 150m, a sign points right down away from the drive through the woods. At a path crossroads shortly afterwards, bear

SOUTHERN WOOD ANT

These aggressively territorial ants thrive in the Teign Gorge's sun-dappled woods but are rare UK-wide. They do have one tender relationship, however, with aphids, whose abdomens they stroke to extract and consume the honeydew aphids obtain from plant sap.

right, joining the **Hunter's Path**, the name given to the gorge-top path that gradually descends around the hillside, opening up magical views of the Teign Gorge to the left.

2) At a short out-and-back detour to **Hunter's Tor** (worth doing for more great gorge views) your onward path swings sharp right, keeping the woods fringing Castle Drogo on the right. Descend steeply north-northwest to a gate, a footpath sign to the Fisherman's Path and a tarmacked track. Turn left, downhill on the track. Your route branches left at a footpath sign after 300m on a path presently forking left again down to meet the River Teign.

3) You are now on the **Fisherman's Path**, the river-hugging path. Just left, a suspension bridge crosses the river on a short out-and-back detour to visit **Whiddon Park**, an ancient deer park sporting spectacular specimens of old oaks and beeches. Afterwards, re-cross the bridge to proceed along the Fisherman's Path by the light-filled wooded banks of the River Teign for just over 2.5km. On this enchanting stretch you may sight kingfishers and herons through the riverside trees.

4) The path emerges through a gate at a delightful 17th-century packhorse bridge, **Fingle Bridge**, with **Fingle**

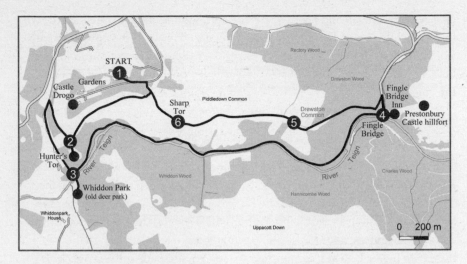

Bridge Inn opposite. **Prestonbury Castle**, a huge Iron Age hill fort, is above. Turn left on the lane past the lay-by parking on the right to presently reach a wooden footpath sign pointing the way acutely left up through the wood. The path almost doubles back along the lane initially, before swinging right through **Drewston Wood**.

5) Your route meets another path near **Drewston Common**. You are now back on the Hunter's Path: follow it through Hunting Gate to where the woods open up onto moor, views of both sides of the Teign Gorge sweeping away. Over the years, the gorge became conifer-dominated but the Woodland Trust and National Trust are together taking on the mammoth task of restoring the deciduous woods here. At a path divide, both routes

ultimately return you to Castle Drogo, but this walk takes the left-hand fork to visit **Sharp Tor**.

6) The tor is not just another lovely viewpoint but is also a stronghold of the rare pearl-bordered fritillary butterfly. Surrounding Piddletown Common often reveals common lizards and slowworms, while nonchalant Dartmoor ponies graze the scrub. After the tor, take a flight of steps to meet a path ascending over the heath to meet your outward route around 200m later at a path junction. Climb through the woods to the Castle Drogo entrance drive, turning left to reach the car park.

6. St Agnes & Gugh Circular

Explore the UK's extreme southwest edge, a fauna and flora frontier of seals, cetaceans, seabirds and singular plants

NEED TO KNOW

START/FINISH: The Quay, St Agnes, Isles of Scilly

DISTANCE: 8.75km (5½ miles) (circular)

TIME: 2½–3 hours

KEY SPECIES: Ocean sunfish, harbour porpoise, least adder's-tongue

MAP: OS Explorer 101

TRANSPORT: Land's End Airport (buses to Penzance/St Just) – 55km (34¼ miles) northwest, on mainland. Then flight to St Mary's Airport – 6.25km (4 miles) northwest and transfer to Hugh Town pier – 3.5km (2¼ miles) northwest. Then take ferry to start.

WALK ACCESSIBILITY: Not wheelchair/pushchair accessible; dogs allowed

DIFFICULTY: Easy–Moderate

SPECIFIC EQUIPMENT: Swimwear

MORE INFORMATION: visitislesofscilly.com and ios-wildlifetrust.org.uk

Great Britain's southwestern-most inhabited land, the island of St Agnes greets you with an embrace that is wild even by the Isles of Scilly's already remote standards. With less settlement and fewer visitors than the main islands St Mary's and Tresco, you feel closer to nature here. For such a far-flung Atlantic outpost, scenery is surprisingly green and benign, yet offshore the magical marine fauna of this AONB-designated archipelago still creates a spectacle. Grey seal, common dolphin and harbour porpoise sightings are regular, while ocean sunfish are not unusual and deep-water specialists Risso's dolphins are sometimes seen.

A few things, however, distinguish St Agnes and Gugh, linked via a sandbar at low tide, from wildlife elsewhere on Scilly. Most notably, the islands were the scene of an epic battle in 2013 between the locals … and the local rats. The rodents, which had become prevalent here following umpteen shipwrecks over the centuries, were an increasing threat to the breeding seabirds. An intensive 6-month campaign later, the locals emerged victorious and the islands were declared rat-free. The result? The burgeoning of breeding Manx shearwater and storm petrel populations, and the formation of a critical rodent-less buffer zone protecting the uninhabited seabird sanctuaries of Annet and the Western Rocks just across the water. Scilly's only kittiwakes breed on Gugh too, while the highlight of the plant life is unexceptional-looking least adder's-tongue, a fern found on St Agnes' Wingletang Down and nowhere else in the UK.

Before you plan your trip here, know that the Scillonian III ferry, making the sea crossings from Penzance on the mainland to St Mary's Hugh Town, might not be the speediest way to reach the embarkation point for the St Agnes ferry but is probably Britain's most wildlife-rich regular ferry trip. This and the St Mary's–St Agnes boat are often the best bets for cetacean observation. Late spring is lovely for wildflowers and seabirds; August through November is the endearing seal pupping season. The route round the islands followed here is on decent paths, and never ascends above the 25masl mark.

ROUTE DESCRIPTION

1) From the off on this coast-hugging adventure, keep your eyes trained on outlying coastal rocks for grey seals. Disembarking onto **The Quay** from the passenger ferry (no cars can be brought to these islands), you'll pass a picnic area and public toilets and take the track that leads right, then swings left to cut across the base of a promontory and skirt the horseshoe bay of Porth Killier. Continue ahead northwest at the bay's end to pass **Big Pool** off left. This is fresh water, but storms push seawater up here and give it a distinctly salty dimension. Consequently, wetland meadow plants, including three sorts of clover, share space with salinity-loving saltmarsh rush. Wigeon and pochard ducks are wintertime visitors here. Your route runs across the base of the Browarth headland and turns left along the beach top. Reefs offshore here may yield grey seal sightings.

OCEAN SUNFISH

The second-largest bony fish on Earth, and a strong candidate for the most bizarre-looking, the ocean sunfish favours tropical and temperate environs, but occasionally strays into UK waters between June and September searching for jellyfish. They are often spotted floating on their side on the sea surface, likely warming their body temperatures.

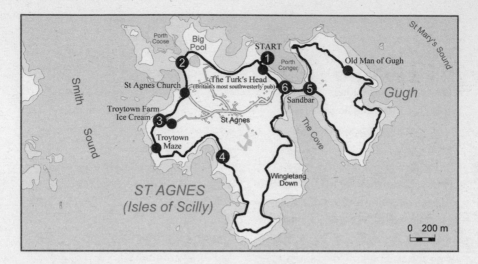

2) Progress onto the rugged crescent bay of Periglis, at the southern end of which you come up onto New Lane with **St Agnes Church** on your right. The 19th-century church was built with proceeds from a shipwreck; the church bell was salvaged from the wreck too. Swing right after the church to **Troytown Farm**, the UK's most southwesterly civilisation, with the path branching slightly right off the main track to run along the campsite's left-hand edge. The farm also concocts legendary ice cream (this walk diverts briefly inland to the hut selling the stuff). At the campsite's far end, the path passes southwest out onto the shoreline.

3) Presently, swing south-southeast to walk by **Troytown Maze**, a pattern likely cut in the 18th century by a lighthouse keeper to represent the fair winds that would protect sailors. A far-older maze was previously carved on the site. The path now meanders along an indented coastline to round Porth Warna. Heading along the bay's eastern shore, negotiate two stiles either end of a rocky beach to reach **St Warna's Well**. Sailors were given a rather less favourable reception on the island at times: here, islanders formerly made offerings to maximise the chances of the sea bringing them a lucrative shipwreck.

4) Southeast of here is SSI-listed **Wingletang Down**, a wind-smacked coastal heath hosting several rare plants, including the least adder's-tongue and golden-hair lichen. There is interesting human history too: many Bronze-Age cairns can be found. There are two small bays at the southern end and many paths:

pick your own route across, then bear northeast to resume your coastal circuit. You'll pass into the island's deepest inlet, The Cove, soon spotting (if the tide is low enough) the lovely sandbar connecting across to Gugh.

5) Start your 2.8km lap of **Gugh** by bearing anticlockwise (southeast) around its shores. The island has a more elemental feel to it than St Agnes, with just a couple of buildings, and is predominantly bracken-clad moor. It's important to stick to the paths to avoid disturbing seabirds, including kittiwakes (Scilly's only colony) and lesser black-backed gulls (Scilly's biggest colony). The main non-natural sight is the colossal standing stone of the **Old Man of Gugh**, seen from the path running northwest across the northern part of the island.

6) Back on St Agnes, a path runs west-northwest from the end of the sandbar to meet Old Lane. Turn right here to presently arrive at **The Turk's Head**, the UK's most southwesterly pub. Beyond this, you hit The Quay again where, as you wait for your boat back, you have a last chance for seal and cetacean spotting.

7. Symonds Yat Rock, the Wye Valley & Highmeadow Woods

Ramble through glorious River Wye woodland renowned for its wild boar and special birds of prey

NEED TO KNOW

START/FINISH: Symonds Yat Rock FE car park, GL16 7NZ – 5.5km (3½ miles) northwest of Coleford (parking charges may apply)

DISTANCE: 14.75km (9¼ miles) (circular)

TIME: 4½–5 hours

KEY SPECIES: Wild boar, peregrine falcon, fallow deer

MAP: OS Explorer OL14

TRANSPORT: Christchurch crossroads bus stop (buses to Coleford/Ross-on-Wye) – 3.25km (2 miles) south of start but only 500m (¼ mile) east of Point 5 on walk

WALK ACCESSIBILITY: Not wheelchair/pushchair accessible; dogs allowed

DIFFICULTY: Moderate

MORE INFORMATION: forestryengland.uk

It was travelling around this wending wooded Wye Valley region in 1770 that inspired William Gilpin to write an account that would become pivotal in the development of British countryside tourism. The work, *Observations on the River Wye*, became a bestseller as 18th-century holidaymakers flocked to clock the picturesque landscapes Gilpin described. This was picturesque, incidentally, not just as an adjective but as an entire new aesthetic concept: it sat somewhere between the two other then in-vogue concepts of the *beautiful* (conventionally pleasing or delightful) and the *sublime* (unquantifiable, sometimes shocking or disquieting greatness). In landscape terms, a riverside meadow would likely be deemed beautiful and a rugged mountain sublime. Gilpin's Wye, then, was the idyll in the middle, with plenty of pleasing scenery but no shortage of the dramatic either.

Looking out from the talismanic walk viewpoint Symonds Yat Rock, a crag protruding over steeply sloping forest down to the Wye's gentle curves, you may think much the same. The rock is a renowned peregrine falcon-watching spot, while the country's biggest wild boar population secretively scuffles in the trees below. You might get sightings of barn owls, tawny owls, sparrowhawks and goshawks too, and encounters with fallow, roe and muntjac deer are frequent. This section of the Wye is also an important salmon spawning area.

Nothing outdoes autumn's glorious russet-gold hues for a trip here. There are some steep ups and downs on this one and, while paths are good quality and well-signposted, they still get mighty muddy.

ROUTE DESCRIPTION

1) From the car park, take the path to **Symonds Yat Rock Log Cabin**, built in 1956 in readiness for Queen Elizabeth II's 1957 visit and still a trusty café serving hungry holidaymakers. From here, make the brief trip across the road on the bridge to **Symonds Yat Rock** and **viewpoint** with its fine panoramas across the Wye Valley: stay long enough and you'll likely spot peregrine falcons too: their favoured nesting point is at Coldwell Rocks, and a telescope is available to watch them. Back in the clearing, follow signs for the Highmeadow Trail, skirting the clearing anticlockwise then making

WILD BOAR

Wild boar might more evoke images of medieval times than of today's fauna, yet unlike bears and wolves, hunted into extinction in the UK several centuries ago, boars can still be found feral in several locales countrywide. The Wye Valley and neighbouring Forest of Dean have the lion's share of Britain's estimated 2600 wild boars.

the steep descent down several flights of steps. About three-quarters of the way down the steps, ignore the cross-path and keep straight on down to swing left (southwest) at the next path junction. Now, go steeply downhill, descending more steps to a track end near The Chalet, turn left and continue downhill to the riverside car park. Veer right here along the river should you wish to experience either the **Saracens Head** pub or the **hand-pulled ferry** across the river in front, likely an important river crossing since Roman times. Otherwise, your route continues with a left-hand turn to follow the path along the forest-fringed River Wye. This river stretch is important for spawning salmon.

2) In 1.75km, as the Wye starts on a large meander and you cross Whippington Brook, prepare to turn left. Climb the track up the small valley deeper into forest, the England-

Wales border at this point (you'll cross between the two several times on this route): ignore one right-hand path and meet a second 525m after leaving the Wye. Turn right on the Wysis Way, ascending steeply with Lady Park Wood on your right. You hit a forest track in 425m: turn right. This track curves left and meets another track junction after 400m. This next stretch is a decent bet for seeing wild boar (although daytime sightings are still rare) as the animals now populating the forest were originally released near the close-by village of Staunton. Turn left then immediately right on the path to forest-ensconced **Near Hearkening Rock**, a quartz conglomerate outcrop with smashing views across to Wales' Skirrid and Black Mountains summits. The path zigzags down to the rock's right and twists back below it: the rock's concave shape, visible here, supposedly amplifies surrounding sound and was allegedly used by gamekeepers to detect poachers. Keep descending to **Suck Stone**, another huge rock hidden in the trees, and afterwards meet a forest track.

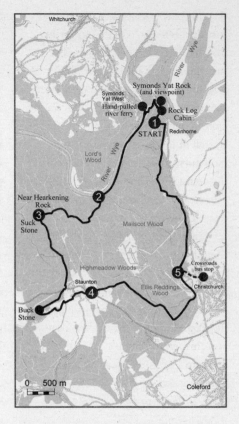

3) Turn left. In 675m, take the diagonal left-hand path uphill, which curves right (south) in 200m and proceeds into Staunton. Cross the A4136 road onto the lane opposite. At the gate soon afterwards bear right and, keeping a wall on your right, climb southwest up to the **Buck Stone** at 279masl – a bulky boulder with enchanting views. You join a grassy track curving left to run southeast down to a lane and turn left back towards Staunton. At a lane junction turn right: the lane then bends sharply left. In the village centre in 250m you turn right at a junction, keeping on the lane to the A4136. Cross, then track the churchyard wall right to a left-hand lane, Whippingtons Corner.

4) This becomes a track ahead and shortly afterwards forks. Keep right (more-or-less straight ahead). Take the minor track fork right in 350m, watching for the forest's trio of deer species as you cut southeast for 725m, curving left (east) at the end of this stretch to join a larger forest track. Now turn right. The track runs southeast for 375m, then veers left (northeast) for 575m. Pass through a barrier and then a house on the left and curve left to pass into the chalet-dotted grounds of Forest Holidays. Keep on the track straight ahead with the forest line on your left: this curves northwest then north past a picnic area to a gate onto the road. Cut through on a path left just before the gate that passes two more cabins, reaches another gate, and then swings right onto the road.

5) The road from Christchurch Crossroads bus stop joins the route here. Head straight across the road (turn right off it if approaching from the bus stop), passing the barrier and selecting the wide path bearing right (north-northeast) through Highmeadow Woods. Stay on this for 1.4km, ignoring several cross-paths and cross-tracks, to where a main forest track runs east-west across your path. Continue ahead here on your path, which shortly afterwards swings left and reaches the edge of Mailscot Lodge in another 175m. Keep the lodge on your left as you skirt the property, after which your path begins swinging to the north. Cross a lane 750m after leaving the lodge perimeter and proceed 600m north. You'll then meet the access road to Symonds Yat Rock car park: turn left for 200m until you reach it.

Wild boar

25

8. Langford Lakes, Grovely Wood & Great Wishford via Little Langford Down & the Handsel Trees

Adventure through age-old woods and chalk downland after a serendipitous wetland start, spotting special birds and insects as you go

NEED TO KNOW

START/FINISH: Langford Lakes Nature Reserve car park, Steeple Langford, SP3 4NH (parking free)

DISTANCE: 22.5km (14 miles) (circular)

TIME: 6½–7 hours

KEY SPECIES: Kingfisher, Adonis blue butterfly, down shieldbug

MAP: OS Explorer 130

TRANSPORT: Steeple Langford bus shelter (buses to Salisbury/Warminster) – 800m (½ mile) northwest

WALK ACCESSIBILITY: Mostly accessible to wheelchair/pushchair users; dogs allowed except at Langford Lakes Nature Reserve

DIFFICULTY: Moderate

MORE INFORMATION: wiltshirewildlife.org and visitwiltshire.com

This walk encompasses a little of everything making Wiltshire's landscape special – undulating grassy chalk downs, mystery-steeped prehistoric sites, secretive ancient woods and a picturesque village or two. But it begins with a set piece utterly atypical of the county in the wetland haven of Langford Lakes Nature Reserve, which sees some 150 bird species stop by annually.

The lakes are excellent for kingfishers, little egrets and water rails. Great crested grebes perform courtship displays in spring and wintertime visitors might include duck family members shoveler, pochard, wigeon and goldeneye. Inky, legend-entrenched Grovely Wood, one of Wiltshire's biggest tracts of woodland, swaddles the higher ground, harbouring ancient oaks, yews and beeches. The woods also wrap around

Little Langford Down, an elusive chalk downland fragment where Adonis blue and dark green fritillary butterflies can be glimpsed along with the extremely rare bastard toadflax plant – and the down shieldbug that feeds upon it.

As most people rush by on the A303 with a stop at the world-famous Stonehenge at most, this northeastern flank of the Cranborne Chase and West Wiltshire Downs AONB feels forgotten and timeless. Visit in June to catch the best of bird and butterfly activity. It's a surprisingly gruelling climb from the lakes up to the woods, but otherwise easy-going.

ROUTE DESCRIPTION

1) Your start point, **Langford Lakes Nature Reserve** is a series of open bodies of water (former gravel pits) seldom seen in Wiltshire and a magnet for many aquatic avians. You can explore the lakes, which are free to enter, as you wish. This path begins by heading along southeast to the Kingfisher Café and on across the divide between Long Pond (right) and Brockbank Lake and Round Pond (left), with some hides for birdwatching en route. You can take the out-and-back path leading straight on and then left to the **hide** at East Clyffe Pond, but afterwards this route continues skirting around Long Pond. Pass a **viewpoint** on the eastern shore, and stroll along the southern shore past another **hide**.

At Long Pond's far end, take the Glebe Walk by turning left, where you might spot stonechats or snipes on your way along the stream, crossing over it twice then cutting across a meadow to return back to the car park.

2) Now, return to the reserve entrance and swing left on aptly named Duck Street into Hanging Langford, turning right at the village hall and presently left at the bridleway sign on a tarmacked lane quickly becoming a tree-enclosed path under the railway line. In another 200m this climbs to a lane. Turn left and keep climbing past Holloway Hedge Barn to where the way splits into two 525m later. Bear left here, curving left around the field edge to then swing right with the hedge on your left.

3) Cranborne Chase possesses one of England's highest concentrations of ancient monuments, and coming up next are several. The clump of vegetation on your left as you begin ascending along the hedge line hides **East Castle**, remnants of a late Iron Age or Romano-British farmstead. Climb 950m to the woodland edge ahead and turn right along it on **Grim's Ditch**, an ancient territorial boundary. Follow Grim's Ditch along the treeline for 1.2km to pass a farm building and reach the entrance to Grovely Wood.

4) Your route now swings left on Second Broad Drive, a Roman road, into **Grovely Wood** on a long, straight path. The wood is a superb assemblage of old-growth trees, with many parts unchanged in centuries, and several associated legends and traditions speak of the wood's ancient past. Its dense cover was used for storing munitions in WW2, and you will find WW2 bunkers along the next stretch too. Proceed for 2.5km and, as fields appear on your right, swing acutely left along the course of Grim's Ditch again to reach a forest track. Now turn right. In 425m, after two right-hand tracks and an acute-angled left-hand track, you reach a left-hand turn.

5) This 1.2km out-and-back route is about the only means of accessing **Little Langford Down Nature Reserve**, the lonesome chalk-grass

upland bastion of bastard toadflax and down shieldbugs, as well as several butterfly species. Turn right at the next junction to reach the open grassland, but remember there is no through path onwards and that you must return. Returning, swing left at map Point 5, then right in 700m on the track running south then southwest along the tree-break to a track junction in 375m. Turn right, then soon afterwards left. You hit Second Broad Drive again in another 100m.

6) Turn left for 300m, passing a turn-off to Grovely Lodge on the right, and where Second Broad Drive swings left keep straight ahead with fields off right, on First Broad Drive. Bear right in 425m to keep on this enchanting avenue through the woods, reaching the turn-off to the **Handsel Trees** in 1.9km. A wood highlight, these three majestic and slightly eerie beeches supposedly mark the graves of sisters accused of witchcraft and brutally put to death. Trinkets adorn the branches of one tree.

7) Back on Second Broad Drive, retrace your steps a few metres, then turn right on the first right-hand track. Turn left in 175m to follow a track running parallel to Second Broad Drive for another 575m, ignoring several side-paths then turning right. At a Y-junction in

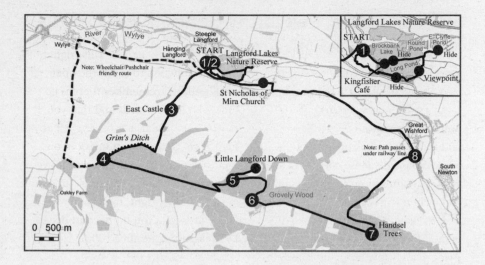

150m bear right again. This distinct path runs northeast, out of the forest, across the slopes of Hadden Hill and then down along field edges to curve under the railway line into **Great Wishford**. This pretty village is traditionally tied to Grovely Wood: the villagers still exercise their right to collect firewood on Oak Apple Day, a medieval custom.

8) Turn left on the road, fork left again on Station Road, bear left in 400m on West Street then turn almost immediately right past the Royal Oak pub on Langford Road. You can follow this quiet lane, twisting over the railway at one point, for the 4.7km back to the right-hand onto Duck Street in Hanging Langford (after which you retrace your outward route to Langford

Lakes). This walk takes one notable deviation from Langford Road after 3.1km: crossing right back over the railway and swinging left to brush the south side of **St Nicholas of Mira church,** then heading west along field edges to rejoin the lane in 475m.

9. Bossington, Selworthy Beacon & Allerford through the Holnicote Estate

Explore the best of Exmoor, from coast to moors to combes

NEED TO KNOW

START/FINISH: Bossington NT car park, TA24 8HQ (parking charges may apply)

DISTANCE: 10.5km (6½ miles) (circular)

TIME: 3–3½ hours

KEY SPECIES: Exmoor pony, red deer, heath fritillary butterfly

MAP: OS Explorer OL9

TRANSPORT: Allerford bus shelter (buses to Minehead/Lynmouth May–Sep) – 1.5km (1 mile) southeast

WALK ACCESSIBILITY: Not wheelchair/pushchair accessible; dogs allowed

DIFFICULTY: Moderate

SPECIFIC EQUIPMENT: Compass

MORE INFORMATION: nationaltrust.org.uk

The Holnicote Estate's 12,000 acres comprise some of Exmoor's most glorious terrain, and this walk runs through the best of it. The route's beauty lies in it touching upon everything that makes this national park special – secretive riverside paths, smashing cliff top vistas, wooded combes (narrow, stream-bisected valleys), eruptions of rolling, bracken-clad moorland hemmed by patchwork-quilt farmland and three enchanting historic villages.

The topographical variety attracts wildlife too. Freely roaming Exmoor ponies and one of England's largest red deer populations favour the moor, while combes entice one of the UK's rarest butterflies, the heath fritillary. Late spring sees the ponies begin giving birth to foals, while woodland combes are brightened by bluebells. Warm summer days bring out butterflies, late summer purples the moors in heather and September marks the start of the red deer rut.

The walk is waymarked and on distinct paths throughout, but a compass helps with navigation on the moorland sections. One steep ascent awaits near the start.

ROUTE DESCRIPTION

1) The walk crosses a footbridge over the River Horner into the woods bounding the car park. Immediately turn left, following the coast path through woodland. The path initially keeps the river on the left before curving away to the right, tracing the wood's edge to pass through a gate and ascend onto gorse- and bracken-dotted moor.

2) You soon reach a stone marker demarcating the NT-owned land at Hurlstone. From here, a short out-and-back walk visits **Hurlstone Point** with its ruined coastguard tower and

fabulous coastal views. Back at the stone marker, the walk now ascends more steeply on the grassy path up Hurlstone Combe on the coast path's inland route. Follow the coast path southeast up over Bossington Hill, avoiding several less distinct side-turnings.

3) Near where the open moor meets a field corner, almost 2km from the stone marker, the coast path forks left. Take the right-hand fork, your broad path ascending east to **Selworthy Beacon** (308masl), a beautiful viewpoint from where much of Exmoor is visible. Continue past the trig point, down to Hill Road.

4) A few metres along the road, a broad bridleway on the right, signposted to Selworthy, brings you down to meet a track. Turn right.

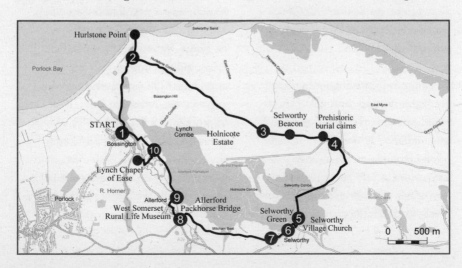

Shortly afterwards, turn right at another footpath sign to descend into Selworthy Combe's beguiling woodlands. Upon reaching a path junction, take the path heading down the combe with the stream on your right.

5) Pass through a gate onto a lane. Selworthy's 14th-century **Church of All Saints,** with its exquisite roof carving and 17th-century pulpit hourglass, is on your left. Turn right through a gate by a cross, descending through picturesque **Selworthy Green**.

6) Explore the green, rejoin the main lane through Selworthy village and, soon after, take a dead-end lane bearing right, signposted 'Selworthy Farm B&B'. The lane passes between barns and terminates. Straight ahead, a hedged track with tracks into fields on either side is your onward route.

7) Continue, ignoring paths off to the right, passing through a belt of woodland to reach a lane at a bend by a thatched house. Carry straight on along the lane, which soon curves left to cross a ford at the medieval and much-photographed **Allerford Packhorse Bridge**.

8) Turn right through charming Allerford village, passing **West Somerset Rural Life Museum**. At the village's end, turn right on the approach lane to Stokes Farm, also marked by a footpath sign to Bossington. Proceed past several buildings and cross a footbridge. A footpath sign to West Lynch and Bossington then points the path left.

9) Your path initially keeps the stream on the left, then climbs the edge of Allerford Plantation woodlands. Bear left at the next path junction, signposted to Bossington. Emerge from the woods, passing Bossington Hall to the left. Keep along the lower path at a fork, negotiating a stile to a gate and path crossroads.

10) Here, an out-and-back path leads left down a lane into West Lynch, where you'll find the comely 16th-century **Lynch Chapel of Ease**. Returning to the path crossroads, go through the gate, crossing a field to pass through a gap into the following field. Turn immediately left along this field edge to a gate, which ushers you down steps to a woodland path. Turn right. Descend the woods through another gate to reach the footbridge back to the car park.

10. Lundy Island Circular

Stretch your legs around this Devon island's seabird-swarmed island cliffs, staying tuned for seals, sika deer, endemic plants and more

NEED TO KNOW

START/FINISH: Lundy Island ferry terminal, Lundy

DISTANCE: 14.5km (9 miles) (part circular, part out-and-back)

TIME: 4–4½ hours

KEY SPECIES: Puffin, Manx shearwater, Lundy cabbage

MAP: OS Explorer 139

TRANSPORT: Ropery Road bus stop, Ilfracombe (buses to Barnstaple/Bideford) – 39.5km (24½ miles) east, on mainland. Then walk 350m (¼ mile) east to Ilfracombe ferry terminal and take MS Oldenburg ferry to start

WALK ACCESSIBILITY: Not wheelchair/pushchair accessible; no dogs

DIFFICULTY: Moderate

MORE INFORMATION: landmarktrust.org.uk and nationaltrust.org.uk

Lundy is a popular destination for the *Springwatch* team, with many visits over the years. With sailings just a few times a week between April and October connecting it to North Devon's coast at Ilfracombe and Bideford, Lundy is likely the most cut-off locale you can visit in Southern England, and the wealthiest in wildlife, too. In a 2013 episode of *Springwatch*, the island was celebrated as Britain in miniature. A former stronghold of the Knights Templar, numerous pirates and even a self-proclaimed king, the Bristol Channel's biggest island subsequently became Britain's first Marine Conservation Zone. This designation, together with its SSSI status, helps protect the area's 200-odd breeding grey seals, common dolphins and basking sharks.

The knobbly, imposing cliffs bring in ten breeding seabird species between April and July, including guillemots, razorbills, kittiwakes and Manx shearwaters. The stars of this cliffhanger of a show are those after whom the island is named, puffins: *lund* means puffin in Old Norse. Lundy's craggy sides, meanwhile, top out in gently rolling grassland and wetland ideal for the likes of skylarks and water rails. Britain's two smallest mammals, pipistrelle bats and pygmy shrews, are also native to Lundy, but introduced creatures like sika deer inhabit the island too. Flower-lovers will be enthralled by the presence of a plant found nowhere else: the Lundy cabbage.

This route encompasses the best of the island by looping right around its coast. It's a steady climb from the pier onto the so-called plateau, where most of the walk takes place, and fairly level thereafter.

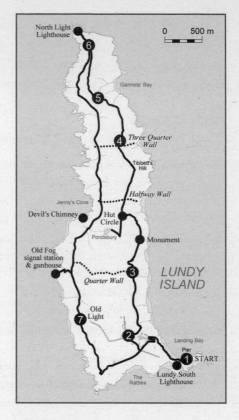

ROUTE DESCRIPTION

1) The limited sailings to Lundy mean booking ferry tickets in advance is advised. From where the ferry docks, with Rat Island off left across reefs, bear right on gravel track Beach Road, bending along low cliff edges with 1897-built **Lundy South Lighthouse** on the cliffs towering above on the left. Afterwards, the track gradually curves inland as it climbs onto the Lundy plateau: look for the extremely rare yellow-petalled Lundy cabbage hereabouts. The track swings hard left, making two hairpin turns and rises to meet the main south-north island track, Lundy Road, 1km after the ferry pier. Turn right, pass St Helen's Church and reach **Marisco Tavern**, the

Lundy community's focal point. Besides being a welcome refreshment stop, you can also record your nature sightings here in a logbook, thus helping island staff monitor wildlife activity.

2) Turn right along the far side of the tavern, passing through a gate. This sheltered area of the island welcomes birds like stonechats and the retiring water rail in soggier areas. You'll see Millcombe House down on the right ahead, yet after a second gate and slight descent you veer up left on Upper East Side Path. This is a beautiful stretch for wildlife-watching, with scrub dropping away to the eastern cliffs off right: look for grey seals and possibly orcas. After 850m, you hit **Quarter Wall**, the first of three dry-stone walled boundaries dividing the island east-west (at this point tumbledown). Cross this at a gate.

3) You now reach Lundy's old quarry remains. Pass Quarterwall Cottages (ruins), skirt left of a small tarn, then bear down right to a lower path following the quarry railway, passing grassed-over quarry faces. This swings up left (northwest) then briefly southwest, avoiding a prehistoric hut circle and joining Lundy Road 850m after the tarn. Here, take the short out-and-back detour left along the track, turning right after 250m to **Pondsbury**, a lake where orchids thrive. Afterwards, proceed north on the track through a gate in **Halfway Wall**, then fork right on the branch-

off path up to reach **Tibbett's Hill**, crowned by its granite holiday cottage, in 400m. Afterwards, take the path descending diagonally northwest to hit Lundy Road again by **Three Quarter Wall**.

4) Bear right after the wall: this path picks up a route running roughly parallel to and 100m from Lundy Road. On these gorse- and bell heather-bedecked grasslands, skylarks are spotted. You might sight sika deer too. Follow this path 800m, views to off-shore Gannet Rock off right, as you eventually curve round left (northwest) around crags to meet Lundy Road. Turn right.

5) For 800m keep on Lundy Road as the track nears the island's north. You'll meet your return path along Lundy's west side but first, continue on the dramatic path which crosses a weather-battered walkway over a gully, negotiates a rise then descends steps to **North Light Lighthouse** (1897), the island beautifully framed tapering to its northernmost point.

6) This drama sets the tone for the more rugged west coast path, your return route. It's all thrilling craggy cliff scenery off right now, but reaches the height of spectacle around **Devil's Slide**, a renowned rock-climbing route, after 1.5km. Pass

Three Quarter Wall and Halfway Wall via stiles to reach seabird central around **Jenny's Cove** and **Devil's Chimney**, where puffins, guillemots, kittiwakes and others nest from April to July. Several paths off right get you closer to the cliffs and cliff-side avian antics but add extra distance to this walk. Cross the stream outflowing from Pondsbury and hit Quarter Wall, crossed via stile, after 550m. Just afterwards make the short out-and-back detour out to the **Old Fog signal station** and **gunhouse** ruins, where canons would once be fired every ten minutes in the frequently occurring poor visibility. Today in good visibility, this is an excellent viewpoint for watching seabirds and marine life further out to sea.

7) After 650m, your next objective is **Old Light**, the original Lundy lighthouse built in the early 1800s. Pass this to the right, continuing 825m to reach South West Point at a sculpture. Now, swing left (northeast) 625m, St Helen's Church soon visible ahead, to a track crossroads at Lundy Road/Beach Road, afterwards continuing straight on your outward route to the ferry pier.

11. Lyme Regis to Axmouth along the Undercliffs

Delve into densely wooded, landslipped cliffs with their own microclimate, rare plants and a menagerie of creatures

NEED TO KNOW

START/FINISH: Lyme Regis Cobb Gate car park opposite Rock Point Inn, DT7 3QD (parking charges may apply)/Ship Inn, Axmouth, EX12 4AF (parking free)

DISTANCE: 11.75km (7¼ miles) (one-way)

TIME: 4–4½ hours

KEY SPECIES: Grass snake, cliff tiger beetle, hazel dormouse

MAP: OS Explorer 116

TRANSPORT: The Square bus stop, Lyme Regis (buses to Axmouth/Seaton/Bridport/Dorchester/Weymouth) at start

WALK ACCESSIBILITY: Not wheelchair/pushchair accessible; dogs allowed

DIFFICULTY: Moderate

SPECIFIC EQUIPMENT: Swimwear

MORE INFORMATION: publications.naturalengland.org.uk

Undercliffs are areas of land caught between sea cliffs and inland cliffs, typically formed due to drastic landslips, and the crumbly Cretaceous coast between Lyme Regis and Axmouth comprises Britain's outstanding example. This is a murky, mythical place, where collapsed cliffs have been colonised by ash, field maple, sycamore, beech and dense scrub. But a wonderland of rocks from different geological periods has also been laid bare and, consequently, the Lyme Regis area has long been a famous fossil-finding destination.

Hazel dormouse

What you see on this walk is a work-in-progress, too, as landslips continue: in fact, this is one of Europe's largest active coastal landslide systems.

Wildlife is as drawn as humans to this bizarre swathe of seaboard, part of West Dorset and East Devon's Unesco World Heritage-listed Jurassic Coast and an NNR besides. Slumped cliffs create a toasty microclimate beloved by basking grass snakes, and the easily eroded ground helps make this one of the UK's key places for seeing cliff tiger beetles. You could also spot the hazel dormouse and three shrew species: common, water and pygmy. Rare flowers include yellow horned poppies along slumped sections, while the big birds commonly glimpsed are peregrine falcons and ravens.

The often slippery, muddy, up-and-down Undercliffs paths are the main challenge on this one: stick to key routes, as foliage can conceal steep drops.

GRASS SNAKE
Britain's largest native snakes, up to 1.5m long, love moisture and warmth in equal measure, hence their presence in the Undercliffs. They are green-brown in colour with distinctive black-and-yellow collars.

ROUTE DESCRIPTION

1) Your walk start point ensures you'll get grandstand vistas of undeniably attractive little beach town **Lyme Regis** early on. It's also handy for excellent **Lyme Regis Museum**, focussing on the area's extraordinary geology, with its impressive fossil exhibits, and the town's rich literary connections: Jane Austen's *Persuasion* and John Fowles' *The French Lieutenant's Woman* are partly set here. Post-museum, follow Lyme Regis' seafront along Marine Parade, running behind **Front Beach**, for 225m. At Boylo's Watersports, take the right-hand set of steps up into **Langmore and Lister Gardens** – worth the clamber for the views, particularly in the direction you are heading southwest towards The Cobb, the harbour wall. Follow garden paths southwest to return down onto the seafront by **Jane Austen's Garden**. Turn right, then left on Cobb Road to the lifeboat station at the beginning of **The Cobb**.

2) Your walk continues right along the seafront, but it's a rite of passage and rather pretty to first walk ahead out along The Cobb. Near the end is **Lyme Regis Marine Aquarium**, with fascinating insights into the local marine life. Afterwards, proceed along the seafront behind **Monmouth Beach** to the car park. Now turn right with the coast path, up steps between chalets ahead into woodland. The path climbs close to a stream northwest to a gate where you turn left. Keep on the well-signposted coast path, bending through tree-flanked but more open ground to meet a northeast-southwest-running track by a house.

3) Turn left. Follow the track 350m to the right-hand 350m-long out-and-back path up to **Chimney Rock** near Underhill Farm. You'll negotiate some steep steps to see this somewhat incongruous rocky pinnacle protruding from the vegetation.

4) You officially entered the **Axmouth to Lyme Regis Undercliffs NNR** just prior to the Chimney Rock path and back on the coast path, the wooded Undercliffs begin in earnest ahead. The next 6.75km traverses the NNR and is a gruelling, muddy, up-and-down walk with many steps. Nor is there really any get-out from

this point on save returning the way you came: there are no public rights of way either to the coast or inland until the NNR exit this walk takes. You do not walk this section for the coastal views (there are few) but for the magical, primordial-seeming world you pass through. Landslips between 1765 and 1840 formed the first section around **Whitlands and Pinhay Cliffs**; The Great Landslip of 1839, which even Queen Victoria came to behold, the third: **Bindon and Dowlands Cliffs**. Here are the more undisturbed centuries-old woods: in the middle, around **Rousdon Cliffs**, the 19th-century-created Rousdon Estate had many exotic species planted that infiltrated the Undercliffs and are now being managed. Towards the end of the Undercliffs, the way cuts across an area of wood-surrounded chalk grassland, then passes along or close

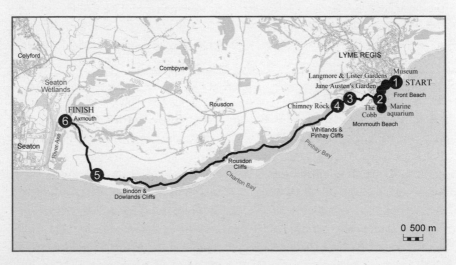

to the edge of the farmland for 825m before departing the NNR.

5) Your route – still on the coast path – heads into fields once more. Upon exiting the NNR, bear diagonally left (northwest) across a field before swinging right (north-northwest) across more farmland. You meet the track of Barn Close Lane 600m after leaving the NNR but know as you go that these chalky, grassy fields can support flowers like early gentians and butterflies such as chalk-hill blues.

6) Go a few metres left, then right over the field to the stile onto Stepps Lane, which you follow left for 675m into **Axmouth** village. Turn left on Chapel Street, along to the T-junction with Church Street. Just left is the finish: the Ship Inn with its bus stop back to the start. Waiting for the bus? Wander west through Axmouth to gaze out over the wader-frequented Seaton Wetlands.

RETURNING TO START: Buses X51/ X53/378, car or bike

12. Rame Peninsula around Cremyll, Cawsand & Rame Head

Make a foray into Cornwall's 'forgotten corner', where fantastic fauna and flora thrive

NEED TO KNOW

START/FINISH: Cremyll ferry pier, Cremyll, PL10 1HX

DISTANCE: 21.75km (13½ miles) (part circular, part out-and-back)

TIME: 6½–7 hours

KEY SPECIES: Dartford warbler, ring ouzel, fulmar

MAP: OS Explorer 108

TRANSPORT: Cremyll ferry bus stop (buses to Plymouth) and Cremyll ferry pier (passenger ferry to Plymouth) at start

WALK ACCESSIBILITY: Not wheelchair/pushchair accessible; dogs under close control

DIFFICULTY: Moderate

MORE INFORMATION: southwestcoastpath.org.uk and mountedgcumbe.gov.uk

Back when Plymouth was Britain's port of choice for launching epic voyages of discovery, Rame Head was the last land mariners would see on journeys sometimes lasting years. Rame Peninsula today is a green, lonesome place, especially contrasted with bustling Plymouth across the River Tamar. Everything about this hike along the peninsula's extremities exudes adventure, starting with the estuary boat trip from Plymouth to the start point. Then there is picturesque Mount Edgcumbe Country Park, atmospheric smugglers' havens Kingsand and Cawsand and the raw wave-bashed majesty of Rame Head itself.

The combination of cliffs and heath provides avian sanctuary for the rare Dartford warbler and ring ouzel, plus fulmars, gannets, buzzards and kestrels. Grey seals bask on rocks around Rame Head. In springtime, the colours of Mount Edgcumbe Country Park's camellias enthral en route.

There are some minor climbs and mud on many stretches, but what takes the time is the sheer amount to see. Curtail the route to a 10km circular by starting/finishing at Cawsand, also with a high-season ferry to Plymouth.

ROUTE DESCRIPTION

1) Just reaching the start point, by ferry from Plymouth, is spectacular. Maritime greats from Sir Francis Drake to Charles Darwin have passed through these waters, while vistas of Plymouth's coastline and the snaking Tamar Estuary are far-reaching. From Cremyll ferry pier, turn left, then left again to the entrance of **Mount Edgcumbe House and Country Park**.

2) The country park, a 3.5km² green swathe splayed along the Rame Peninsula coast, is among Britain's grandest landscaped gardens. While it does boast formal gardens, the surrounding parkland with its woods, temples and lakes already hints at the peninsula's innate wildness. The coast path, your route for much of this walk, runs around the park's edge. The way first skirts the **formal gardens** and **Cornish Black Bee Reserve**, followed by arcing **Barn Pool Beach**, where Darwin's *HMS Beagle* moored before conveying the naturalist to South America, where he would develop the Theory of Evolution by Natural Selection that changed how the natural world was perceived.

3) On open grassy ground with **Milton's Temple** ahead, a lakeside path forks right to the park's impressive **collection of camellias**. Pass more woodland to more open ground studded by the **Folly**, a late-18th-century ruin. Dip into more woodland, descend to a stony beach then climb to an old folly and viewpoint. Next, swing inland to round Picklecombe Fort apartment complex. From **Picklecombe Seat**, another elaborate garden feature, your route swings back towards the coast to come down through woods alongside Picklecombe Fort approach road. Turn right on the road, then after 50m leave it through a barrier-cum-gate on the left. The path now runs largely through wood-fringed meadows for 1.75km to a gate onto the lane at **Kingsand**. Both Kingsand and adjoining Cawsand, typically ravishing Cornish smuggler's ports, are worthy of exploration.

4) Turn right onto Devonport Hill, then immediately left on a narrow lane sporting an 'Unsuitable for Motors' sign. Thread through houses onto Heavitree Road, another narrow thoroughfare that bends around to the beachfront. Turn right on Market Street and left on serpentine Garrett Street, which climbs away from the beach then descends into **Cawsand**. Keep straight ahead onto The Square,

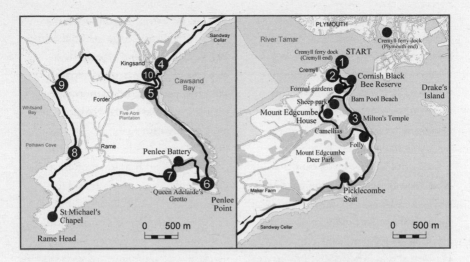

passing the left turn down to Cawsand Beach, to reach St Andrew's Church. Here, turn left on Pier Lane.

5) Pier Lane ascends, becoming a tarmacked path through coastal woodland. Pass some houses after 200m and bear left on a driveway after a further 500m to reach Bayfield Cottage, with gated private property ahead. Your path climbs right of a security fence through woods to Earl's Drive. Turn left, soon emerging at a viewpoint with benches by **Queen Adelaide's Grotto**.

6) Your route then pivots sharp right on a track soon reaching a gate. The coast path continues ahead but first, divert up to **Penlee Battery**, a good birdwatching location. This entails taking the track almost doubling back acutely to the right: it presently

swings left, crossing a field and twisting up through woods onto the thickly vegetation-covered battery fortifications. Turn left along the top of the battery, looking for rare flowers like the bee orchid, continue to the car park entrance then take the zigzagging path down to the left, rejoining the coast path.

7) Turn right. The path cuts onto exposed coastal heath with jagged rocky coast below. Pass a house up to the right as, ahead, **Rame Head** headland looms large, crowned by 14th-century **St Michael's Chapel**. Climb the headland, which offers fabulous birdwatching: peregrine falcons, fulmars and gannets might be descried. Then descend again, afterwards climbing towards the lofty mast near Rame Head car park. Some way below the mast, bear left along the coast path at a wooden sign. Pass two inaccessible sandy coves far below; the path then swings right (northeast), descending to a lane at Polhawn Fort with huge, tempestuous Whitsand Bay ahead. Dartford warblers and ring ouzels frequent this area.

8) The path squeezes straight over the lane, down to the right of a house: turn right on the driveway then left at a double gate onto the path above Whitsand Bay. After 650m this starts clambering the grassy cliff, then veers sharp right up to a lane.

9) Cross the lane onto a triangular junction island. Then turn left: this lane climbs towards New Wiggle Farmhouse. At a bend just before the farmhouse, branch right on a path. This swings through woods, past an old military ruin and diagonally down across a field to a hedged path that meets a driveway by Wringford Cottages. Turn left, heading straight over to a lane junction and field beyond. Descend across a field on a clear path to a stile with Cawsand drawing closer below. Through the stile, take the lower path down to New Road. Turn left, following the road curving left around Cawsand Fort. At a streetlamp below the fort, turn right down steps to Garrett Street in Kingsand.

10) You now rejoin your outward route. Once you reach the Folly in Mount Edgcumbe Country Park, you can vary your return route to the park entrance and Cremyll ferry pier just beyond via any number of pretty pathways.

13. The Wilderness Trail around Helman Tor

Trek through old tin streaming territory that inadvertently fashioned upland wetlands perfect for birds, butterflies and dormice

NEED TO KNOW

START/FINISH: Helman Tor car park (2.5km/1½ miles southeast of PL30 5HP, the closest postcode for sat-nav purposes) – 2km (1¼ miles) east of Lowertown (parking free)

DISTANCE: 11.5km (7¼ miles) (circular)

TIME: 3½–4 hours

KEY SPECIES: Hazel dormouse, nightjar, adder

MAP: OS Explorer 107

TRANSPORT: Lostwithiel railway station – 6.75km (4 miles) by foot/11.25km (7 miles) by car

WALK ACCESSIBILITY: Not wheelchair/pushchair accessible; dogs on leads May–Jul around Helman Tor, otherwise under close control

DIFFICULTY: Moderate

SPECIFIC EQUIPMENT: Compass

MORE INFORMATION: cornwallwildlifetrust.org.uk

Moorland around central Cornish town Bodmin is invariably associated with bleakness – these are the barren environs made famous by Daphne du Maurier novel *Jamaica Inn* – so Helman Tor's rocky outcrop and its surrounding woodlands and wetlands come as a fecund surprise, albeit not an entirely natural one. Tin streaming, the ancient method of washing tin from streams, was practised here for centuries, creating many pools and wetlands in the process. Today these soggy spots act as wildlife magnets.

Of the three separate nature reserves here, the elegant small red damselfly and unusual butterfly species favour Breney Common's water-filled tin streaming hollows; the scrub and woods of Red Moor work wonders for the elusive nightjar and hazel dormouse; and Crift's grasses coax out sun-seeking adders and common lizards. This is also Cornwall's biggest nature reserve. Summertime sees purple devil's-bit scabious flower lure in the butterflies, while dusk shortens your odds of spying dormice and nightjars.

Paths on the area's specially designed Wilderness Trail this walk mostly follows are wild in feel and occasionally boggy, overgrown and hard to find, despite waymark posts: bring your compass.

ROUTE DESCRIPTION

1) The hike starts by clambering up titular walk feature **Helman Tor** (209masl), scaled via the path leading north from the car park. Among the elaborate piles of granite on top are three logan stones (finely balanced boulders). Clear days should scoop views north to the Atlantic and south to the English Channel, and it's also a vantage point to observe the interesting surrounding landscape, much moulded into humps and hollows by tin streaming. A path winds left (west) from another scattering of

HAZEL DORMOUSE

Being nocturnal and found in only a few locations across Southern England and Wales, the dormouse is surprisingly tough to spot. Look for flashes of ginger near tree bases in winter and tussocky moors come spring and summer.

rocks behind the first back down onto the car park access road.

2) Turn left for 200m towards the car park, then branch right on the track towards Breney Farm. In 450m, turn right along a path running beside a field hedge. Across the field, pass through into the tree belt signifying your arrival onto **Breney Common**, its small lakes' hollows enticing rare small red damselflies and marsh and pearl-bordered fritillary butterflies. The main path bears northwest, west and northwest across the common for 675m, after which you reach a lane by houses.

3) Turn right, following the lane curving left past a church to a wooden double gate on the right 275m later. Pass through the gate and emerge beyond the trees onto more open ground on Lowertown Moor. Your path now bears left (west) around the edge of tree-dotted moor, presently swinging right (north) to run close to field edges on the left. The route veers gradually left and, just after the end of the second left-hand field (and before a pylon line), you swing sharp right (east) along a treeline beside fields on the left. Pass alongside three fields before your path meets a hedged track. Turn right along this, reaching a lane in 250m.

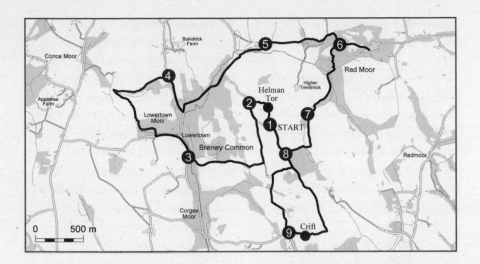

4) Turn right, then at the T-junction turn sharp left along another lane that passes the car park access road and reaches a sharp left-hand bend after passing under the pylon line. Here, take the muddy right-hand path winding through woodland south of Little Trevilmick Farm and emerge on a path directly east of the farm.

5) Now follow the path east, through a section of meadow and then more woods, where you'll steer left of a pond and presently reach a lane. Turn left, then right at a double gate to enter the woods of **Red Moor**. This is a stronghold of birds like yellowhammers and nightjars and also a key hideout of the surprisingly uncommon hazel dormouse. Trace the track along to a dividing of ways at a Wilderness Trail marker. The official trail swings left; you bear

right. In 150m, your track passes a right-hand path with a marker post. You later take this path but first continue on the 600m out-and-back route along the track to the lake, another result of tin streaming, to maximise chances of wildlife sightings. Back at the path with the marker post, now fork left.

6) You soon pass an information board, then cross a stile to enter dense woodland. Zigzag through the woods along boardwalks and over a footbridge to meet a path junction, where you turn right. The Wilderness Trail soon bears left and can also be taken but is hard to follow in places; this walk proceeds down the path and with open fields ahead, then bears left close to the edge of the woodland. Bear south then southwest through the woods to where the first field on the right ends, then continue straight on to meet a path junction 150m later.

7) Turning right here returns you to Helman Tor. Turning left, on this route, ushers you south over an expanse of woodsy scrub for 350m. Swing left before a lake to pass through trees and reach the continuation of the track from the car park, here the Saints Way long-distance path.

8) Turn left for 950m, passing a picnic site to enter the reserve's southern zone, **Crift**, at a right-hand gate. Here, much of the medieval field layout has been preserved and a 12th–14th-century longhouse uncovered. Common lizards and adders are sometimes caught sunbathing, too. Cross the field beyond the gate, entering scrubby woodland ahead. Your route now twists through this, bearing generally west and right of a group of buildings ahead to reach a lane bend by the access track to Whistow Farm.

9) Turn right along the track, presently passing the farm on the right. The route then swings slight left, traces the right-hand edge of a field, crosses a stream and another field and reaches Breney Farm. Here, immediately after a farmyard, bear right across a field and pass through more woods to rejoin the Saints Way track. It's now a 525m walk left back to the car park entrance.

14. Porthgwarra, Gwennap Head & Nanjizal

Take in tantalising coast and outstanding bird- and sealife-spotting along the English mainland's southwestern edge

NEED TO KNOW

START/FINISH: Porthgwarra car park, TR19 6JR (parking charges may apply)

DISTANCE: 7.25km (4½ miles) (circular)

TIME: 2–2½ hours

KEY SPECIES: Basking shark, red-billed chough, Balearic shearwater

MAP: OS Explorer 102

TRANSPORT: Tresco bus stop (buses to Porthcurno/Penzance/Land's End/St Ives Apr–Sep) – 3km (2 miles) north

Red-billed chough

WALK ACCESSIBILITY: Not wheelchair/pushchair accessible; dogs allowed

DIFFICULTY: Moderate

MORE INFORMATION: visitcornwall.com and southwestcoastpath.org.uk

Giving Land's End a run for its money as mainland Britain's southwestern extremity, Gwennap Head and environs go in for crowds of birds rather than holidaymaking hordes, and the entire entrancing coastline of this walk, an SSSI as well as being part of Cornwall AONB, forms one of England's foremost birdwatching sites.

The secret to this area's avian abundance lies in it being first and last landfall in some while for many feathery migrants making their journeys across the Irish and Celtic Seas from and to the Mediterranean and Africa. Rarities spied here include the red-billed (or Cornish) chough and Balearic shearwater. Cliffs also provide a vantage point for spotting basking sharks, dolphins and grey seals. May and October are key months for watching migrant birds, while May also kick-starts three months of primetime for watching basking sharks.

Rollercoasting a cove-carved seaboard from cute-as-a-button seaside hamlet Porthgwarra to the wild Nanjizal Beach, and looping back across the mix of farmland and maritime heath behind, this walk rarely gets busy due to its distance from major tourist facilities. It gets its main climb over with at the start, too. A well-trodden route, it's prone to muddiness in parts.

ROUTE DESCRIPTION

1) From the car park, walk back down the few metres into **Porthgwarra**. At the sharp lane, bend with the track to **Porthgwarra Beach** ahead, turning right onto the South West Coast Path at a signpost. The initially narrow path rises steeply above Porthgwarra along a stunning stretch of coast, lofty broken cliffs soon plummeting below. The path then levels somewhat. Pass the **Gwennap Head daymarks**, two large conical structures warning vessels of dangerous offshore rocks, off to the right, then draw alongside **Gwennap Head NCI** (National Coastwatch Institute – a voluntary organisation supporting the HM Coastguard) 800m after leaving Porthgwarra.

2) Gwennap Head could easily be labelled Great Britain's southwestern-most point, but for want of the marketing that gives Land's End, 6.5km north, the honour. Nature lovers do not mind, though, as this is one of Cornwall's best locations for observing basking sharks, cetaceans and a wide range of migrant birds. Your route swings north after Gwennap Head NCI around the bay of Porth Loe.

> **RED-BILLED CHOUGH**
> Red-legged, red-billed and also known as the red-billed chough, this crow family member's habitat is now confined to the fringes of the country: the Cornish, Welsh, Scottish and Irish coasts. Its place in British legend is interesting: King Arthur supposedly departed this world in chough form.

3) Passing rugged headlands Pellitras Point and Black Carn on the cliffs off left, the coast path meets the first of two paths diagonally intersecting from the right, swinging northwest. Lying 400m after the second intersecting path is a fork: the coast path bears right while another lower, hairier path runs around the clifftops of Carn Barra before rejoining the coast path further on.

4) After the paths rejoin, it's another 650m skirting above the Pendower Coves to **Carn Lês Boel**, an Iron Age promontory fort.

5) From here the coast path bends northeast, a white house visible ahead. The path soon drops steeply down steps to meet another main path at a valley bottom. Just left are the wooden steps onto Nanjizal's ruggedly handsome beach, rocky at high tide but sandy at low tide.

6) Nanjizal is regularly touted as one of Cornwall's finest hidden beaches.

The beach's southern end ruptures into **Song of the Sea Cave**, a narrow but lofty rock arch with sea crashing through from either side. You're also still in the SSSI here, so the aforementioned wildlife might also be glimpsed. Re-climbing the wooden steps, it's decision time. This walk makes a round trip of it, returning inland, but you can also retrace your outward route along the coast, where wildlife sightings are likely to be better.

7) Return to the junction of the coast path and the valley bottom path. This round-trip route ignores the coast path climbing to the right, ascending the valley bottom path and passing the previously seen white house. Past the house, the route becomes a broader track, heading east, becoming a lane and reaching Higher Bosistow Farm. Skirt the farm's southern side on the drive, with the farm buildings to your left. Just before the outlying outbuilding on the right, turn right on a short grassy track to a field edge.

8) Head across the field, picking up a grassy track running past one field boundary to turn left midway along the following field edge. Now follow the path crossing three fields in an easterly direction to emerge on a driveway just northeast of a house and southwest of Ardensawah Farm.

9) Turn right. The drive becomes a rougher track running southwest or west through farmland onto open heath. As the track then swings south, it forks. Take the left-hand, south-leading fork and 40m later, do the same again at another fork, branching left to encounter a small lake after 250m.

10) Passing the lake on your left, it's a straightforward run southeast to meet the approach road to Gwennap Head NCI. Turn left. This road soon curves down to the car park.

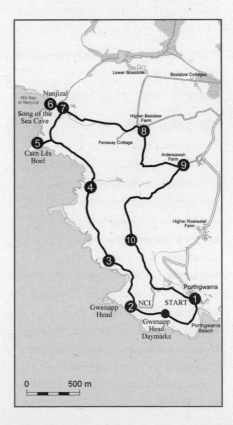

15. Horner Wood & Dunkery Beacon

Ascend some of England's greatest ancient oak woods to Exmoor's highest point through rich bat- and bird-spotting territory

NEED TO KNOW

START/FINISH: Horner Wood NT car park, TA24 8HY, behind Horner Tea Gardens (parking charges may apply)

DISTANCE: 17.25km (10¾ miles) (part circular, part out-and-back)

TIME: 5–5½ hours

KEY SPECIES: Oak, barbastelle bat, red deer

MAP: OS Explorer OL9

TRANSPORT: Horner Turn bus stop (buses to Minehead/Lynmouth May–Sep) – 1.25km (¾ mile) north

WALK ACCESSIBILITY: Not wheelchair/pushchair accessible; dogs under close control

DIFFICULTY: Moderate–Difficult

MORE INFORMATION: nationaltrust.org.uk

The Holnicote Estate's second entry in this walk book sinuously navigates one of England's largest ancient oak woodlands, a bewitching, primeval-feeling place where 15 of 17 UK bat species, including the rare barbastelle and Bechstein's bats, can be found alongside some 320 lichen species and hundreds of different beetles. Yet nor can it resist climbing to Exmoor's highest point, Dunkery Beacon, from where panoramas across the NP to the Bristol Channel are exceptional and prehistoric sites litter the wine-coloured bracken. There are also likely sightings of red deer and Exmoor ponies. And it is the picture-perfect transition between wood and moor that makes the walk such a joy. It's all protected as a SSSI and NNR too.

April to June, when pied flycatchers, wood warblers and redstarts join the woodland bird chorus with lesser spotted woodpeckers providing percussion, is especially enriching. Save some woodland walking until late evening to bat-spot. You'll climb 450m en route to Dunkery Beacon, and negotiate several steep, often muddy, always rooty combe paths.

ROUTE DESCRIPTION

1) From the car park's public toilets, a path cuts through onto the lane by idyllic **Horner Tea Gardens**. Turn right, passing the tea gardens and cottages, then left on the track at the grassy triangle. This runs initially with meadows off left before **Horner Woods** press in, with burbling **Horner Water** as your guide onwards and inwards. Look out for venerable sessile oaks and ashes, often mythically bearded in lichen, plus dippers and grey wagtails on the stream. It's only 400m after the last field fades on the left that you turn left to cross Horner Water at the next footbridge on Tucker's Path.

2) The path zigzags up out of the wood to a path crossroads with the Windsor Path; head straight across. Contours bunch together for a steep ascent over tree-dotted hillside to the **Jubilee Hut**, a pleasant viewpoint over the woods. Turn right here on the Coleridge Way long-distance path. At the fork in 200m keep right and 400m later, after passing through thicker woodland again, reach the car park at **Webber's Post** (238masl). A bench marks an excellent raptor-viewing point (buzzards, kestrels and

> **BARBASTELLE BAT**
> If you're a chiropterologist, this is the big British find: an elusive bat that loves wet southern woodlands. It has a distinctive flattened face and large ears meeting in the middle.

hobbies) can be seen here and classic all-round Exmoor viewpoint.

3) A broad stony track leads from the car park's far (southern) end to cross the lane to Cloutsham and heads straight across (south) onto the slopes of Easter Hill. Climb steadily south to the 300m contour. Then continue south along the contour to round Hollow Combe. Switch direction to west along the top of these woods, then veer southwest to descend and ascend Aller Combe. Just after the woods here is a path crossroads. You can take the short out-and-back right-hand detour here to view **Sweetworthy**, an Iron Age hillfort and former medieval village. Afterwards return to the crossroads and proceed straight up ahead (south) for the 140m ascent to **Dunkery Beacon** (519masl).

4) Besides being Southern England's highest land outside Dartmoor and a great viewpoint, this is a top spot for sighting red deer and Exmoor ponies. The many prehistoric monuments hereabouts include Bronze Age burial mound **Little Rowbarrow**, which you pass descending due west from the summit. Beyond Little Rowbarrow is **Great Rowbarrow**, another burial mound, and the path down to the road at a small car park and NT marker stone.

5) Turn left a few metres, then right on the minor path through the heather with Lang Combe opening up off right. This soon bears northwest gradually down 1km to meet a lane near two small lay-bys. Turn right and, 625m later, a fence on your right is your prompt to swing acute right. Stay on open moor now to descend on the path to the next combe's treeline. Several streams have sources near here, soon converging into the stream that will flow into Horner Water and you swing round three of them, south, east then northeast. You then branch left on a path easing down to follow the east bank of the stream descending through Bagley Wood and Oak Wood. From the point your path comes alongside the east stream bank, it's a 600m descent to a sharp lane bend south of Wilmersham hamlet. Here, consider the 1km out-and-back detour up to **Stoke Pero church**, Exmoor's highest church (included in the walk distance).

6) Your descent of the thickly wooded combe now continues (to the right, if

coming from Stoke Pero church). The path crosses the stream several times on a 1km descent before swinging away from the stream left (northeast) to pass a left-hand turn and then cross Horner Water at a footbridge. Turn right on the gentle woodland track. There are other paths exploring upper Horner Wood but this walk traces Horner Water for 1.3km east southeast or east. It then swings north for 900m to reach Tucker's Path footbridge and your outward route, which you follow 975m down Horner Water to the car park.

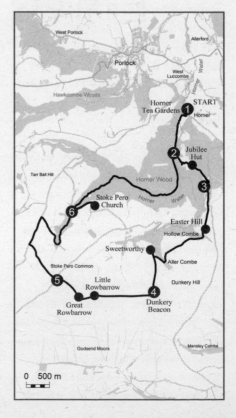

SOUTHERN ENGLAND

16. Blackwater Arboretum & the Tall Trees Trail

Enjoy some of England's most epic trees on this easy and enchanting amble

NEED TO KNOW

START/FINISH: Blackwater car park, SO42 7QB – 5.5km (3½ miles) northwest of Brockenhurst (parking free)

DISTANCE: 3.25km (2 miles) (circular)

TIME: 1–1½ hours

KEY SPECIES: Douglas fir, giant redwood, oak

MAP: OS Explorer OL22

TRANSPORT: Brockenhurst railway station – 5.5km (3½ miles) southeast

WALK ACCESSIBILITY: Accessible to wheelchair/pushchair users; dogs under close control

DIFFICULTY: Easy

MORE INFORMATION: newforestnpa.gov.uk

Douglas fir

This walk is all about trees: some of Southern England's greatest, grandest trees, no less. Native oak and sycamore there are, but the route also visits some fantastic foreigners: Douglas firs and giant redwoods dating from the 1850s. It really is a magnificent introduction to the arboreal paradise that is the New Forest, with information boards throughout helping you learn more about the mighty specimens here. The walk includes an optional extension to the Knightwood Oak, so old it was reputedly visited by Henry VIII, who hunted hereabouts.

DOUGLAS FIR
This especially straight-trunked conifer is native to North America, but botanist David Douglas introduced the tree to Britain in 1827. They can live for over 1000 years.

ROUTE DESCRIPTION

1) In the car park, you will see a chunky wooden signpost towering above an information board and, nearby, a wooden archway onto

Rhinefield Ornamental Drive. Cross the road onto a broad track. Your outward route soon reaches the path right along the Tall Trees Trail, indicated by another chunky wooden sign (where this walk will later go). First, however, continue along the track to Blackwater Arboretum, the arched gate into which is visible ahead.

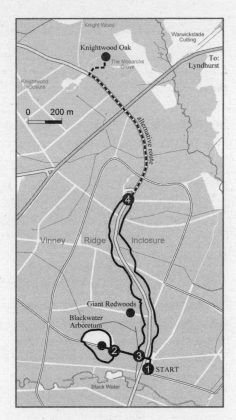

2) Inside **Blackwater Arboretum**, turn immediately left off the main track at a gravestone-shaped information sign. The path curves clockwise through this delightful grassy woodland passing splendid Douglas fir, oak and other trees, some planted during Queen Victoria's reign. The path crosses the main track further on, curving back through woodland on the track's other side to the arboretum entrance. Afterwards, retrace your steps to the turn-off (now on the left) onto the Tall Trees Trail.

3) The path crosses a small bridge, meandering through more enchanting woodland. It soon passes another gravestone-shaped sign behind which stand some **giant redwoods**. The Tall Trees Trail continues, meeting Rhinefield Ornamental Drive 1km from its start point.

4) From here, there is an optional (1.4km) out-and-back detour, following Rhinefield Ornamental Drive to cross the A35 road, 300m after which a short right-hand path leads to another famous tree, the **Knightwood Oak**. This fenced-off behemoth is over 500 years old with a trunk girth of over 7m (you could alternatively drive here after completing this walk). Back at the Tall Tree Trail's junction with Rhinefield Ornamental Drive, cross the drive (turn left if coming from Knightwood Oak). Return via the woodland path on the drive's other side, which curves back to your car park after 1km.

17. Le Catioroc Headland to Fort Grey via Shingle Bank, L'Erée Headland, Lihou Island & L'Erée Beach

Stroll by seabirds, wading birds, seals and sought-after molluscs on Guernsey's storied shores

NEED TO KNOW

START/FINISH: Le Catioroc Headland car park by Mont Chinchon Battery (200m northeast of GY7 9LT, the closest postcode for sat-nav purposes) – 550m (¼ mile) northwest of Perelle (parking free)/Fort Grey, St Pierre du Bois, GY7 9BY (parking free)

DISTANCE: 8.75km (5 ½ miles) (part one way, part out-and-back)

TIME: 2 ½–3 hours

KEY SPECIES: Ormer, aquatic warbler, orchids

MAP: States of Guernsey's/Digimap's Bailiwick of Guernsey Map

TRANSPORT: Guernsey Airport (flights from London Gatwick/Manchester/Birmingham/Bristol/Southampton) – 6km (3¾ miles) southeast, then bus to Le Croix Martin bus stop, 200m west)

WALK ACCESSIBILITY: Mostly accessible to wheelchair/pushchair users; dogs not allowed on L'Erée Beach May–Sep

DIFFICULTY: Easy

SPECIFIC EQUIPMENT: Swimwear

MORE INFORMATION: visitguernsey.com

Guernsey has an unusual concoction of influences: France (the Channel Islands of which Guernsey is a part are far closer to French shores than English ones, and the territory once belonged to the Duchy of Normandy) and Germany (the island was occupied by German troops during WW2) have left their marks here alongside those of the UK. In fact, Guernsey is a bailiwick: a crown dependency that sets its own laws and holds its own elections. The island's wildlife is varied too. In the southwest, the coastal zone is a potpourri of sandy shores, rocky reefs, saltmarshes, reedbeds, vegetated shingle bank, grasslands and the causeway-accessed island Lihou – all in especially close proximity – and this piques the interest of some diverse fauna and flora.

Many separate nature reserves along this coast make up the overarching Lihou Island and L'Erée Headland Ramsar site. La Claire Mare reserve is one of Guernsey's prime birdwatching locales, where breeding reed warblers and stonechats are joined by scarce aquatic warblers in autumn, plus overwintering snipes, water rails, ducks and gulls. Lihou, meanwhile, sports a remarkable 214 seaweed varieties besides its contingent of seabirds and waders. You can also expect to spot grey seals as well as common and bottlenose dolphins, while special mention goes to locally celebrated sea molluscs the ormers, Guernsey

delicacies beloved by gourmands. Later on in the walk, some of the loveliest orchid meadows in all the British Isles are a draw in April and May, February through July is seabird breeding time and October and November oversee overwintering birds arriving and the likelihood of sighting dolphins rise.

The only thing likely to tire you on this straightforward shoreside walk is the number of things to see. Roads follow the walk around the beach stretches, just not on Lihou and L'Erée Headland, so wheelchair and pushchair users can experience most of this. To walk out to Lihou Island, you'll need a low tide: check tide times beforehand.

ROUTE DESCRIPTION

1) From the car park, occupying a lonely headland northwest of Perelle Bay, a path a short distance southwest along the road leads to **Mont Chinchon Battery**, part of the 18th-century defences built by the British to quell any invasion likely to result from the French Revolution. Alongside is **Le Trépied dolmen**, an impressive Neolithic chambered tomb. Historic sights seen, continue along the shore or the road until you reach the parking at the northeast end of **Shingle Bank Nature Reserve**.

ORMER

Their unique taste makes these sea snails a gourmet Guernsey food, and they are often exposed on low-tide rocks. But many rules restrict the harvesting of them and incur hefty penalties if broken: the world's first recorded underwater arrest happened on the island in 1968 after a scuba diver was spotted ormer-foraging.

2) The vegetated shingle bank, a rare habitat UK-wide, forms a natural barrier protecting land just behind from the sea and forging a haven for wading birds like oystercatchers. As you progress southwest along the path beside it, though, keep an eye out for a left-hand path leading alongside a red-roofed house to **Claire Mare Nature Reserve** and a well-placed hide providing excellent birdwatching, particularly in autumn and winter. The big spots are autumn's aquatic warblers: only 40-odd of these birds are known to stop off in the British Isles annually. Also watch out afterwards for another left-hand path across the road, this time after the houses, to **Colin Best Nature Reserve**. Here, a transitional habitat between the saltwater marshes and freshwater ponds, along with coastal grassland, allows ducks and waders to thrive.

3) Up ahead rears **L'Erée Headland**. The route veers briefly inland to the left of houses to a junction where a left-hand turn runs the short distance to **Le Creux es Faies**, a passage tomb dating to at least 2500 BC. Afterwards, climb the headland itself on a zigzag path passing **Fort Saumarez** off right. Then curve left around the grassland where plants scarcely seen on the UK mainland, like sand crocus, are found. On the headland's far side,

you'll see the causeway leading out to **Lihou Island Nature Reserve**.

4) If tides permit, the out-and-back walk to Lihou from here – 2.75km, including circuiting the island – transforms this route into a real adventure. The westernmost point in the Channel Islands has a ruined monastery, abundant birdlife, a tidal pool where you can swim at its western end and, above all, a remote, peaceful feeling. Back at the Guernsey end of the causeway, you now turn right to continue skirting the headland and proceed southeast onto beautiful, sandy **L'Erée Beach**.

5) After taking time to enjoy the beach, your route runs along the sand only about 300m before coming up onto the Route de la Rocque Poisson road at the beach car park. You're heading inland now to see some exquisite orchid fields: if you don't wish to see them or Fort Grey at the end, there are several bus stops along the road for returning back to the start. For orchid-oglers and fort fanatics, turn right along the road, staying beachside, for 150m, then swing left on Rue de Marais. Next, take the first right and follow the lane along: continuing straight ahead, this becomes Rue des Vicheris in 250m. After this, you'll soon spy the fields of **Les Vicheries Nature Reserve**, traditionally managed to preserve their wildflowers. The fascination for many visitors is the loose-flowered orchids: the flower spikes have several widely separated flowers, almost unheard of among UK mainland orchids. Other wildflowers also grow here, and paths maintained around field edges let would-be photo-takers get close. Follow Rue du Douit du Moulin back to the beachfront afterwards.

6) Bearing left on beachfront-running Route de Rocquaine, you can keep on the grass on the right for around 375m. After this, it's 400m more along the road to **Fort Grey**, the walk's end, jutting distinctively into the sea and home to a compelling maritime museum.

RETURNING TO START: Bus 91, car or bike

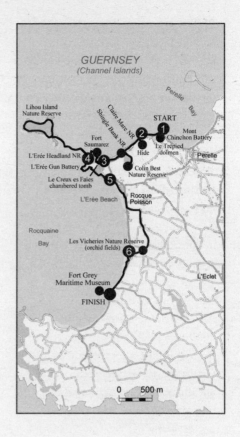

18. Acres Down & Bolderwood from Millyford Bridge

Scout for goshawks and deer on woodsy heaths across this fetching old royal hunting ground

NEED TO KNOW

START/FINISH: Millyford Bridge car park, SO43 7GR – 3.25km (2 miles) west of Lyndhurst (parking free)

DISTANCE: 10.25km (6¼ miles) (circular)

TIME: 2½–3 hours

KEY SPECIES: Goshawk, honey buzzard, fallow deer

MAP: OS Explorer OL22

TRANSPORT: Lyndhurst Fire Station bus shelter, 4km (2½ miles) east

WALK ACCESSIBILITY: Not wheelchair/pushchair accessible; dogs under close control and on leads at Bolderwood Deer Sanctuary

DIFFICULTY: Easy–Moderate

MORE INFORMATION: newforestnpa.gov.uk

Goshawk

Protected since 1079 when William the Conqueror decreed it a royal hunting ground, the ancient New Forest probably offers today's best insight into what the English medieval rural landscape was like. The forest's blend of widely dispersed, well-preserved mixed woodland and tussocky heath (the greatest expanse of heathland remaining in Europe, no less) is splendidly showcased on this time-lost trail.

The goshawks that were fixtures of country life for centuries but subsequently got hunted to UK extinction are now back breeding in the New Forest and a sight to behold in the skies above the springtime heath. Rare honey buzzards haunt the heath in summer, while great and lesser-spotted woodpeckers, treecreepers and, near woodland streams, kingfishers and firecrests, are other avian highlights. Special mention also goes to the forest's fallow deer: this walk takes you to one of the best places to observe these creatures in the wild.

This route is all on well-defined paths, tracks or lanes, and contour lines change little, but paths do get muddy.

ROUTE DESCRIPTION

1) From the car park at the route's beginning, the northbound track beyond the vehicular access barrier is clear. Follow this across **Highland Water**, a pretty peaty stream you will cross twice on the walk, where lesser-spotted woodpeckers and kingfishers are spotted. After 300m, where the main track continues, branch right (north-northeast) on a smaller path climbing serenely through magnificent mixed woodland of oak, beech and conifer.

2) After 600m, emerge onto the open tree-dotted heath of **Acres Down** (89masl) with wonderful views as far

GOSHAWK

Breeding in the New Forest once more as of 2002, after a 120-year absence, goshawks are now found in several scattered locations across Britain. They are larger than the closely related sparrowhawks, while shorter wings and longer tails distinguish them from the more-common buzzards.

south as the Isle of Wight (location of walk 19 in this book). Watch out here for displaying goshawks in spring, plus redstarts and woodlarks. You'll wind through a second patch of woodland before swinging slightly left (north) to join the main track traversing the down.

3) Bear left. The track trundles across the heath top, ignoring several cross-paths, and into another tract of woodland to meet a wider track leading to Acres Down Farm campsite. Turn left, soon reaching a 4-way track junction by the farm buildings.

4) Turn left, immediately taking another left-hand track fork, to reach Acres Down car park. Through the vehicular access barrier, proceed on the gravel forest track leading for almost 2km southwest. You cross the Bagshot Gutter stream and, eventually, Highland Water again. Just afterwards, the main track swings hard right and you continue straight ahead (still southwest) on a dirt path. This meets another broader track after 500m.

5) Turn right. Your track curves left, then right, then gently climbs to bear acutely left at a junction marked by a wooden post. From here it's 375m to the road gate at **Bolderwood Deer Sanctuary**.

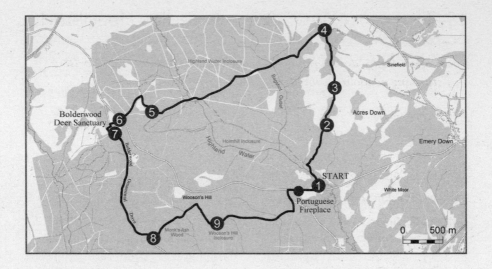

6) The sanctuary is the New Forest's best spot for observing wild deer. To see the fallow deer herd and continue the walk, cross the road and the car park beyond to Bolderwood Ornamental Drive, turning left and then right through the trees and following signs to the **viewing platform** overlooking a meadow the herd frequent. Afterwards, take the path running right of a wooden bench to loop back onto Bolderwood Ornamental Drive.

7) Turn right on the drive, at this point marked by wooden fences on both roadsides, for 1.5km. The drive bears southeast, passing the entrance to Bolderwood Cottage, swinging south then southeast again. Despite this being a trafficked road, the wood-fringed verge makes pleasant walking.

8) After 1.5km, at a low vehicular access barrier on the right, a broad path entranceway ushers you left and beyond a barrier on a path running northeast through Monk Ash Wood. Bridge a stream and, 200m later at a clearing and path junction, swing sharp right (southeast) as your route enters Wooson's Hill Inclosure. Almost 300m later, bear left at a path junction and soon reach the inclosure's main forest loop track.

9) Your route now turns left, running 1km to a 4-way crossroads with a wider, well-metalled track. Turn left here then 70m later, fork left to presently meet a road. Turn right along the roadside, passing the distinctive **Portuguese Fireplace** war memorial and arriving at Millyford Bridge car park after 400m.

19. Tennyson Down & the Needles Headland

Coast over chalky downland where rare birds and flowers, butterflies and stunning seaboard provided a famous poet's muse

NEED TO KNOW

START/FINISH: Tennyson Down NT car park (325m/ ¼ mile south of PO39 0HY, the closest postcode for sat-nav purposes) – 1.25km (¾ mile) south of Totland (parking charges may apply)

DISTANCE: 12km (7½ miles) (circular)

TIME: 3–3½ hours

KEY SPECIES: Dartford warbler, kestrel, purple hoary stock

MAP: OS Explorer OL29

TRANSPORT: Southampton ferry terminal – 43.75km (27¼ miles) northeast, on mainland. Take ferry to East Cowes – 29.75km (18½ miles) northeast, then bus via Newport to Golf House – 1.5km (1 mile) west

WALK ACCESSIBILITY: Not wheelchair/pushchair accessible; dogs under close control

DIFFICULTY: Easy–Moderate

MORE INFORMATION: nationaltrust.org.uk

The Isle of Wight's Needles Headland is not short of claims to fame. It sports one of Britain's most distinctive landmarks in its trio of chalk stacks stepping out into the English Channel, it is where one of the country's fabled poets, Alfred, Lord Tennyson, lived and drew inspiration and it is where wireless telecommunications began. It is also home to important grass-and-chalk downland, being restored to exude its natural abundance of past centuries. Downland flora includes the purple hoary stock, found only in a few locations countrywide, plus vetches attracting Adonis blue butterflies. June, when flowers and butterflies brightly colour the clifftops,

> **DARTFORD WARBLER**
> Distinguished by a ruddy breast and striking red-ringed eyes, this warbler is making a comeback, due to factors such as milder winters. The bird had previously declined to just a few pairs UK-wide by the 1960s.

is sublime. Dartford warblers perch on gorse and the cliffs provide sightings of kestrels, peregrine falcons and fulmars. In 2020, *Autumnwatch* followed the story of the Isle of Wight's very own sea eagles, reintroduced to the island in 2019 after an absence of 240 years.

Chalk paths swiftly get slippery: what with the strong winds and exposed clifftops too, take care when walking.

ROUTE DESCRIPTION

1) The car park is in a former chalk quarry: facing the quarry face, take the track left, soon reaching a bench and steps on the right. Continue straight, following the signposted T24 path. Pass through a bridle gate, proceeding on a path at the bottom edge of the trees. Emerge onto open ground after 600m, ignore a path branching right soon after and, about 1.25km from the bridle gate, arrive at a 4-way marker post.

2) Make a 90-degree turn left onto Green Lane, a bridleway. About 300m later, reach a T-junction. Turn left here for the short out-and-back detour to **Farringford House and Gardens**, residence of landscape and nature poet Tennyson from 1853 to 1892. The gardens here are kept faithful to the 'careless-order'd' way the Tennysons liked them, the poet so loving the flora that he permitted

none to be cut. Back at the T-junction, your route continues straight on 375m to Gate Lane in Easton.

3) Turn right, passing the beautiful thatched **St Agnes Church** and **Dimbola Museum** on the right, then following a roadside path to a toilet block and Freshwater Bay bus stop (buses to Newport). Turn right. This dead-end lane passes a country house, continuing straight at the drive end onto chalky cliffs, swinging right along them over magnificent **Tennyson Down**.

4) This is one of Britain's most important chalk downland habitats, being restored to open grass-topped downland by removing trees and allowing rabbits and cows to graze, thus returning it to its state a century ago. Consequently, wildlife is making a comeback: watch for kestrels, the rare Dartford warbler and butterflies like the Adonis blue. There are several paths across the down and as long as you keep the coast fairly close on your left, it doesn't matter which you take.

Dartford warbler

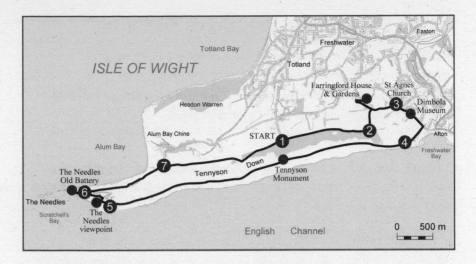

Continue past **Tennyson Monument** on the highest point (147masl) and, 4.5km after coming onto the clifftops, approach The Needles headland as cliffs on your left now swerve to cut in front of you.

5) Pick up a path bearing right that becomes a concrete track. As this track bends sharply right before the fenced-off NCI station, a path leads down to a good **viewpoint** of The Needles. Back on the track and just after the NCI station, swing left on a concrete path descending with The Needles dead ahead. This swoops down to the entrance of **The Needles Old Battery** (entrance fees may apply), a 19th-century military fort that, more significantly today, boasts the best views of **The Needles**. These chalk stacks, the outermost crowned by a lighthouse, make up one of Britain's most iconic

natural sights. Your path descends steps to a car park on a road by the battery.

6) Turn right along the road for 1.25km, a path alongside or near it for most of the distance. At a left bend before **The Needles Landmark Attraction** park (encompassing the monument to Guglielmo Marconi's world-first wireless transmission, made here in 1897), keep straight on the signposted T25 path, climbing steps and going through a kissing gate.

7) Keep on the path along the lower end of the slope, a fence on your left. Pass Warren Farm off left. Shortly afterwards, at a path junction, your route bears diagonally uphill (southeast) on a track to a beacon. Pass through a gate, then take the T24 path downhill to the left (northeast) back to the car park.

20. Abbotsbury to the Isle of Portland along Chesil Beach

Behold Britain's biggest tidal lagoon, abundant birdlife and curious insects on a talismanic tract of Dorset seaboard

NEED TO KNOW

START/FINISH: Grove Lane car park, Abbotsbury, DT3 4JH – 650m (½ mile) south of Abbotsbury village centre/Chesil Beach car park, Portland, DT4 9XE (parking charges may apply)

DISTANCE: 16.75km (10½ miles) (one-way)

TIME: 5–5½ hours

KEY SPECIES: Swan (mute and whooper), scaly cricket, little tern

MAP: OS Explorer OL15

TRANSPORT: Ilchester Arms bus stop, Abbotsbury (buses to Dorchester/ Weymouth) – 825m (½ mile) north

WALK ACCESSIBILITY: Not wheelchair/pushchair accessible; dogs allowed but not in swannery and on leads along Chesil & Fleet Nature Reserve restricted access zone Sep–Apr

DIFFICULTY: Moderate

MORE INFORMATION: dorsetwildlifetrust.org.uk and fleetandchesilreserve.org

Chesil Beach is a 29km-long strip of shingle shore running from West Bay near Bridport to Portland but the special stretch from Abbotsbury onwards is this walk's focus. Here the shingle stack becomes a barrier beach (or spit), with the UK's largest saline lagoon, West Fleet and East Fleet, opening behind. This makes a magnet for all manner of birdlife and other unique creatures besides. Protection of this environment is rigorous. The beach and lagoons are enfolded in the Jurassic Coast Unesco World Heritage Site, the Dorset AONB and Chesil and Fleet Nature Reserve – and this helps the fauna to flourish.

Anticipate dunlins, ringed plovers, oystercatchers and some of Britain's largest concentrations of little egrets among the year-round waders, while whooper swans and Brent geese

MUTE SWAN

What would city park lakes, village ponds and rural riversides be without the promise of these white waterbirds with their orange-and-black beaks and wide wingspans. Despite their large size, we humans have long associated swans with elegance and mystery. In Britain, it is a criminal offence to kill them.

overwinter with other wildfowl. A colony of little terns also breeds beachside. The habitat supports more unexpected species too: brown hares and seldom-seen insects like the scaly cricket. Wintertime lets you get quite close to the lagoon wildfowl and has none of summertime's access restrictions, but May still edges it, when sea thrift, sea campion and yellow horned poppy brightly bedaub the Chesil Beach pebbles. Augmenting this wildlife blockbuster is Abbotsbury's swannery, hosting the world's only managed colony of mute swans.

The walk's downside? Its access restrictions: Abbotsbury Swannery opens spring to autumn only and much of Chesil Beach prohibits access May through August to allow reserve birds to breed. The upside? The coast path cuts an alternative route on the lagoon's landward side, from where you'll still see ample lagoon birdlife,

and you get two walks in one, as each route is utterly different. Whichever way you walk, first check Chickerell Firing Range times (gov.uk): when operating, the map-marked zone is out-of-bounds. The shingle walking can be hard going but it's fairly level.

ROUTE DESCRIPTION

1) This walk leads south from the car park when aforementioned restrictions are not in force and for both wildlife-watching and novelty – it follows the country's longest barrier beach after all – is recommended. The alternative is pretty good too, though. This leads east, following the coast path into low hills southeast of Abbotsbury and then back coastwards to still trace the inland West and East Fleet shore for over half its length. Both routes have the same end point: the alternative route is 2.5km longer than the way

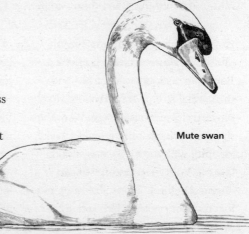

Mute swan

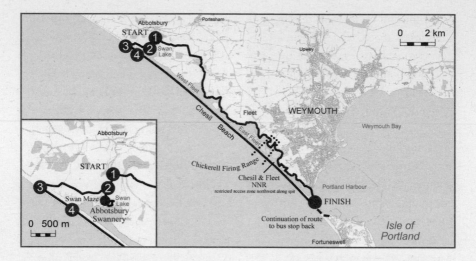

along the beach. Should you select the route described below along Chesil Beach itself, begin by heading south on Swan Lane to **Abbotsbury Swannery**. Nowhere else on Earth can you wander through a breeding mute swan colony and because the 600-strong flock are constantly monitored, there are fascinating insights into the species that can be gleaned here. Further piquing interest is the fact that the site was formerly the turf of a generously endowed abbey: Benedictine monks established the swannery, probably in the 11th century. There is an admission charge, however. If you wish to pay to see the swans, this walk's distance includes circling the swannery's main lake, named – can you guess? – **Swan Lake**. If you do not wish to pay, you need only proceed 275m along Swan Lane to pick up a right-hand track

(swannery visitors need to return to this point afterwards too).

2) The track runs across a field to a gate. Then take the path cutting diagonally left across the field corner to steady a course along the field edge. Follow this field edge and then another, meeting the coast path 800m later. Turning left, you soon hit the **Chesil Beach** shingle.

3) Turn left (southeast) along the beach. This really is a formidable assemblage of pebbles, sculpted into several levels by the sea: the difference between beach top and lower foreshore is up to 15m. Going can be arduous, and for the next 14km this walk sticks along the shingle. Civilisation may be close across the water but is absent from this route until the very end. In 750m you reach the anti-tank blocks marking the start of the NNR's restricted access zone. Between this line and the Portland boundary stone at the zone's southeast end it is birds only between May and August.

4) Continuing along Chesil Beach you get nice views across to the swannery as the saline lagoon opens up on your left. Afterwards, a surprising sense of isolation kicks in. The landward side is quiet farmland with few houses visible and you are walking hemmed in by sea and lagoon, as likely to hear squawking birdlife as any human sound. Halfway along on the lagoon's landward side, the shore juts out noticeably further. Across the water, you'll spy the houses in Fleet, the village on which J. Meade Falkner's *Moonfleet* was based. Along the shore ahead, meanwhile, you'll already see your endpoint, the Isle of Portland, linked to the mainland only by a road bridge and by this beach. Mainly, though, this is somewhere to enjoy some unforgettable lagoon birdwatching. The lagoon narrows after East Fleet with the Weymouth conurbation looming off left; the walk's end is in another 3.25km at the car park immediately after the lagoon end. If you are taking public transport back to the start, continue a little further along the beach to Portland Beach

Road roundabout, then head inland along Hamm Beach Road to reach the bus stop back: an extra 1.5km.

RETURNING TO START: Bus 1 (Castletown National Sailing Academy–Weymouth King's Statue), then bus X51/X53 (Weymouth King's Statue–Abbotsbury Ilchester Arms), car or bike

21. Cerne Abbas Giant Circular

Check out Britain's largest chalk figure, bewitching butterflies and a mightily impressive badger-watching spot

NEED TO KNOW

START/FINISH: Buckland Newton village hall car park, DT2 7BZ (parking free)

DISTANCE: 16.5km (10¼ miles) (circular)

TIME: 4–4½ hours

KEY SPECIES: Badger, Adonis blue and Duke of Burgundy butterflies

MAP: OS Explorer 117

TRANSPORT: Saw Mills bus stop (buses to Dorchester/Sherborne/Yeovil) – 4.5km (2¾ miles) northwest of start and New Inn bus stop , Cerne Abbas – 250m (¼ mile) southwest of Cerne Abbey en route

WALK ACCESSIBILITY: Not wheelchair/pushchair accessible; dogs not allowed at Dorset Badger Watch, otherwise on leads or under close control

DIFFICULTY: Moderate

MORE INFORMATION: cernevalley.co.uk, nationaltrust.org.uk and badgerwatchdorset.co.uk

Rolling chalky green hills above, historic villages with fine taverns and tearooms below, this Wessex ramble through rolling inland Dorset runs like an illustrated excerpt from a novel by local lad Thomas Hardy. It loops Britain's largest chalk figure the Cerne Abbas Giant, a 55m nude club-wielding male etched into hillside above Cerne Abbas village. It's been variously interpreted as a Middle Ages depiction of Hercules and a 17th-century slight at Oliver Cromwell: you decide.

Plenty ogle the giant, but precious few know his chalky surroundings coax out some extraordinary butterflies, including the radiant Adonis blue and the elusive Duke of Burgundy. Near journey's end, meanwhile, is Dorset Badger Watch, an outstanding opportunity for badger observation. Hides take you close to the stripy mustelids as they emerge from their setts in the evening to scout for food. Springtime is special, when badger cubs first venture above ground and orchids tint the grassy slopes.

There are four moderate climbs, two short main road walking sections and muddy paths aplenty on this walk.

ROUTE DESCRIPTION

1) From **Buckland Newton** village hall, turn right along the B3143 road. Opposite The Old Chapel Stores, a grassy path branches right. Curve around a field edge and through a gate, then 120m along, a second gate in the left-hand hedge leads to a path crossing the following field to a gate. Now head down another field to a 5-bar gate onto a lane junction.

2) You are still in Buckland Newton here. Keep straight, immediately passing the **Gaggle of Geese** pub. Turn left on Lockett's Lane, passing the turn-off to the business park and the farm buildings thereafter, and swing right on the muddy, stony bridleway of Rousiball Lane.

3) Climb Bladeley Hill on this track, ignoring three turn-offs, for 1.75km to Old Sherborne Road. Turn left along this sometimes-busy road, reaching a track signposted 'Beech Tree House' on the left after 35m.

4) Here turn right through a gate into woodland. Immediately pivot right on a path branching away from the road at an acute angle and pass through a gate along a field bounded

BADGER

Dorset's chalky, woodsy countryside is ideal badger sett-building territory, where ground is easily excavated and roots offer protection. Up to 12kg in weight and 75-100cm long, Eurasian badgers are chunky creatures, their distinctive face stripes warning potential predators against attack.

by woodland on the left. After this long field, turn left on an enclosed track and, a few metres later, swing left through a gate on a pretty track bearing you down the woodland edge.

5) Exit the woods at a gate, following the hedged track between fields to a track junction before buildings at Minterne Parva. Turn left. The track twists around a field edge to a 'Private' sign on the right. Continue straight on a path with the hedge on your right, climbing to a fingerpost at another field entrance. Here it's easiest to trace the hedge up to the left to reach the footpath gate along the field top. The way here is part of the Wessex Ridgeway long-distance path, showcasing the chalky uplands between Marlborough, Wiltshire and Lyme Regis, Dorset.

6) The path climbs right, ploughing through scrub after a waymark post, passing through trees and reaching a 4-way path junction. Turn right on the path signed 'Cerne Abbas 1¼ miles'. This narrow, unkempt path hits a gate after 400m. Beyond, turn left through woods to cross into a field. The path crosses the field higher up, but it's often easier to follow the field edge right, reaching a stile onto Giant Hill.

7) Delightful **Giant Hill** is, with all its exposed, undeveloped chalky grassland, a butterfly haven for Adonis blues and Duke of Burgundies. Short-eared owls also favour the hilltop. Your path now bears slight left and down, descending the west slopes of Giant Hill. The giant himself is fenced off to prevent erosion, but you'll get your chance to see him. Continue along the giant's protective barrier, then off Giant Hill down steps through woods, passing a 4-way footpath sign and reaching a gate below.

8) Ignore the paths to Cerne Abbas village for now, first detouring to Giant View. Continue west through the gate on a path soon reaching farm buildings. Skirt these to the left, cross the River Cerne, pass a car park, reach Duck Street and turn right: ahead is **Giant View**. After appreciating the giant in all his glory, retrace your steps to the River Cerne. Now, turn right on the riverside path. After 200m cross the river onto Andrew's Lane, leading to Abbey Street in Cerne Abbas.

9) Charming **Cerne Abbas** village lies to the right but your path turns left to the duck pond and entrance to **Cerne Abbey**. Pass through the stone-arched gate into the abbey burial ground. The path leads straight across, past Commonwealth war graves, exiting through another gate. Now bear diagonally right across the

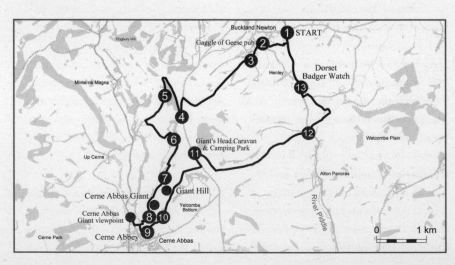

tree-dotted field, gently climbing to some woods. With the woods on your left, continue along the top of the next field to a bench and gate.

10) Pass through onto a path ascending northeast through woods and then grassland, offering impressive views. The path eventually encounters a 5-bar gate. Proceed along the hilltop to a bridleway sign, then swing right along a field hedge to meet Old Sherborne Road again. Turn left and 300m later right into Giant's Head Caravan and Camping Park.

11) Head straight down to the bottom field hedge then turn right, ascending through woods and out of the campsite at a gate. Trace the following field edge to a Wessex Ridgeway sign and gate. Turn left. Follow this track 800m down to Black Barn, then continue 1.25km to join the B3143 after some farm buildings.

12) You now turn left, and can follow the road the entire way back. Yet this walk swings right after several metres through the lower of two field gates. Ascend this field and another, hedges on your left, to a path junction where the Wessex Ridgeway and Hardy Way meet. Turn left on the Hardy Way, down and around to meet a lane at a house. Turn left, then right on the B3143.

13) After 175m along the road **Badger Watch Dorset** appears, a fantastic place to observe badgers. Watch the creatures by arranging in advance to meet here at 6.15pm daily between April and October. You'll be led to hides where you can see badgers leaving their setts to forage: a wonderful spectacle. Foxes, rabbits and bats can be seen too. Afterwards, return along the B3143 for 1km into Buckland Newton and the village hall.

22. Studland Bay to Kingston via Swanage & Worth Matravers

Sample the best track on the Dorset coast's greatest hits – a wildlife paradise of heath, dunes, chalk cliffs and coves

NEED TO KNOW

START/FINISH: Knoll Beach car park, BH19 3AQ – 1.25km (¾ mile) north of Studland (parking charges may apply)/Scott Arms bus stop, Kingston, BH20 5LH

DISTANCE: 33.5km (20¾ miles) (one-way)

TIME: Full day

KEY SPECIES: Smooth snake, Dartford warbler, Lulworth skipper butterfly

MAP: OS Explorer OL15

TRANSPORT: Studland Heathland House bus stop (buses to Swanage/Bournemouth) – 1.5km (1 mile) south

WALK ACCESSIBILITY: Not wheelchair/pushchair accessible; dogs allowed but on leads May–Sep on Studland Bay beaches

DIFFICULTY: Difficult

SPECIFIC EQUIPMENT: Swimwear

MORE INFORMATION: nationaltrust.org.uk, durlston.co.uk and visit-dorset.com

If Dorset's coastal walks were a greatest hits album, this might be Queen's *Bohemian Rhapsody*: long, lavishly operatic, full of hugely varying sections that seamlessly combine and good enough to keep replaying. This kicks off circling an internationally important wildlife habitat, Studland and Godlingston Heaths NNR, where heath, dunes, bog and *carr* (waterlogged forest) form environs conducive to all six native British reptiles, including the endangered smooth snake. Then there are iconic Old Harry Rocks, a grand assembly of chalk cliffs and stacks, Durlston Country Park NNR with its wonderful wildflowers and gigantic guillemot colony, and postcard-worthy curving cove Chapman's Pool. Oh, and one of Dorset's finest pubs, which the route diverts unabashedly to sample.

April to May is when Studland Bay's reptiles emerge from hibernation, when Durlston's guillemot colony is mustering and when most of the area's 500+ recorded flowering plant species are at their blooming best. The route is mainly along the Jurassic Coast Unesco World Heritage Site and is well marked, but there are enough steep ascents and descents that, combined with the distance, make this a challenging day's walk.

ROUTE DESCRIPTION
1) Knoll Beach car park is the furthest **Studland Bay** car park from Studland village. The bay is a popular beach destination, but this walk is primarily concerned with the **Studland and Godlingston Heaths NNR**, and begins by looping round some of it. Heading north on the track from the car park delivers you to the Little Sea lake, meaning you'll see this site's astonishingly diverse terrain types (coastal heath, freshwater lake and sand dune). You could sight rare smooth snakes and sand lizards as well as common lizards, slow worms, adders and grass snakes, plus Dartford warblers. There are numerous paths: venturing about

halfway along Little Sea, then circling back beach-side to pass the start car park is 2.25km.

2) Passing Knoll Beach Café on the right, the route continues south, then southeast beside the beach. Pass Sandy Beach, then South Beach, after which the coast path diverts slightly inland to round woods by Harry Warren House wedding venue 1.5km southeast of your start point.

3) Turn left at the path junction to reach your next objective, Handfast Point and its remarkable views over **Old Harry Rocks**, deeply indented chalk cliffs with broken chalk formations trailing out in front into the sea. Afterwards, proceed southwest along the cliffs, views of enviably situated resort town **Swanage** opening up ahead, and 3.25km later, at the town's first houses, swing right inland onto the Ballard Estate. This temporary swerve away from Swanage Beach avoids the groynes (timber barriers erected to prevent longshore drift) retaining the sand. Follow the main estate road south, taking the second right and passing onto Ballard Way. Swing left on Redcliffe Road, then continue straight onto Ulwell Road: this hits **Swanage Beach** again in 425m. Follow Shore Road along the beach.

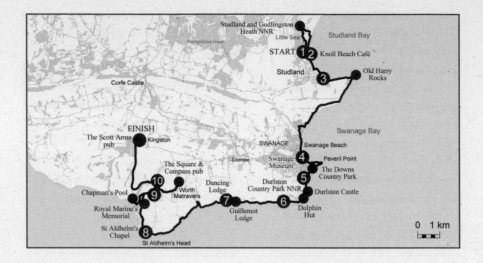

4) At the beach's southern end, skirt left around Mowlem Theatre to walk Swanage's prettiest section of waterfront. Pass **Swanage Museum**, swinging right by The Stone Quay onto High Street and turning left. Do not take the left-hand turn onto the pier but continue slightly further along the road to branch left on the coast path by Swanage Amphitheatre. It's now a straightforward run east to Peveril Point, then southwest over pleasant The Downs Country Park. Turn left when the path meets curving Belle Vue Road and left on Durlston Road in 175m.

5) Next, turn left on Isle of Wight Road, delivering you into **Durlston Country Park NNR**. This fabulous place is much more than an urban green escape. Landscaped grounds

wrap a Victorian **castle** housing a **visitor centre** displaying live images from the park's clifftops: a unique way to watch Southern England's second-largest guillemot colony, plus razorbills and fulmars, breeding here in spring and summer. Wilder areas comprising meadows, heath and woods support one of the UK's greatest varieties of flowering plants (springtime highlights are early spider orchids and early gentians). Therefore many butterflies are present too, including the extremely rare burnt-orange Lulworth skipper. Round Durlston Head with its **Great Globe**, one of the world's largest spherical stone sculptures, and **Dolphin Hut**, an excellent dolphin observation point, and continue to Anvil Point Lighthouse. The coast path departs the NNR after the third field on the right.

6) It's now 2.25km along the coast to first **Guillemot Ledge**, Swanage area's highest cliffs, and shortly afterwards **Dancing Ledge**. This flat cliffbase wave-cut platform exhibits an unusual phenomenon when certain tides wash across, with the seawater appearing to 'dance' as it moves.

SMOOTH SNAKE
Inhabiting just a few heathland sites countrywide, the smooth adder-like snake is a constrictor: it crushes prey to death. Fortunately for most living things, it favours the also-rare sand lizard for its meals.

7) Some especially lovely coast path follows, rimmed by spectacular limestone cliffs: look for 'strip lynchets', ancient terrace-like field systems, en route. Forge southwest via Seacombe Cliff, descend to Seacombe Bottom, deviate inland to avoid old Seacombe Quarry before turning left up steps back onto clifftops. Next, descend to Winspit Bottom, then climb **St Aldhelm's Head** (108masl). Besides smashing views, the headland has the comely Norman **St Aldhelm's Chapel** on an out-and-back path north from the coastguard station.

8) Next is the 1.9km northbound tramp to the grassy slopes above Chapman's Pool cliffs. This features the steepest descent (and, then, ascent) of the walk with steps to help. Keep straight at the pretty stone-walled **Royal Marine's Memorial** and in 400m reach a path crossroads. Left here, this walk includes the steep out-and-back 1.6km descent/ascent to **Chapman's Pool**. The cove is spectacularly ramparted by a semi-circle of cliffs and is great for rock pooling and wild swimming. Back at the path junction, bear inland over a stile. Keep along the right-hand edge of the following field, cross a stile, bear diagonally across the next field and cross another stile onto a track.

9) Turn left. This becomes a lane by a junction at some stone houses. Your onward route bears left here at the footpath sign. However, following Renscombe Road right brings you into Worth Matravers and one of Dorset's best country pubs **The Square and Compass**, welcome refreshment after your long walk. It's 2.3km out-and-back. Returning from Worth Matravers, it's right at the previously mentioned lane junction, soon curving to a gate.

10) The initially paved way is squeezed between the steep contours of North Hill (right) and West Hill (left) as it descends left below glorious gorse-clad slopes. After passing some houses and woods lower down, a track swings southwest for excellent views of Chapman's Pool before veering north for a steady climb on a paved lane to a gate by the approach to Westhill Farm. Keep straight on, following South Street 925m to a road junction in Kingston. Turn right. Presently pass the Scott Arms pub on the left and, just beyond along West Street, the bus stop for buses back to the walk start.

RETURNING TO START: Car, bike or bus 40 (Purbeck Breezer) to Swanage bus station then X50 to Heathland House in Studland village

LONDON & SOUTHEAST ENGLAND

23. Richmond Park via the Tamsin Trail & Pen Ponds

Find solace in the wildness of this London nature haven

NEED TO KNOW

START/FINISH: Richmond railway station, London, TW9 1EZ

DISTANCE: 17km (10½ miles) (circular)

TIME: 3–3½ hours

KEY SPECIES: Red and fallow deer, skylark, cardinal click beetle

MAP: OS Explorer 161

TRANSPORT: Richmond railway station at start, plus stations/bus stops around the park periphery and car in the park car parks (parking free)

WALK ACCESSIBILITY: Accessible to wheelchair/pushchair users; dogs on leads May–July, at other times follow local signage (there are dog-free, dogs-on-leads and dogs-under-close-control areas)

DIFFICULTY: Easy–Moderate

MORE INFORMATION: royalparks.org.uk

The largest of the Royal Parks, Richmond Park is among the capital's most important zones for fauna and flora. Established as a deer park by King Charles I in the 17th century, the park's show-stealing creatures are still the 600-odd red and fallow deer. Grey squirrels, foxes, rabbits, voles and three bat species reside here too, alongside woodpeckers, skylarks and even escaped parakeets! Over 1000 beetle species are also supported, including national rarities like the cardinal click beetle. And that is not forgetting the

CARDINAL CLICK BEETLE
Richmond Park's venerable oaks are a lifeline for this nationally scarce beetle, red or orange in colour, that lays its eggs in rotten oak wood.

legions of resplendent trees, especially the oaks, many of which predate the park's creation. But this walk's greatest appeal, perhaps, lies in discovering how pristinely wild somewhere so close to Central London can be.

In 2018, *Springwatch* captured the wild beauty of this park across the seasons. The park is at its loveliest ablaze in autumnal hues. The deer rut also takes place then.

Paths are well-surfaced and generally level throughout, with plenty more park trails besides the below, enabling you to tailor this route into a choose-your-own adventure.

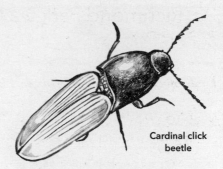

Cardinal click beetle

ROUTE DESCRIPTION

1) Turn left out of Richmond Station on The Quadrant/A307 road. Turn right at Lloyds Bank; this lane heads straight on, becoming a cut-through alongside Richmond Library Annexe onto Little Green. Take the path heading diagonally left across Little Green park opposite; follow the path across onto Richmond Green beyond. On Richmond Green's far side, near the site of the former Royal residence **Richmond Palace**, turn left on the road, then right at the triangular green onto Friar's Lane. When the lane hits the River Thames, turn left.

2) Follow the Thames-side path under Richmond Bridge, past Rotary Gardens and on to Buccleuch Gardens. At the end of Buccleuch Gardens with Petersham Meadows ahead, at black iron railings and a gaslight-topped sign, turn left to proceed onto the A307, crossing the road then entering the gate onto Terrace Field just to the left. Take the right-hand path in the park beyond,

cutting onto Nightingale Lane near the junction with Richmond Hill road. Follow Richmond Hill to the right, reaching a double mini roundabout with Richmond Park's Richmond Gate entrance ahead.

3) Through the gate, turn left to follow the blue arrow-signed Tamsin Trail clockwise around the park periphery. This broad path generally hugs a treeline of resplendent oaks, staying close to the park boundary, and passes many of the deer's favourite spots. The path curves east around to Sheen Gate, running in front of Sheen Lodge, skirting Adam's Pond and again largely following the treeline to cross Beverley Brook on a footbridge, reaching Roehampton Gate.

4) The Tamsin Trail now sticks alongside the left-hand (east) side of Priory Lane, the golf course on its left. At a prominent tree stump on the right, the trail curves left away from Priory Lane, crossing Beverley Brook

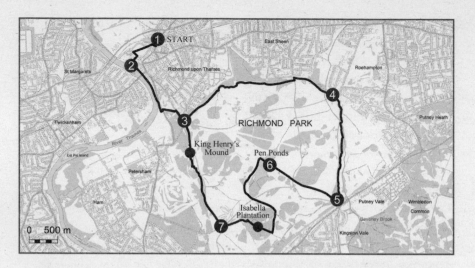

on its own bridge. Next, follow the broad, surfaced path through Killcat Wood, with another path more closely hugging Beverley Brook to the left and Priory Lane off to the right. This path ambles south through tree-dotted parkland to reach a car park near Robin Hood Gate.

5) Leave the Tamsin Trail here, before Robin Hood Gate, by turning right and crossing the car park at a legend board. Cut through onto Priory Lane, which you cross onto a track through trees leading northwest. You are now on the Capital Ring Walk. Keep straight ahead in the same direction at the subsequent path crossroads, heading into open parkland. The grassy path makes for the left-hand side of the woods ahead, meeting Spanker's Hill Car Park and continuing northwest

to reach **Pen Ponds**. This is the site of an ongoing conservation effort to attract herons and skylarks, which are often seen here.

6) Cross between the two main ponds. Turn left, tracing the path along the shore and around the south of Pond Plantation to a metalled park drive. Continue straight over the drive onto a wide path. As this soon curves left, your route bears a slight right on a grassy path meeting the north edge of Isabella Plantation. The path follows the plantation edge clockwise to reach its entrance at the black-metal Broomfield Hill Gate. Follow the main path through **Isabella Plantation**, a woodland garden renowned for its dazzling spring-flowering azaleas, to Peg's Pond Gate. Then head west across grassland to Ham Cross.

7) Here, back on the Tamsin Trail, your path follows Queens Road northwest, presently veering away from the road to draw alongside Petersham Park car park. Deviating briefly from the Tamsin Trail, turn left here into Pembroke Lodge grounds, its entrance between two hedges. Bear right in front of the house to spot a wooden sign for King Henry's Mound. This indicates the path through Pembroke Lodge Gardens to the **King Henry's Mound** viewpoint, from where there are brilliant views of Central London. Your route then proceeds north, re-joining the Tamsin Trail, which runs parallel to Queens Road back to Richmond Gate. Return on your outward route to Richmond Station; alternatively, follow Richmond Hill 1km straight on (northwest) to where it meets the A307, which soon curves right to reach the station.

24. Chesham to Chorleywood via Chess Valley

Board the London Underground to check out Chess Valley and some of the capital's closest 'real' countryside

NEED TO KNOW

START/FINISH: Chesham railway station, HP5 1DH/Chorleywood railway station, WD3 5ND

DISTANCE: 13.5km (8½ miles) (one-way)

TIME: 4–4½ hours

KEY SPECIES: Water vole, kingfisher, banded demoiselle damselfly

MAP: OS Explorer 181/172

TRANSPORT: Chesham railway station at start

WALK ACCESSIBILITY: Not wheelchair/pushchair accessible; dogs allowed

DIFFICULTY: Easy–Moderate

MORE INFORMATION: chilternsaonb.org

The Chilterns AONB is 883km^2 yet Chess Valley, threading along its fringe close to where London's suburban sprawl begins, is reckoned to number among its loveliest parts. It's a thrill to be able to hop on the Metropolitan Line in Central London to start this surprisingly rural walk, which traces the River Chess, a nationally rare chalk stream. Shallow, warm water replete with brown trout and grayling fish feeds an ecosystem of woods, water meadows and fields. These support a notable population of water voles and fashion a home for kingfishers, grey herons, green sandpipers and stonechats.

With local human populations also reliant on the river's water and the London periphery nearby, jeopardy is never far away either. The upside to close-by conurbation, though, is that as a critical component of London's green belt, the Chess' course has become a conservation focal point, with a string of nature reserves en route.

This gentle walk (while stretches are suitable for pushchairs/wheelchairs, the route overall is not) is undeniably at its finest on a clement spring day, when plants like purple loosestrife and water forget-me-not bedeck the riverside.

ROUTE DESCRIPTION

1) Turn left immediately outside Chesham station entrance down steps onto a tarmacked path and turn left. This feeds into Punch Bowl Lane in 225m: follow this to the T-junction with Red Lion Street and cross the road with care, briefly turn left, then take the path on the right, which runs parallel with Red Lion Street and then Amersham Road (the A416) through Meades Water Gardens. Return onto Amersham Road at Wheelhouse Veterinary Centre, turning right along it until a roundabout. Take the first exit onto Moor Road and follow it under the railway bridge along to a junction after tennis courts. Here, continue straight onto the Moor, the grassy parkland ahead, between two squat red-brick buildings. Turn left to follow the Moor's edge to the **River Chess**.

2) Follow the riverside path, soon entering woodland. After the Moor's end, the path reaches a weir, with a fishery through the trees on the right. Cross the river here, turning right along the other bank. Cross back over again in 350m after the fishery lakes. The path heads straight, then swerves left into an industrial estate. Turn right after the first group of buildings on the right, heading southwest for the trees beyond and the path on their far side. Swing left with the treeline on your left

BANDED DEMOISELLE DAMSELFLY
One of only two damselflies with coloured wings, the banded demoiselle is a beauty: males are metallic blue with a dark-blue wing spot; females metallic green with pale green wings. They love slow-flowing lowland waterways like the River Chess.

to meet Hollow Way Lane 325m later. Here, bear left (more-or-less straight ahead). At Latimer Road, turn left for 175m, past the recycling centre to a right-hand lay-by. Your path leads back from here to curve right with the river on your right through two tree-flanked fields. The path veers away from the river to feed into trees onto Blackwell Lodge drive. This soon swings right onto Blackwell Hall Lane; turn left. The lane curves left ahead: keep straight on the track at a Chess Valley Path sign.

3) Passing a house on the left and at the track fork afterwards bearing right, you now strike across open countryside and the walk's prettiest scenery. Hit the right-hand edge of woodland ahead, then head along its edge for 1.5km with fields on the right: lovely **Latimer Park**, designed by Capability Brown, opens up, and you'll soon see **Latimer House** on the left. After passing the house and more woods alongside, continue on the parkland path straight ahead to Stony Lane at a kissing gate. The comely houses of **Latimer** village are just left here; your route heads straight across.

4) Continue through open grassy fields with Baldwin's Wood off left and the river below right. In 1.25km, pass just right of Mill Farm Barns onto the lane at Chenies Hill. Turn left, then swing right through a metallic 7-bar gate with a walker's gate alongside. This path delivers you to **Frogmore Meadows Nature Reserve**, an SSSI where traditionally managed meadows hemmed by woods make a fine location to watch for barn owls, water voles and a springtime patchwork of wildflowers from lady's bedstraw to southern marsh orchids. The path passes briefly into the woodland here, then curves right to a short right-hand path which leads to a **wildlife-viewing platform**.

5) It's now 375m with fields on the left and riverside woods on the right to where the path crosses Holloway Lane. Afterwards, a track continues straight on past watercress beds (the Chess' water has optimal watercress-growing conditions) to Moor Lane, where you swing right. The damp grassland of **Sarratt Bottom Nature Reserve**, where hedgehogs are often spotted, is now off right. Continue straight at the dead-end sign.

6) The way ahead (track, then path) over the next peaceful 1km comes close to the riverside, maximising chances of kingfisher sightings. Near the end of this section, the river swings further from the path and you pass a house off right before reaching New Road.

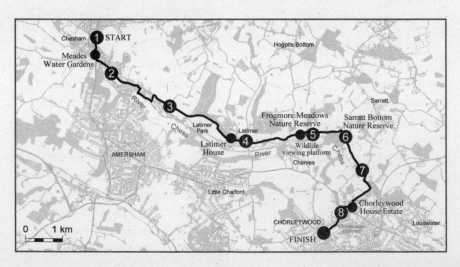

7) Continue straight across the field ahead to the hedge, then swing right to cross the river, afterwards turning left on a wider track. Presently, at a junction with a house drive, bear right (more-or-less straight ahead) but then turn right in another 175m. Next, proceed with woodland initially on the left for 575m to a parking area near the corner of a metalled lane ahead. Turn left on the lane through **Chorleywood House Estate** grounds. Pass some tennis courts on the right, swing right through woodland to brush the tennis courts and reach Chorleywood House Drive after skirting a car park. Turn left, briefly right on Rickmansworth Road and left on Common Road beside some ponds.

8) Instead of taking Common Road into Chorleywood, follow the paths parallel with it back through **Chorleywood Common** off left. You might see muntjac deer, foxes or badgers. The common's main path eventually winds southwest to a car park: turn left on the road beyond the car park, then right on Betjeman Gardens. As this cul-de-sac bends left near its end, spot the cut-through on the left through houses: a twisting flight of steps leading down to Chorleywood station.

25. Blean Woods

Saunter through centuries-old broadleaf woods, being serenaded by
nightingales and surprised by heath fritillary butterflies

NEED TO KNOW

START/FINISH: RSPB Blean Woods car park, CT2 9DD – 525m (¼ mile)
northwest of Rough Common (parking free, entry charges may apply)

DISTANCE: 11km (6¾ miles) (circular)

TIME: 3–3½ hours

KEY SPECIES: Nightingale, lesser spotted woodpecker, heath fritillary butterfly

MAP: OS Explorer 150

TRANSPORT: Lovell Road bus stop, Rough Common (buses to Canterbury) –
525m (¼ mile) southeast

WALK ACCESSIBILITY: Accessible to wheelchair/pushchair users; dogs on leads

DIFFICULTY: Easy–Moderate

MORE INFORMATION: rspb.org.uk and kentwildlifetrust.org.uk

The Blean Woods NNR, a string
of different woods forming a long
and lovely expanse just northwest
of Canterbury, is Kent's finest
place for nature lovers to make a
pilgrimage. This dendrologists'
delight is Southern England's most
extensive tract of ancient broadleaved
woodland and a veritable mosaic
of various arboreal areas. Expect
deciduous and conifer, mixed, mature
and coppiced, cleared zones of
farmland and heathland and canopy-
obscured ones, which wrap you in a
wild and time-lost woodsy embrace –

the combination of which appeals to
a broad spectrum of wildlife.

The woodland's mascot is the
heath fritillary butterfly, only just
saved from extinction in Great
Britain, in large part due to the
efforts that made these woods an
agreeable environment for the insect.
The continuation of the practice of
coppicing here helps these butterflies
and other creatures flourish. A
nationally significant nightingale
population also appreciates the
coppiced woods, hedgerows and
scrub to make their spring and

summer music. Nightjars and lesser spotted woodpeckers, the UK's rarest woodpeckers, reside here too within trees that are predominantly sessile oak, as well as hornbeam, birch, beech and coppiced sweet chestnut.

A clement late spring day is when you want to stop by. Nightingales perform sweet melodies, and you can linger later into the evening for the chance of spying nightjars or a woodcock roding (making breeding display flights). This route, largely following the waymarked black trail around the heart of the RSPB-managed part of the woods, lets you experience all the above-mentioned types of woodland. There are so many paths that wheelchair and pushchair users will have no problem finding a route to suit. And if this walk isn't a sufficient leg stretch, take on all or part of the Big Blean: a 40km trail circuiting all the Blean woodlands.

Nightingale

NIGHTINGALE

The plain but spectacular-sounding nightingale has one of its decreasing English strongholds in Blean Woods. Almost all the UK's nightingales are found in Southeast England, where they can be heard (and, more seldom, seen) singing their hearts out in scrub, hedgerows, thickets and coppiced woods between April and August.

ROUTE DESCRIPTION

1) Routes here are well waymarked. From the car park, take the path from the northwest corner (the one beside the noticeboard, not the one between benches) through **Church Wood** for 300m to a path crossroads. Continue straight over: the way forks just beyond and you follow the black trail waymark left. It's 475m across a stream to the next path crossroads: continue straight again. You'll soon pass through a large heather-clad clearing, heading northwest. After this at a fork in the trees, bear left (southwest), about 225m after the previous crossroads. This path soon converges with a broader, grassy path and here you leave the black trail, heading left 225m to hit the pleasant forest track of New Road.

2) Turn right, and bear right at the gravel track fork immediately ahead. Follow the broad track 500m to a crossroads and then take the wide grassy path left. Keep on this, again briefly the black trail, for 975m to another path crossroads. Next, swing right to cross the Sarre Penn stream. Ignore side paths and continue 200m to a T-junction where you turn left. This path soon curves around right (northwest). Then, where it makes a 90-degree right-hand turn northeast, you again leave the black trail that leads away left. The northeast leg takes you back to the main forest track in 675m.

3) Swing left into **North Bishopden Wood** (the suffix 'den' suggests the place was originally for keeping pigs). Open trackways or rides like this, which let in ample sunlight, are good spots to search for heath fritillaries in late spring. The track curves around right and reaches a left-hand path in 800m where you turn left through the trees to rejoin the black trail briefly, bearing right (northeast) along the woodland's northwest edge.

4) Stay tuned on the next section, which passes several farmland hedgerows, for nightingale song. In 550m, bear left on the track a few metres to the lane at Denstroude Farm. Turn right along the lane for 325m, passing the mobile coffee stop and glamping site at Brook Farm. You then make a 90-degree right-hand turn, ignoring the angled right-hand track by the white bollards alongside. The track runs 400m south-southwest past several buildings to re-enter the woodland ahead at a left-hand stile just after the first trees.

5) Bear left after the stile to pick up the black trail once more, walking east-southeast along the north of **Grimshill Wood**. Bear left (northeast) at a junction, staying close to the woodland periphery, then swing right in around 275m to follow a path southeast to a wider, rutted forest track. You brush the track, but instantly veer northeast on a path between a break in the woodland. Hold this course for 525m, bear right at the T-junction and then take the next right again to bear southwest along Grimshill Wood's main track.

6) In another 450m, turn left on the path forging southeast back through Church Wood to another division of ways at a red trail marker post. Bear left. Continue on a light woodland path with fields through the trees to your left. Turn right in 300m. Your path now bears south for 375m, crossing Sarre Penn and then ignoring two right-hand paths,

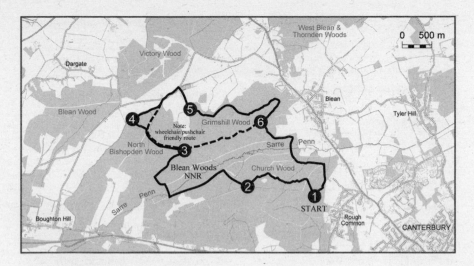

before bearing left at the third path junction. Proceed on this path, crossing a stream and keeping ahead immediately afterwards, to hit the next path crossroads in 525m. Here, turn left then in a few metres right before a bench. Now a red/green/black-waymarked post points the way right. A long straight down the east edge of Church Wood sets you on course for the 625m walk south then southwest to the car park.

26. Devil's Punch Bowl & Hindhead Commons

Admire one of nature's most astonishing reclamation acts in Surrey's hilly wooded heaths

NEED TO KNOW

START/FINISH: Devil's Punch Bowl car park, next to Devil's Punch Bowl Hotel in Hindhead, GU26 6AB (parking charges may apply)

DISTANCE: 5.25km (3¼ miles) (circular)

TIME: 1½–2 hours

KEY SPECIES: Lesser spotted woodpecker, woodlark, roe deer

MAP: OS Explorer OL33

TRANSPORT: Hindhead Crossroads bus stop (buses to Aldershot/Haslemere) – 450m (¼ mile) west

WALK ACCESSIBILITY: Mostly accessible to wheelchair/pushchair users; dogs allowed

DIFFICULTY: Easy–Moderate

MORE INFORMATION: nationaltrust.org.uk

Woodlark

One of the British countryside's greatest-ever comebacks was orchestrated when the engineering feat of the Hindhead Tunnel opened through the Surrey Hills AONB in 2011. Beforehand, the busy London to Portsmouth road, the A3, ran right through the midriff of this woodsy heathland. Now the tunnel takes the road underground, and nature has made a triumphant return.

The Devil's Punch Bowl itself is an almighty, mostly wooded depression in the ground resulting from underground stream erosion and has long been a visitor attraction: now it's an SSSI reunited once more with the encompassing heath of Hindhead Commons and bisected by quiet tracks rather than a traffic-snarled A-road.

Wildlife appears to appreciate the change. The full trio of UK woodpeckers, including the rare lesser spotted, tap their rhythms in the woods. Feathered heathland hangers-out include Dartford warblers, woodlarks and nightjars. This terrain is also perfect for rabbits and roe deer:

you can catch both nibbling grass on the heath where Exmoor ponies also graze and where occasional adders will soak up the sun in warm weather.

Late summer here, when the heath heather and gorse beguile with radiant purples and yellows, is best. Decent paths mean wheelchair- and pushchair-users could manage most of the route, except perhaps the part up Gibbet Hill.

ROUTE DESCRIPTION

1) There are two main tracks ostensibly continuing on in the same direction beyond the car park's vehicular barrier posts: take the grassy one leading off directly behind the sculpture. It's odd to think that this is the former course of the A3, and that the trunk road now runs far beneath this peaceful spot. In 175m, where paths intersect with your track at an angled crossroads, bear right to shortly turn left on a broader tarmacked byway open to all traffic. Follow this 625m, passing the **Sailor's Stone**, remembering a sailor murdered by rogues in this thoroughfare's darker past, to reach an unmarked path branching right.

2) Here, the trees fall back to reveal cracking views of the **Devil's Punch Bowl** but the best panoramas come by taking the right-hand path up to **Gibbet Hill** (272masl), highest

WOODLARK

The woodlark, while not nationally rare, should get birdwatchers' hearts beating faster: in the UK it only breeds on Surrey heaths and a handful of other locations. Streaky brown on wings and back, it sports a distinguishing white eye stripe running back and around its neck, resembling a visor pushed too far down.

point on the punch bowl rim and Surrey's second-highest summit too. You can see the London skyline in clear weather. From certain angles, the higher curving edge of the Punch Bowl where you now stand resembles a natural amphitheatre, the bottom over 100m below. One legend relates that the bowl was gouged by the devil scooping out earth to throw at the Norse god Thor, but there are myriad other stories about the bowl's formation too. The **Celtic Cross** near the top interestingly commemorates the three fellows found guilty of the aforementioned sailor's murder.

3) Departing Gibbet Hill, take the path descending southeast (seemingly straight ahead from the angle you approach the top on this walk) to meet a track in the woods below. Continue straight over on a tree-lined track, watching and listening out for woodpeckers. This track too runs southeast for a time, then veers left (northeast) to reach **Temple of the Four Winds**. Here are the scant remains of the hunting lodge of William James Pirrie, the British shipbuilder whose Harland & Wolff firm built the White Star Line ships, including *Titanic*.

4) Pick up the solid forest track running southwest for 975m. Just before buildings at Combe House you swing right, the buildings on your left. The way forks just beyond the buildings: fork left, proceeding west-northwest 375m to hit open ground with houses off right. You presently reach the drive, which curves up to join a metalled lane. Turn left. The lane tunnels through the trees, bringing you alongside houses on the left and, in 575m, an acutely angled right-hand gated track.

5) The track delivers you straight up northeast onto a lovely stretch of bracken- and tree-scattered **Hindhead Commons**. The straightforward route here means you can revel in the views, with the South Downs clearly showing off south, and concentrate on wildlife-spotting the creatures featured in the introduction. Exmoor ponies were introduced to restore the heath's health: it had become clogged by scrub and pine after commoners stopped grazing the land. After 525m, you deviate slight left (north-northwest) from the northeast-bound route but remain on a distinct track. Meet the Greensand Way long-distance path 225m later and turn left. The broad sandy track carries you west-northwest across to the corner of the heath and, ignoring side-turnings, you'll reach the car park approach road after 625m.

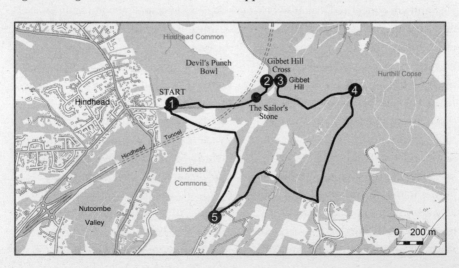

27. Harting Downs

Take a trip back in time to this ancient woodland-swaddled downland, bastion of rare butterflies, birds and curious molluscs

NEED TO KNOW

START/FINISH: Harting Down NT car park, GU31 5PN – 1.5km (1 mile) southeast of South Harting (parking charges may apply)

DISTANCE: 6km (3¾ miles) (circular)

TIME: 1–1½ hours

KEY SPECIES: Duke of Burgundy butterfly, cheese snail, short-eared owl

MAP: OS Explorer OL8

TRANSPORT: Uppark bus stop (buses to Chichester/Petersfield) – 1.25km (¾ mile) northwest

WALK ACCESSIBILITY: Not wheelchair/pushchair accessible; dogs on leads

DIFFICULTY: Easy–Moderate

MORE INFORMATION: nationaltrust.org.uk

Downs, so far as citizens of Southeast England are concerned, can also be ups: they are chalky, grassy hills that roll across Sussex, Kent and Surrey and elsewhere and, most significantly, make up the South Downs National Park. The vital vestige of chalk downland at Harting Downs has a time-lost feel, its blend of grassland, scrub and woodland embosoming one of the most pristine, species-rich locales in the Southeast. This walk elevates you onto verdant, flower-quilted ridges framed in far-reaching views, dips you down into centuries-old pockets of woods and brings you close to some enchanting and downright eccentric wildlife in the process.

Late spring is a radiant time for visiting. Rare butterflies emerge, like the Duke of Burgundy with wings patterned like fragments of terracotta. By summer, flowers like pyramidal orchids dot the grasslands, carpenter bees drone and skylarks chirp overhead. You may well sight roe (late summer) and fallow (autumn) deer rutting and a wintertime walker may descry a short-eared owl or, on the woodland floor, that nationally rare mollusc the cheese snail. Buzzards, sparrowhawks and kestrels boss the skies year round.

Paths are clear, well defined and well signed throughout. There is one climb of note (up Beacon Hill); the others are gentler ascents.

> **CHEESE SNAIL**
> With a known UK range limited to the hills of South and Southeast England, cheese snails are distinguished by the fine hairs that young and some adults have on their shells. Find them in deciduous and mixed woodland leaf litter and on rotting wood.

ROUTE DESCRIPTION

1) The car park near the top of Harting Hill (229masl) is flanked by open grassland, along the northern edge of which runs the South Downs Way long-distance footpath, which this walk initially follows. The easiest route onto the South Downs Way is by crossing the grassland to the northeast and passing through a gate. The views opening up on this first section are fantastic: all the way to the North Downs. Continue on the South Downs Way along the grassy top of the downs, skirting a clump of woods on the left and slightly descending towards a larger spread of woodland ahead.

2) Just before the woodland to the right are **Cross Dykes**, Iron Age mounds that perhaps originally functioned as boundary markers and today enable a fascinating mix of insects to survive. The mounds retain the sun's heat, which makes attractive conditions for yellow meadow ants to build anthills. Usually during April and July, common blue butterflies seek out these ants to help extract the butterflies' secretions; in return, ants care for the common blues' caterpillars in earthen annexes of their colonies. Also look out hereabouts for Duke of Burgundy butterflies, cheese snails and violet-tinted carpenter bees. By now you will have noticed the other path running parallel to your own over on the right. Switch to this path now, keeping the woodland edge on your left for 150m before passing through it on a well-defined chalky-white path to a gate onto more open downland. Beacon Hill now looms ahead. Ascend it by heading east-southeast through the field fence at a gate.

3) Rounding the top of **Beacon Hill** (242masl) on a minor deviation from the main path, continue southeast down the other side to see the chalky track bearing the South Downs Way threading up the hill ahead and the same track also curving to your right at an acute angle. Turn

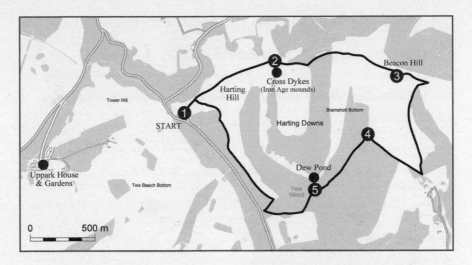

right on the track. This then curves left with the slopes of Beacon Hill on the right and a long finger of woodland immediately left. Swing south, slightly veering away from the woodland edge, and skirting the lower slopes of Beacon Hill. Meeting more woodland, your path next swings northwest for 500m with Beacon Hill still to the right and woodland on the immediate left.

4) At a signpost, you veer away from Beacon Hill and descend southwest, woodland now on either side, to reach the **Dew Pond** on the right on the valley bottom, the happy domain of frogs and dragonflies.

5) Your route then proceeds southwest, passing into a yew wood. This climbs back up the contours of Harting Hill, bending west then northeast to meet a long, open grassy area between two bands of woodland. It is now a gentle ascent, staying close to the woodland on your left and swinging slightly left (northwest) at the end of the treeline to gradually descend onto the South Downs Way. Here, turn left on your outward route back to the car park.

Cheese snail

28. Goring, Great Chalk Wood, Hartslock Nature Reserve & the Thames

Perambulate a portion of chalky Chiltern Hills escarpment esteemed for its orchids

NEED TO KNOW

START/FINISH: Goring & Streatley railway station, RG8 0EP (parking charges may apply)

DISTANCE: 10km (6½ miles) (circular)

TIME: 2½–3 hours

KEY SPECIES: Orchids, grey heron, red kite

MAP: OS Explorer 171

TRANSPORT: Goring & Streatley railway station at start

WALK ACCESSIBILITY: Not wheelchair/pushchair accessible; dogs allowed

DIFFICULTY: Easy–Moderate

MORE INFORMATION: bbowt.org.uk and chilternsaonb.org

Grey heron

The Goring Gap is no boring blank, but a divide between the AONB-designated chalky uplands of the Chiltern Hills and the North Wessex Downs, renowned for its array of wildlife. This walk winds through the woods and chalk grasslands of the Chilterns AONB, a topography propitious for some of the country's most magical orchid displays come spring and summer. Such rich flora in turn encourages butterflies like the chalkhill blue, as buzzards and red kites coast above. You'll take in an idyllic stretch of the River Thames on this one too, where you might spot swans or grey herons, before ending in genteel Goring with its trove of historic red-brick and timber-framed houses.

May through July are the loveliest months, when the orchids carpet woods and hillsides and when waterbirds on the Thames are breeding.

ROUTE DESCRIPTION

1) Turn left out of the railway station on Gatehampton Road, then right onto Reading Road. Take the second right onto Whitehills Green, a housing development and cul-de-sac. Follow Whitehills Green around to the left, then at the far line of houses aim for a yellow parking restriction sign on the right, beyond which your path squeezes through a gap in a hedge onto Sheepcot Recreation Ground.

2) Here, make for the far left-hand corner ahead. A hedge gap leads onto the Chiltern Way long-distance

path. Turn left, following the path up over the chalky rise. Pass two field boundaries. At the end of the third field, the path swings right, dropping to a gate with **Great Chalk Wood** ahead. Go through the gate, along the field edge and enter the wood.

3) Yours is the main woodland path, trundling southeast. Ignore two paths and a muddy track that branch off from it. Chiltern Way signs point the way as you reach the eastern boundary of the wood. At a connecting path, turn right to gently ascend up the eastern boundary, then near the garden of Chalkwood House on the left, turn right (east) at a sign along the south of the wood. Leave the wood at the southwest corner on a tree-lined path between fields, reaching two large barns at a lane.

4) Turn left, charming views of the Thames valley unfolding below. Approaching a clump of woodland, the lane kinks right, then left soon after. At the left-hand kink, take the track branching right to a field gate, before which a muddy tree-lined path snakes down the chalky slopes. After 725m this reaches the gate of **Hartslock Nature Reserve**.

5) This wood-fringed chalk grassland is famous for its fabulous flowers. Orchid species including the bee,

ORCHIDS

For all the excitement wild orchids generate among nature lovers, they are part of the largest family of flowering plants, Orchidaceae, boasting some 28,000 species. With colours ranging from white to pink to purple, it's thought their popularity with humans is due to their perfectly symmetrical blossoms.

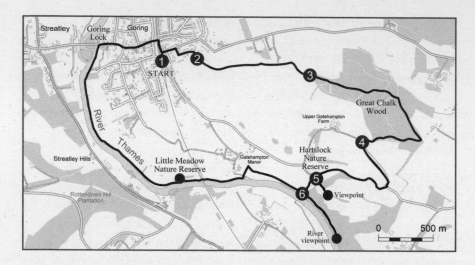

monkey, pyramidal, lady, common spotted and twayblade thrive here, as well as the rare pasque flower. Looking at the wood ahead, you'll see two gates. Climb up the wood through the first, arriving on a chalky grassy ridge with a **viewpoint** showing off one of the prettiest stretches of the River Thames below. Look for red kites: their reintroduction in the Chilterns AONB was pivotal in re-establishing the raptor's UK-wide populations. Descend via the grassland path that returns through the second gate. Back by the reserve entrance, turn left down through the meadow onto the Thames Path.

6) This walk briefly journeys left along the Thames Path to a **river viewpoint** by a WW2 bunker, where swans and grey herons can be observed. Then follow the Thames Path back in the other direction into Goring for the final 4.25km. Passing under the railway bridge, you walk through **Little Meadow Nature Reserve**, a creepy-crawly haven home to the rare clubtail dragonfly. At the beauty spot of Goring Lock, leave the riverbank, turning right onto Goring High Street. Follow the High Street through Goring to cross the railway bridge after 500m. Turn right to return to Goring & Streatley railway station.

29. Cuckmere Valley, Cuckmere Haven, Seven Sisters Country Park & Friston Forest from Alfriston

Marvel at what a melange of unsullied river, wetland, chalk grassland and beech forest can do for animals and plants

NEED TO KNOW

START/FINISH: The Willows car park, Alfriston, BN26 5UG (parking charges may apply)

DISTANCE: 23.25km (14½ miles) (circular)

TIME: 6½–7 hours

KEY SPECIES: Little egret, short-snouted seahorse, beech

MAP: OS Explorer OL25

TRANSPORT: Market Cross bus stop, Alfriston (buses to railway stations at Berwick and Seaford) – 225m south (and also en route)

WALK ACCESSIBILITY: Not wheelchair/pushchair accessible; dogs allowed

DIFFICULTY: Moderate

SPECIFIC EQUIPMENT: Swimwear

MORE INFORMATION: nationaltrust.org.uk, sevensisters.org.uk, forestryengland.uk and publications.naturalengland.org.uk

All that is green and pleasant in rural England has been distilled into the Cuckmere Valley around Alfriston: ambling rivers and rambling beech forest, village greens and venerable buildings and chalky hillsides presiding over glimmering saltmarshes. Crucially, in Sussex's sole undeveloped river mouth, what you see is a landscape where wildlife has been more or less left to 'get on with it'.

And the wader-frequented wetlands enfolding the river's lower course duly combine with chalk grasslands, heath and cliffs to provide year-round fauna and flora delight.

On riverside meadows, scan above for skylarks and bankside for kingfishers. Wintertime wetland shenanigans star curlews and wigeons, while in summer you could spot dunlins and black-tailed godwits. Little egrets, a bird this area has excelled at protecting, fish with grey herons in marshland back from Cuckmere Haven beach as seabirds nest on the cliffs. The seawater, meanwhile, contains an important population of short-snouted seahorses, threatened worldwide as fishing industry bycatch. And those chalk grasslands secrete many surprises: adders, several less-common butterflies and green-winged orchids among the floral rarities. Rabbits, meanwhile, appear to be everywhere at all times.

May, when wildflowers bedeck the grasslands, takes some beating. This is when you'll clock breeding seabirds and summertime waders and find Friston Forest's fine beech trees fully leafed. This walk's terrain, variously protected as an SSSI or NNR, gets a little up-and-down in Seven Sisters Country Park but is generally pretty level.

ROUTE DESCRIPTION

1) From the car park, turn left along North Street into charming historic **Alfriston** village, where you'll pass Sussex's only surviving **Market Cross**. Continue straight onto High Street and make a left along an alley with a brown signpost pointing to **St Andrew's Church**. The church is a handsome, 14th-century spired affair: this walk branches right across the green for a closer look at this and timber-framed, also-14th-century,

Alfriston Clergy House, the first property ever acquired by the NT, alongside. Afterwards, follow the village green's left-hand side along River Lane briefly, keeping straight at the bend to cross **White Bridge** over the River Cuckmere.

2) Follow the east riverbank 1.75km, a fine stretch for spotting kingfishers, then pass Litlington village off left. Turn right to cross the signpost-marked wooden footbridge, then continue along the west riverbank. Almost 2km along is the 1.1km out-and-back path to **Litlington White Horse** on High and Over hillside, cut in 1924 and visible for some distance beforehand. If you do climb up, there are fantastic views back over Friston Forest. Back along the riverside, it's more comely chalk grassland meadows, bounded by pockets of woodland and low hills. Despite the benign inland location, the river is already tidal here and will soon meet the sea in dramatic style.

BEECH
If oak is king of British broadleaves, so beech is regarded as queen. The tree's dense domed canopy means beech woodland is often linked with rare, retiring wildlife. Identify beeches through their oval, wavy-edged leaves. Britain's tallest native tree is a 45m-high Derbyshire-based beech.

3) Another 1.4km and you hit the A259 road, where you turn left to reach Exceat Bridge by Cuckmere Inn. A pavement then helps walkers along around a right-hand bend to **Seven Sisters Country Park** entrance on the right, with a **visitor centre** on the left.

4) The country park is an interesting mix of the sinuous River Cuckmere with its surrounding saltmarsh, alongside which your route runs south, and undulating chalk hills. Staying near the water, you will likely see considerable wader action. Branch left immediately inside the country park entrance at a signpost to presently join the South Downs Way. You follow this 1.75km to the sea but, at a signpost and gate after 900m, you have the out-and-back option to venture off right out over river channels on raised paths: very handy for wader-spotting.

5) The park guards the approach to **Cuckmere Haven**. Just before the beach, marsh and river channel flank you on both sides: a great opportunity to look for little egrets and grey herons as they fish amicably together. Bulky chalk cliffs rear up off left. Turn left along the shingle beach, watching out for plants like yellow horned poppies. At the cliff base, take the chalky path gouged in the steep slope up to the clifftops and clifftop path. Turn right,

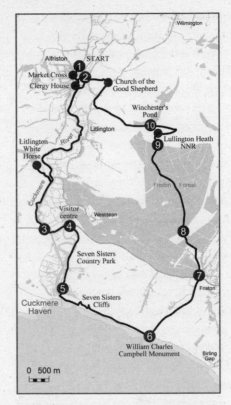

skirting the more tangled heath off left across noticeably shorter grass. After 325m, this path curves around left to rejoin the South Downs Way, where you turn right. Spring is grand here, when you might sight fulmars, kittiwakes and jackdaws cliffside and green-winged orchids on the unimproved chalk grassland behind.

6) Proceeding along the rolling, pearly-white chalk cliffs for 1.75km, you reach **William Charles Campbell Monument**, wrapped by a seat for appreciating the exquisite cliff views.

105

Now fork left and inland on a grassy path. This meets a metalled drive by a cattle grid and Crowlink NT car park in 1.5km. Pass the car park on your left, continuing along the lane to the A259 by a church at Friston village edge. Across the road, on the grassy junction triangle's left side, spot a hedge-recessed gate and pass through.

7) Take the right-hand of the two route options behind the hedge, on a north- and then north-northwest-running path skirting downhill left of a building in a clearing and then diagonally across a field. Head straight over the drive of Friston Place with its impressive ornamental garden, continuing across a field to turn left on another track inside the treeline ahead. At a track junction in 250m, do not take the track hard right but the path ahead and slight right (north-northwest): this soon emerges into the open, crossing Friston Hill.

8) Meet another track at the treeline of **Friston Forest** ahead and keep straight over. Follow this route north 475m to a track junction, north-northwest 775m to another junction, then northwest 400m to a third junction, where you keep straight to presently curve right (northeast) to the next track junction in 800m. You're traversing Southeast England's most extensive beech forest planted in modern times as you go.

9) Continue straight into beautiful **Lullington Heath NNR**. One of Britain's largest remaining expanses of chalk heath sharing space with spreads of chalk grassland, this is home to numerous flowers and butterflies alongside foxes, badgers and several mice, vole and shrew species. The reserve entrance point is a notorious adder sunbathing spot. The path curves left (northwest), then right (northeast) up to a crossroads, then sharp left on the track along to **Winchester's Pond** – good for spotting dragonflies, damselflies and birds like whitethroat having a drink.

10) Continue straight at the next track junction, forking right at the junction 575m later to descend into Lullington village. Turn right on the road for 500m, passing the left-hand lane to Alfriston and arriving at an entrance to some houses on the left. Turn left. A path squeezes through to pretty **Church of the Good Shepherd**, one of England's smallest churches, swinging in front of the church, then through a field hedge gap. Next, continue along the field with the hedge on your immediate right to reach Lullington Road by a house. Continue straight to rejoin your outward route, keeping straight again, over White Bridge, back into Alfriston.

EASTERN ENGLAND

30. Dedham Vale's Constable Country

Meander riverbanks that inspired Britain's great landscape painter and still entice outstanding birdlife

NEED TO KNOW

START/FINISH: Dedham Riverside car park, CO7 6DH – 450m (¼ mile) north of Dedham (parking and entry charges may apply)

DISTANCE: 10.75km (6¾ miles) (part circular, part out-and-back)

TIME: 2–2½ hours

KEY SPECIES: Redshank, teal, pollarded willow

MAP: OS Explorer 196

TRANSPORT: Marlborough Head bus stop, Dedham – 400m (¼ mile) south (and also en route)

WALK ACCESSIBILITY: Not wheelchair/pushchair accessible; dogs allowed

DIFFICULTY: Easy

MORE INFORMATION: nationaltrust.org.uk and rspb.org.uk

With its lush meadows fringed by mature oak, willow and alder, threaded by the sinuous River Stour and sprinkled with venerable historic properties, the Dedham Vale AONB resembles the landscaped parkland of a rambling centuries-old English country estate. It was here on the bucolic Suffolk-Essex border that John Constable lived and gleaned inspiration for the magnum opuses that would become regarded as the foremost examples of British landscape painting. On this magical maunder through Constable Country, the sleepy countryside scenes he captured are not just canvases, but still-living, still-breathing things.

Birds are just as enamoured with this environment. The riverside might treat you to grey herons or the blue flash of a kingfisher, while the SSSI-designated

Redshank

POLLARDING

The River Stour sports exquisite examples of pollarded willows. Pollarding, an ancient rural management strategy, is now ingrained in the countryside's fabric. Historically, pruning upper tree branches created dense, high-quality, accessible timber and formed distinctive land boundaries. But it also aids wildlife; encouraging new growth and often letting trees live longer.

marshland beyond harbours waders galore. An early springtime morning is perfect for enjoying the courtship displays of lapwings and redshanks, as cowslips and yellow rattle paint riverbanks gold.

This walk is level and well signposted but does get muddy.

ROUTE DESCRIPTION

1) From the car park, turn left on the B1029 road. Cross the River Stour, turning right through the gate onto winsome riverside meadows. Pass through one field hedge, then at a footpath sign on a tree guard bear gradually left, cutting across the meadow away from the riverbank. The path arrives at a kissing gate 100m back from the riverbank.

2) Follow the tree-lined path to a path junction. Turn left. The path crosses an arm of the Stour, dividing into a path (branching right) and a track (branching left). Take the track, bending around a house onto Fenbridge Lane, which gently ascends to a lane junction.

3) Turn right on Flatford Road for 850m, a footpath running alongside the lane most of the way, to a 4-way junction where Flatford Road swings sharply left. Turn right here, descending through NT Flatford Mill car park and then past the welcome hut down steps to a sunken lane by Flatford Mill.

4) This is the enchanting heart of Constable Country. Here is a **Constable Exhibition**, the **RSPB Flatford Wildlife Garden** where swallows, goldfinches and other birds busy themselves in the foliage, a riverside tearoom and shop in charming **Flatford Bridge Cottage** and, down the cul-de-sac along the near riverbank, **Flatford Mill** and **Willy Lott's Cottage**, scene of Constable's best-known painting *The Hay Wain*. Flatford Mill itself is now a field centre offering courses in various aspects of the arts and the environment. Constable was born in nearby East Bergholt, son to a corn merchant who owned Flatford Mill. Most of his paintings depicted rural life hereabouts, where he grew up.

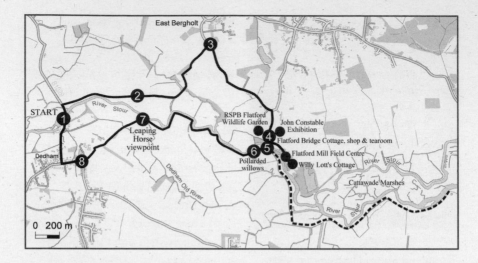

5) Cross Flatford Bridge over the Stour to where your return route leads through a kissing gate across riverside meadows. Beforehand, this walk proceeds on an out-and-back path to the left to **Cattawade Marshes.** This important wetland, enfolded by arms of the Stour, attracts redshanks (spring), teals and wigeons (winter) and year-round lapwings and oystercatchers. This path along the reserve's southern edge is the closest you can get to the wader wonderland. It is your choice how far you walk; this route ventures 2.25km before returning to the Flatford Bridge kissing gate.

6) Through the gate, proceed along the river's southern bank across meadows studded by beautiful pollarded willows. Pass (but do not cross) Fen Bridge after 1km. The riverbank path then bends to arrive at a short enclosed stretch bounded by kissing gates, the setting of Constable's painting *The Leaping Horse.*

7) After the second gate, the path bears diagonally left across the meadow to a copse. Continue onto a tree-lined path running past a kissing gate and information board on the left. Walk straight on, swinging slightly right (southwest) along a widening path now on open ground. This soon kinks left by a house and 'Private' sign on a track meeting Brook Street in Dedham at a bend.

8) Bear right into **Dedham** village's attractive centre, replete with Georgian and medieval timber-framed buildings. At the pink-hued Essex Rose Tea House, turn right on the B1029. Walk out of Dedham, reaching the start car park after 400m.

31. Hickling Broad

Catch great crane sightings in winter and special summertime peeps at rare butterflies within this watery Norfolk Broads wildlife paradise

NEED TO KNOW

START/FINISH: Hickling Broad NWT car park, NR12 OBW – 2km (1¼ miles) east of Hickling Heath (reserve entrance fees may apply)

DISTANCE: 5km (3 miles) (partt circular, part out-and-back)

TIME: 1–1½ hours

KEY SPECIES: Common crane, swallowtail butterfly, marsh harrier

MAP: OS Explorer OL40

TRANSPORT: Bus stop at junction of Heath Road/Sutton Road – 3.25km (2 miles) west

WALK ACCESSIBILITY: Wheelchair/pushchair accessible to jetty (Point 3); no dogs

DIFFICULTY: Easy

MORE INFORMATION: norfolkwildlifetrust.org.uk

Broads are large, shallow bodies of water, interconnected by rivers and dykes and surrounded by marshland, which form a web of more than 300km of inland waterways across Norfolk and Suffolk. They are a lure for human water lovers from boaters to walkers and a critical habitat for a gamut of birds, insects and mammals. Head to Hickling, the biggest of the Norfolk Broads, if you want to experience the wildlife here but have time to do so in just one place.

Due to the latticework of streams and channels around Hickling Broad, complete circuits

Swallowtail butterfly

by foot are surprisingly convoluted, but excellent NWT Hickling Visitor Centre is a base for one of the broad's finest wildlife walks.

Following well-maintained trails, and via five prime wildlife-viewing spots, this little amble can lead you to some mighty big bird and butterfly sightings. Many of the country's common crane population roost here between November and February, during which time marsh harriers also overwinter. Bitterns, barn owls and kingfishers are glimpsed year-round, Chinese water deer have been introduced, otters are more elusive residents and the summertime glory is the swallowtail butterfly, found only in the Norfolk Broads.

ROUTE DESCRIPTION

1) From **NWT Hickling Visitor Centre**, head across the picnic area to the south and, beyond, through two sets of gates on an all-ability path heading south. This runs between small ponds and later another double set of gates to **Cadbury Hide**. This

SWALLOWTAIL BUTTERFLY

This extremely rare butterfly has its only UK sanctuary in the Norfolk Broads. Its mosaic-like wing patterning, buttercream with black veins and blue margins, dazzles Hickling Broad visitors in summer, when it feeds on plants like ragged robin and thistle.

is a good area for catching glimpses of swallowtail butterflies in summer.

2) Your path now arcs with broads off to the left to a path junction at a wooden bench in the reeds after 250m. Turn left, then soon turn left again on the short out-and-back path to **Secker's Hide**, with great views out over the water and reedbeds. Back at the beginning of the Secker's Hide path, turn left to reach Hickling Broad's shoreline after 200m. Turn left. Now trace the edge of a patch of woodland along a path presently curving around to the right and reaching a jetty.

3) At the jetty, the all-ability path ends: wheelchair and pushchair users can backtrack on the outward route to the Cadbury Hide path junction at the wood bench, then take the left fork to return through the reeds to the visitor centre. This walk continues with the woodland on the left and Hickling Broad off right. Your path swings left 200m after the jetty.

4) The path now runs straight along an inlet of Hickling Broad for 400m, passes a **viewing hut** and soon bends right to curve round in front of a house. Reaching the house drive, cross it, proceeding on a track that curves left to run parallel to the drive. Almost immediately, ignore a path to the right

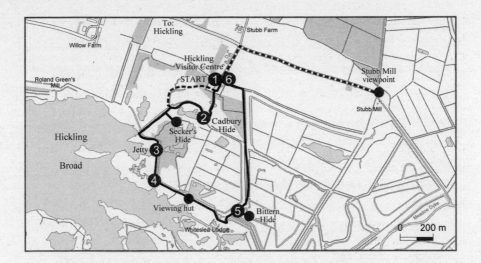

then take the second out-and-back path to **Bittern Hide**.

5) Back at the beginning of the Bittern Hide path, turn right. Your track initially keeps running parallel to the house drive, swinging left then reaching a track junction after 400m. Continue straight on, following the house drive until it bends left back to the visitor centre.

6) The final out-and-back stage of this walk takes you back up the visitor centre approach road until this curves sharp left. Here, turn right on narrow, scenic Stubb Road. After 850m the road ends at **Stubb Mill viewpoint,** the perfect place for viewing cranes and marsh harriers between November and February. Afterwards, return along Stubb Road to the visitor centre.

32. Woodwalton Fen

Discover the watery wonderland of one of Britain's first nature reserves

NEED TO KNOW

START/FINISH: Woodwalton Fen reserve car park (parking along Great Raveley Drain near corner with Chapel Road), PE26 2RS – 2.5km (1½ miles) southwest of Ramsey Heights (parking free)

DISTANCE: 5km (3 miles) (part circular, part out-and-back)

TIME: 1–1½ hours

KEY SPECIES: Kingfisher, marsh harrier, scarce chaser

MAP: OS Explorer 227

TRANSPORT: Chapel Road bus stop, near Ramsey Heights (buses to Peterborough/Ramsey) – 1.5km (1 mile) east

WALK ACCESSIBILITY: Not wheelchair/pushchair accessible; no dogs

DIFFICULTY: Easy

MORE INFORMATION: greatfen.org.uk

Welcome to a tale of conservation past and conservation future. In 1910 wealthy banker and nature-lover Charles Rothschild, concerned by how British countryside was disappearing, purchased land at Woodwalton Fen to create Britain's second modern-day nature reserve (the first, Wicken Fen, had also been a Rothschild brainchild). The wet woodland, meadowland and marsh here, bisected by drains (ditches), is among Britain's last tracts of wild fenland. Home to a staggering 5000 species, this fen's ecological importance is clear. And it is part of the much bigger Great Fen project that will link this reserve with fellow nearby NNR Holme Fen, preserving more fenland for generations of wildlife and humans to come.

For now, though, there is plenty for nature-loving walkers to do. This walk combines aspects of the reserve's Marsh Harrier and

KINGFISHER

Britain has just one kingfisher species: the common kingfisher. Its bright blue and orange colouring stands out as it darts along water surfaces like Great Raveley Drain, scouting for small fish.

Waterbirds Trails, where three bird hides enhance wildlife-watching conditions. Spring and summer see reed buntings and reed warblers foraging in path-side reeds and marsh harriers nesting, while rare flowers like fen ragwort and fen violet bloom. Dragonflies, including the rare scarce chaser, emerge from May to August, soon attracting the hobbies who feed on them. Glimpse a blue flash and it could be a kingfisher: this is one of the UK's most reliable places to spy them.

Kingfisher

This route is flat but although paths are well defined, they can get very boggy.

ROUTE DESCRIPTION

1) Cross Great Raveley Drain into the reserve. Turn right alongside the drain on the Marsh Harrier Trail, soon reaching the sluice. Turn left along another intersecting drain immediately ahead. Follow this path for 400m, passing one path/drain crossroads to a bridge at a second path/drain crossroads.

2) Turn right over the bridge, following the east side of the drain, to where the path crosses to follow the drain's west side after 175m. Cross another path ahead, then the drain beyond on a bridge and continue to the boardwalk to **North Hide**, a prime location for spotting marsh

harriers. When you are ready, retrace your steps to Point 2.

3) Back at the second path/drain crossroads, make the short 300m out-and-back walk to see the **Rothschild Bungalow** built by Charles Rothschild in 1911.

4) Returning to the second path/drain crossroads once more, turn left. Continue with the drain on your right to meet a grassy track at a T-junction. Open farmland is ahead.

5) Turn left, then left again at the next path/drain junction, away from the farmland. Follow this, the reserve's main path, in a west-southwest direction with the drain on your right. At the second path/drain junction, with the path to the reserve entrance

115

ahead, turn right. You now follow the reserve's Waterbird Trail.

6) The path runs almost due south for 750m, with a drain on the right, crossing three intersecting drains. You pass a lake, **Rothschild's Mere**, on the right and, at the lake's southern end, make the short (250m) out-and-back walk to the **Rothchild's Mere bird hide**.

7) Back on the main path, turn right, with a second lake, **Gordon's Mere**, now on your left. You pass the left-hand fork to **Gordon's Mere bird hide**, reaching a path/drain crossroads soon afterward. Turn left, with the drain on your right. This path meets Great Raveley Drain again at the reserve's eastern boundary: turn left (north) to follow it 900m back to the reserve entrance.

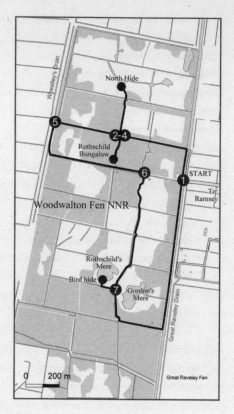

33. Minsmere, Dunwich Heath & Westleton Heath

Whet your appetite for avian life in dazzlingly diverse forms on this East Anglian wetland and heathland epic

NEED TO KNOW

START/FINISH: RSPB Minsmere Visitor Centre car park, IP17 3BY – 2.75km (1¾ miles) northeast of Eastbridge (parking free, entry charges may apply)

DISTANCE: 18.5km (11½ miles) (circular)

TIME: 6–6½ hours

KEY SPECIES: Avocet, barn owl, marsh harrier

MAP: OS Explorer 212/231

TRANSPORT: Leiston Library bus stop (buses to Ipswich/ Aldeburgh/Saxmundham) – 6.75km (4¼ miles) southwest

WALK ACCESSIBILITY: Not wheelchair/pushchair accessible; no dogs

DIFFICULTY: Moderate

MORE INFORMATION: rspb.org.uk

Marsh harrier

A flagship RSPB nature reserve for over 75 years, Minsmere has a privileged position within Suffolk Coast and Heaths AONB: titanic wetlands are embosomed by dunes, beach, woodsy heath, farmland and precious little civilisation. Because of how the reserve merges into quiet surrounding countryside, wildlife-watching here reaps extraordinary sightings: small wonder *Springwatch* had a base at Minsmere for 3 years.

Farmland, woodland, heathland and wading birds all make this their home. In the wetlands' heart around the hallowed avian address of the Scrapes, avocets and common terns arrive in summer, curlews and sandpipers pass through in autumn and gigantic duck flocks gather in winter. There is a dedicated hide for observing bitterns, nightingales sing in the woods and barn owls, marsh harriers and Montagu's harriers – Britain's rarest raptors –

patrol farmland-marshland boundaries. Otters are the reserve's non-avian highlight. Further north, Dunwich Heath counts Dartford warblers as its residents and with adjoining Westleton Heath constitutes one of East England's biggest remaining heathlands. Westleton is also the autumnal arena for Great Britain's largest red deer rut outside Scotland.

Paths are in good nick, although mud-prone, throughout and terrain low-lying: the longer-than-usual time given above is for wildlife-watching. Many of Minsmere's paths *are* wheelchair- and pushchair-friendly – ask visitor centre staff – but this walk is too muddy to be so.

ROUTE DESCRIPTION

1) A heads-up: there is a charge (worthwhile for the birdlife you'll see) to enter the Minsmere reserve. If you don't wish to pay, start the walk in Eastbridge, take the path (later taken on this walk) running east below Minsmere New Cut and join the walk by the coast at Point 4. A public viewpoint looks onto the reserve's East Scrape from the coastal side anyway. Begin this walk by passing through the **visitor centre** (ask about binocular hire and guided walks) then onto the path leading out beyond onto the end of Sheepwash Lane, the reserve's approach road. Cross the small lake on the walkway

and turn right to visit the first of the walk's six wildlife hides: **North Hide**. Afterwards, backtrack along Sheepwash Lane to pass the car park entrance on the right. Then continue another 100m to a left-hand path running parallel to the lane along the woodland edge. This feeds onto **Whin Hill**, from where *Springwatch* regularly broadcast between 2014 and 2017: great views sweep over tussocky heath down to Island Mere and the reserve's southern wetlands.

2) A broad grassy path arcs cross-heath down to the wetland edge. Here, there are two paths: the short out-and-back to **Island Mere Hide**, bedecked by rare southern marsh orchids in late spring, and your onward route, bearing left along the heath-wetland divide. This runs 650m southeast, dipping into mixed woodland to reach **Bittern Hide**. Here, peep out over reedbeds to watch these booming-voiced waders, then swing northeast through the woods to a path crossroads 250m later.

BARN OWL

Barn owls are taken for granted as one of England's talismanic countryside birds, with their distinctive white heart-shaped faces. But although widely distributed, places with likely sightings are scarce, and the Eastbridge side of Minsmere is one of the best.

3) Turn right. Your route now heads 1km southeast, out into the open and along to meet the line of Minsmere New Cut, a drainage channel. On the way, though, you pass coastal lagoon **West Scrape** on your left. The birdlife mentioned in the introduction can be seen here. **West Hide** is best for spying summertime avocets: the birds became a breeding British species again at the reserve in the year it opened, 1947, having not bred in the UK for a century beforehand. At Minsmere New Cut, swing left to reach the beach by the red-brick **sluice**, which helps regulate Minsmere's water levels.

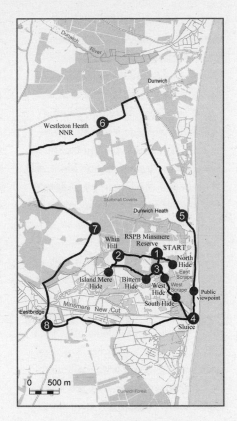

4) Turning left, your route trundles north through grassy dunes between wetland and beach. After 475m is the **public viewpoint** onto the reserve's East Scrape; another 1km afterwards and you bear left (inland) at a path crossroads toward **Dunwich Heath**, its car park and tearoom. Left of the tearoom, spot a blue sign for Heath Barn and a left-hand path demarcated with white posts. Track this to a picnic area where two broad barrier-marked paths appear ahead: here, take the right-hand path.

5) Now follow Sandlings Walk, a long-distance path designed to showcase this lowland heath, which is among Britain's rarest habitats. Continue for 1.25km, watching for uncommon birds like Dartford warblers, on a path heading northwest. Where Sandlings Walk branches right at a path crossroads, continue ahead north-northwest another 875m, passing Mount Pleasant Farm along to a road. Turn left for 250m, left again on a track and before a house swing right along the edge of more heath. The heath is divided into two distinct quadrants and delivers you to **Westleton Heath NNR** boundary in 400m at a path T-junction.

6) Turn left, then in 75m swing right to cross the NNR's southern limit. England's largest red deer herd are often seen hereabouts. The straightforward path hits a lane at a gate in 1.3km. Turn left, passing a parking lay-by, to a T-junction in 975m with a track continuing ahead. Turn left on dead-end lane Vault Hill. In 1km, you reach a green footpath sign and take the bridleway right, edged here by logs.

7) The walk's next stretch heads southwest for 1km, passing into woods near the end and meeting a lane at a bend. Turn right, proceeding 300m to a T-junction, then turning left for 575m, crossing Minsmere New Cut and arriving at where the lane forks in Eastbridge village. The left fork passes **Eels Foot Inn**, where the beer garden also doubles as decent birdwatching turf.

8) By a red-brick house 125m later, take the track left. Barn owls are often sighted on this section, as are marsh harriers. Presently turn right on a path opposite a house: the route then swings left to chart a steady course eastward, parallel to Minsmere New Cut off left. Pass between two lines of trees, brush two plantations to your right and proceed along the pancake-flat, muddy way to reach the sluice at map Point 4, 2.6km after leaving the lane in Eastbridge. Retrace your route back into the reserve to map Point 3. Here at the path crossroads swing right, on a previously untaken path for 175m back to Sheepwash Lane, then retrace your outward route to the car park.

MIDLANDS & THE PEAK DISTRICT

34. Bradgate Park & Swithland Wood

Relish this ravishingly rugged moor and woodland near Leicester, a centuries-old sanctuary for red and fallow deer

NEED TO KNOW

START/FINISH: Newtown Linford car park, Bradgate Park, LE6 0HB – 3.25km (2 miles) northwest of Anstey (parking charges may apply)

DISTANCE: 8km (5 miles) (circular)

TIME: 2–2½ hours

KEY SPECIES: Fallow and red deer, bluebell, little owl

MAP: OS Explorer 246

TRANSPORT: Bradgate Park bus stop, Newtown Linford (buses to Leicester) – 200m southwest

WALK ACCESSIBILITY: Bradgate Park sections wheelchair/pushchair accessible; dogs under close control and on leads near Deer Sanctuary

DIFFICULTY: Easy

MORE INFORMATION: bradgatepark.org

Little owl

A short jaunt outside Leicester is the surprising location of some of the Midlands' most magical countryside. A deer park since the 13th century, Bradgate Park's sweeps of moor, crag and patchy woodland are quite rugged: more redolent of the Peak District than of a suburban country park. The park bounds ancient Swithland Wood, one of Leicestershire's most important native woodlands for wildlife. And the two together make a memorable rural excursion, where wildlife is stringently protected and, as a result, relatively easy to spot.

A 550-strong herd of fallow and red deer, currently three-quarters fallow, is the main animal attraction. The deer roam freely, but also have a large deer sanctuary (no humans allowed) across the south of the park. Birdlife is also quite diverse: look for yellowhammers and Old John's resident stonechats on the open ground, three owl species including the little owl and a medley of aquatic birds at Cropston Reservoir.

Most of Bradgate Park's paths are manageable by wheelchair and pushchair. Ascents are quite gradual and there isn't really any getting lost. All times of year hold promise but autumn's ruddy hues and avian visitors are probably best.

ROUTE DESCRIPTION

1) Start on the main path onto the moorland through the gate from the car park: this runs north-northwest with an expanse of beautiful broadleaf woodland impressing from off on the right. You're bound for **Old John**, the hill crested by the folly of Old John Tower that marks the park's high point. Clambering up here is a rite of passage for visitors and many paths fork off to see it: this route takes the fork 250m after the gate. This grassy way leads northeast and passes through **Tyburn Copse**, one of several spinneys (small

> ### LITTLE OWL
> Spied across England (and less often in parts of Wales and Southern Scotland), the little owl is a 19th-century introduction. It's easier to spot than most of the owl family, being frequently seen by day.

bunched-together stands of trees) hereabouts and one of the few with a path through it: others are preserved as havens for birds, notably rather vociferous rooks.

2) The next objective, straight ahead up over the grassland, is the **Yeomanry War Memorial**. This shares the park's highest ground with 18th-century **Old John Tower**, which stands just beyond after a brief dip to traverse a comely copse. On the open ground around Old John, birds like yellowhammers, skylarks and meadow pipits, plus the stonechats that like the nearby crags, are regulars. The pastoral panorama of Leicestershire is also delightful. The most straightforward descent off the top is north-northwest, aiming for the woods of Hunts Hill at the park corner. Afterwards, though, you're swinging east below Sliding Stone Wood, the next woods visible in a clockwise direction from Hunts Hill. Your path traces the park and the open moorland edge beside field hedges.

3) After 675m along from Hunts Hill woodland, and with Sliding Stone Wood just right, a park information board and wooden kissing gate set in a dry-stone wall usher you left out of Bradgate Park and on a track between fields to Roecliffe Road, with **Swithland Wood** ahead.

4) It does not matter which path you choose through the wood so long as you experience this pretty place: there is no going wrong really. Aim to at least loop around Great Pit lake as this route does. Ahead of you are already two options: the straightforward path following the woodland-farmland divide and, just right along the road, the minor path deeper into the woods that this walk takes. Either way, follow the paths roughly northwest, not straying too far from the woodland edge. Drawing parallel with a wood-flanked corner of Swithland Woods Farm Holiday Camp off left (northwest), you need to swing right (east-southeast) to round Great Pit. The wood is a conservation success story. This series of now-flooded slate quarries was imperilled when a timber merchant purchased the land in the 1920s, felling much of the surrounding woodland, but the remainder was preserved when locals battled to save it. Enjoy the exquisite oaks, birches, alders, limes and rich forest floor, bluebell-cloaked in spring. This route swings back south towards Roecliffe Road after rounding Great Pit lake. However, where the path splits 200m after the southern lakeside near a field corner, turn left rather than keeping straight along the main track towards Swithland Wood South car park.

5) Continue along the woodland edge with a stream and the field on your right, then cross a footbridge and swing diagonally left across the field to reach Roecliffe Road beside Horseshoe Cottage Farm. Turn left for 125m, then right through Cropston car park to take the path alongside **Cropston Reservoir**. The reservoir attracts avians like little egrets and ospreys and, stopping by in autumn, black-tailed godwits and sandpipers: watch them from the **wildlife-viewing area** beside Deer Barn Tearoom at the end of the shoreline, where there is also a **visitor centre**.

6) Keep to the main metalled drive running southwest after the tearoom/visitor centre. In 250m, deviate right to walk through the ruins of 16th-century **Bradgate House**, where Lady Jane Grey, Britain's shortest-reigning monarch (a mere nine days) was born. Little owls seem to like the nearby oaks. Back on the

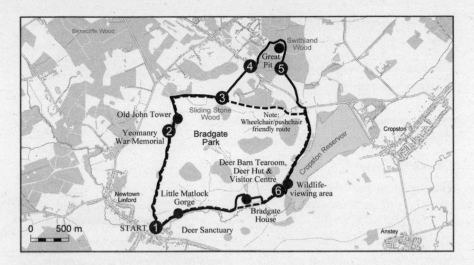

drive afterwards, you're on the park's south side. While deer roam freely park-wide, the area to your left is a **Deer Sanctuary** reserved just for them. The park has another delight in store for you, however: ahead you pass through an area known as **Little Matlock Gorge**. This, romantically named for its supposed similarity to the Peak District beauty spot, is a lovely concluding stretch of grassy riverside dotted with exotic plantings like monkey-puzzles as well as native trees. The start car park beckons just beyond.

35. Rutland Water's Hambleton Peninsula

Get a gander at the fabulous wildfowl and wading birdlife lured to little Rutland's enormous reservoir

NEED TO KNOW

START/FINISH: St Andrew's Church, Hambleton, LE15 8TH (parking free)

DISTANCE: 8.5km (5¼ miles) (circular)

TIME: 2–2½ hours

KEY SPECIES: Osprey, smew, baitballs

MAP: OS Explorer 234

TRANSPORT: Sewage Works bus stop (buses to Oakham/Stamford) – 3.25km (2 miles) northwest

WALK ACCESSIBILITY: Accessible to wheelchair/pushchair users from point 2 onwards; dogs allowed

DIFFICULTY: Easy

MORE INFORMATION: anglianwaterparks.co.uk, discover-rutland.co.uk and lrwt.org.uk

Smew

Rutland Water, among Europe's largest manmade lakes, is proof that humans *can* do much good for wildlife – even with huge construction projects primarily designed to benefit themselves. When this reservoir was created in 1976, it also fashioned what would become one of England's most important inland wetland wildlife sites, and easily the most important in the Midlands.

The main Rutland Water Nature Reserve was where, in 2001, conservationists succeeded in getting an osprey pair to breed in the wild in England for the first time since the mid-19th century. Today many ospreys breed here; many more fledge here and then move elsewhere. The reserve's other important avians include overwintering great egrets, greylag geese, pink-footed geese, curlews, red-crested pochards and smews. An enviable 100-plus bird species have been seen around SSSI-designated Rutland Water. While the reserve itself, a paid-for attraction, has the best close-up birding, many birds can be seen around the reservoir: especially Hambleton

Peninsula, which brushes the reserve's fringes and has a scenic circular ramble – the very one detailed below – beginning and ending by a cracking pub. The peninsula also gets you further out into the middle of an inland body of water on dry land than almost anywhere else in the UK, putting it in a winning position for observing waterbirds.

The non-feathered highlight is undoubtedly Rutland Water's baitballs – phenomena where millions of small fish gather together as defence against predators – subject of 2021's *Winterwatch*. Winter, when some 25,000 wildfowl settle in the reserve, is a particularly wild time, although summer is ideal for osprey observation. Wintertime paths can get muddy but are good enough to cope.

ROUTE DESCRIPTION

1) If driving, park with care so as not to block the narrow lanes close to Hambleton village's **St Andrew's Church**. You embark on your ramble through the churchyard, the path passing out through the back. Next, keep hedges on your immediate right as your route bends around behind the back of some houses and, after 175m, enter a large field. Now, head straight across the middle of the field to a stile onto the Rutland Water Cycle Route (RWCR), the pedestrian- and bike-friendly route you will be following around much of Hambleton Peninsula.

SMEW

For Britain-based wildfowl-watching fanatics, the smew is one of the rarest (and most adorable) discoveries. Estimations are that just 125 of these diving ducks from Europe's frozen north overwinter here. The black-and-white males are most distinctive with fuzzy crests and black eye patches; the ladies are greyer with attractive red-brown heads.

2) At this point, you're still within the bounds of **Rutland Water Nature Reserve**. The reserve has a separate entrance and an admission charge, but with over 30 hides here for observing wildlife up quite close it is one of the best set-ups of its kind in England. It's recommended to first do this walk and see what wildlife you can spot, then separately visit the reserve (there are two reserve entrances, **Anglican Water Birdwatching Centre** and **Lyndon Visitor Centre**, with the latter usually best for watching ospreys). Turn left on the RWCR here and, 500m later, reach a metal gate onto a lane.

3) Turn right along the lane. Off right, grass leads invitingly onto open shore and, for stages of this walk, you may wish to check out the shore outside of the stretches the RWCR visits to maximise potential bird sightings. After 130m on the lane, though,

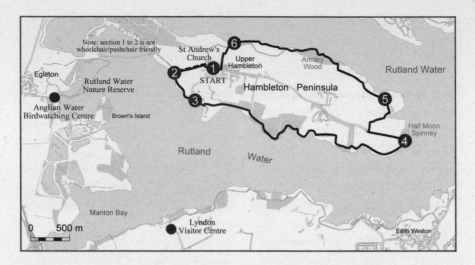

ensure you follow the RWCR as it kinks left at a 'no parking' sign, then immediately right through a gate to resume a course parallel to but further back from the shore. The route runs into **Hambleton Wood** with its resident nightingales ahead. After a sinuous kilometre through the woods, the RWCR bends across some fields and through another smaller wood. Then, at a right-hand gate where the RWCR runs out of the woods, pass through to continue along the grass behind the shoreline.

4) You hit the peninsula's tip at **Half Moon Spinney** after crossing a stile. Turn left on the lane for 475m, then right to follow the RWCR again. As you round the peninsula's eastern edge, there are ample opportunities to scout out wildlife-watching and picnic spots in the tree-dotted grass to the right.

5) Swinging round onto the peninsula's north shore, it's 800m until the RWCR plunges into **Armley Wood**, the vestige of a once far-larger broadleaf wood in pre-reservoir days, and still sporting fine specimens of oak and sycamore. Exiting the wood, the RWCR bends left away from the shore, but you can continue ahead along the grass by the shoreline for a last lovely stretch of birdwatching.

6) Return onto the RWCR by a copse in 700m. The RWCR becomes a track bending left and then right ahead: pass left through the metal gate on the right-hand track bend. Halfway up the ensuing grassy field, look for a kissing gate on the right leading onto a track, which you follow up to Ketton Road in Hambleton. Turn right, with St Andrew's Church now just ahead.

36. Sherwood Forest, the Wildwood Trail & Budby South Forest

Stroll splendid forest festooned with ancient oaks and entrenched in stories of outlaws

NEED TO KNOW

START/FINISH: Sherwood Forest main car park, Swinecote Road opposite Forest Corner, Edwinstowe, NG21 9QB (parking and entry charges may apply)

DISTANCE: 8.25km (5 miles) (circular)

TIME: 2–2 ½ hours

KEY SPECIES: Oak, roe deer, Welsh clearwing moth

MAP: OS Explorer 270

TRANSPORT: Visitor Centre bus stop (buses to Nottingham) – 200m into walk

WALK ACCESSIBILITY: Accessible to wheelchair/pushchair users; dogs under close control

DIFFICULTY: Easy

MORE INFORMATION: visitsherwood.co.uk and rspb.org.uk

Robin Hood knew a good forest when he saw one. The legend of the man and his merry men hiding out here from the Sherriff of Nottingham and other associated baddies is still what lures people in to the Sherwood Forest NNR, and one tree, the Major Oak, is a survivor from the outlaws' old greenwood. But the collection of oaks over six centuries old here (almost 1000) simply beggars belief, and is probably the biggest in Europe.

On this forest foray you'll pass mighty trees aplenty, Major Oak included. You may also perhaps spot purple hairstreak butterflies up in the oaks, Welsh clearwing moths in the birches, the likes of nuthatches and tawny owls and a medley of hedgehogs, rabbits and grey squirrels. This forest is also a treat for the ears; *Springwatch* 2021 captured the awakening of spring with a symphony of wild sound. Listen too for the early spring and winter percussion of woodpeckers, the unmistakable spring call of the cuckoo and the subtle rustle of roe deer in the undergrowth. The walk also provides a flavour of wilder, quieter Budby South Forest, where forest mixes with scrub to make a home for yellowhammers and willow warblers.

The going is level, well marked and manageable by wheelchairs and pushchairs, and there are enough paths to tailor this route according to your fancy.

OAK

No tree could be more emblematic of Britain than the oak: Robin Hood and the future King Charles II used them to hide in, and these kings of the countryside support more life than any other UK tree species. Sherwood Forest's majestic oaks are both sessile and pedunculate.

ROUTE DESCRIPTION

1) Cross the B6034 road with care after leaving the car park, continuing straight over onto Forest Corner. This dead-end lane passes Sherwood Forest Art & Craft Centre and Sherwood Forest YHA to reach the state-of-the-art **Sherwood Forest Visitor Centre**, where you'll find forest information, trail guides and a shop/café. Afterwards, this walk primarily follows the Wildwood Trail, the NNR's longest signed trail. Pass through the visitor centre and take the well-surfaced path bearing left along the car park edge and into the forest. Remember to watch out for fantastic trees and the above-mentioned fauna throughout. Many arboreal wonders have information placards and information boards spotlight forest creatures too. Your way runs close to the forest edge initially, fields visible off left, to a dividing of the ways after 350m. Take the left fork, ignoring a left-hand path soon after, to reach a path junction at Broad Drive after 525m.

2) Turn left here, proceeding 525m to where several paths diagonally intersect your route. Here turn diagonally right (northwest). After 625m this path delivers you onto one of two parallel tracks running straight north; bear right to follow this 450m to a track junction. There are two right-hand paths here: take the second, a path that winsomely

Roe deer

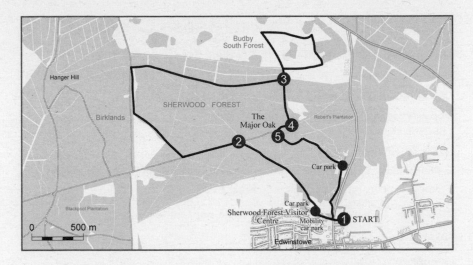

traces the divide between stands of broadleaf and conifer forest. You follow this path for 1.5km, ignoring one route off left and two to the right; just after halfway it becomes wider and passes through charming grassy clearings.

3) At a path T-junction, with the onward route to the Major Oak to the right, turn left for the loop around **Budby South Forest**. You soon reach a broad track. Cross straight over into this RSPB-managed, less-trammelled part of the NNR. The trees are more thinly spread here, meaning heathland habitats can flourish and birds like yellowhammers, linnets and nightjars thrive. Swing right at a path crossroads after 400m, then take the grassy track swinging right in front of thicker forest to the broad track you previously crossed. Turn right and continue for 375m, then left to continue your

onward route. On this path, you reach a broader track after 550m.

4) Turn right on a track at the sign 'Major Oak 5 mins walk.' Take the next left to curve in front of the **Major Oak** 200m later: purportedly a millennium old, the tree is fenced off and supported by crutches.

5) Curve left again after the tree, following the protective fence around and then a fenced track. Keep on this for 700m, ignoring a path left, to arrive at a car park. Just beforehand, you come alongside buildings on the left. Pass through vehicle-preventing bollards and along a path between car park areas, soon coming out at Edwinstowe Cricket Ground. Skirt right around the cricket ground edge, the visitor centre ahead and the return route to your car park just beyond.

37. Eastnor Deer Park to British Camp through the Malvern Hills

Climb one of England's best viewpoints, prettily positioned among wood-bounded, butterfly-rich grasslands

NEED TO KNOW

START/FINISH: Eastnor Deer Park car park (Woodyard entrance), HR8 1RA – 3.5km (2¼ miles) east of Ledbury (parking free)

DISTANCE: 11.5km (7¼ miles) (part circular, part out-and-back)

TIME: 3–3½ hours

KEY SPECIES: Adder, green woodpecker, red deer

MAP: OS Explorer 190

TRANSPORT: Ledbury railway station – 3.5km (2¼ miles) northwest

WALK ACCESSIBILITY: Partly accessible to wheelchair/pushchair users; dogs allowed but on leads in deer park

DIFFICULTY: Easy–Moderate

MORE INFORMATION: eastnorcastle.com and visitthemalverns.org.uk

The Malverns may be small as hill ranges go (just 13km long) but they offer many marvellous things, including British Camp, one of Britain's best-preserved Iron Age hillforts and finest viewpoints. This classic English beauty of a walk makes a less-tramped yet picturesque passage to the hillfort from the southwest.

The walk first runs around a deer park with a resident red deer herd, where a mosaic of mesmeric grasslands and woods sets the tone for the route. In the scrubby grasslands, summertime butterflies include the grayling and small heath, and you might startle an adder soaking up heat, while birdlife includes green woodpeckers and stonechats. The springtime chorus in the woods could feature nuthatches and pied flycatchers; rare barbastelle and serotine bats also inhabit the woodland in this area.

It is a steady climb up Hangman's Hill and British Camp but the going is untroubling overall. Nearby Eastnor Castle does command an entrance fee, but the deer park is free and invariably it is open all year-round.

ROUTE DESCRIPTION

1) The route begins by the broad tarmacked track, also known as The Ridgway, running over the cattle grid from The Woodshed snack bar. Follow this east to a track junction in 225m. This walk now circles attractive **Eastnor Deer Park** keeping left on The Ridgway: you'll get to return via the other track later. Continue north through the park until you see two lakes off right: here, cut across the grass aiming for the far end of the first lake. The path squeezes between the lakes, afterwards following a treeline to reach a track. Much of this area is used as a campsite. Turn left, then right on another track in 50m.

2) Follow the tarmacked track east past Ashen Fields Coppice, in which red deer sometimes lurk, to **Eastnor Obelisk**, a 27.5m-high memorial erected in 1812, and an impressive viewpoint. Proceed along the main track to the cattle grid at the deer park entrance: pass through to three metal gates on your left. Head through the third of these on a track doubling as the Three Choirs Way long-distance path. This soon swings right through Gullet Wood. You initially follow a northeast-bound woodland track, which kinks left in about 425m: continue straight. Afterwards, it's more a path you're following, first northeast and then north with Swinyard Hill off right to reach a right-hand connector path onto a wider, well-beaten path. Turn left. Your path kinks right, then left and reaches another path junction in 75m.

Green woodpecker

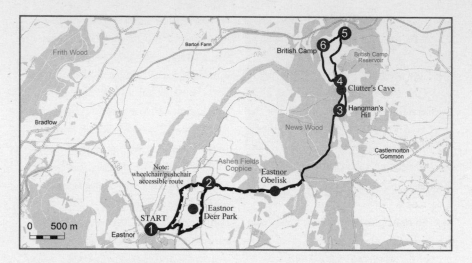

3) Here, you swing right (east-southeast) on a broad path (straight ahead is the way this walk returns from British Camp). This soon curves sharp left (north) onto **Hangman's Hill**, another scenic viewpoint, with the broad grassy ridge denoting your onward route running north, flanked by woods. All these open grasslands are ideal for spotting butterflies and teensy harvest mice.

4) Head on north 400m and there is bulky British Camp hillfort, sloping up in front. It's your choice how you explore it: there are numerous paths, all interesting. This walk takes the obvious Three Choirs Way route up along the eastern side. This ascends initially northwest over adjacent, slightly lower and also fortified Millennium Hill, then becomes leveller for a time, tracing contours northeast with **British Camp Reservoir** below right and the grassy slopes to the top of British Camp still off left. Ahead, the path brushes woods on the right, then meets the main path to the top.

5) Continue straight on here to the close-by car park and the refreshments awaiting just beyond should you need them. To continue the walk, turn left and upwards. Climb some steps, then swing left on a broad, gently ascending path that nevertheless negotiates four more flights of steps before **Herefordshire Beacon** summit. It's understandable why Iron Age peoples constructed **British Camp** hillfort up here: views sweep over 12 counties and the steep, easily defensible sides make this feel far higher than 338masl. While likely dug out to today's extent in the 4th to 2nd centuries BC, this

was probably a defensive site for much
– maybe millennia – longer.

6) Take the path heading south down
from the top, along the hillfort's
western flanks to reach Point 4 on the
map in 750m. Rather than returning
on the ridgetop path south here,
take the lower path running parallel
but along the treeline to the west to
Clutter's Cave. Afterwards, Point 3
on the map is 325m along the treeline.
Now, retrace your outward route
to Point 2. Try the aforementioned
alternative route back through the
deer park: all along tarmacked tracks.
Turn left along the track, curving right
in 625m but ignoring side-tracks, then
in 325m swing sharp right between
metal gates and presently left through
a gate over a stream. Pass Eastnor
Bowling Club, then shortly afterwards
meet your outward route to the start.

38. Stiperstones Ridge & the Bog

Roam an iconic ridge and a nature-reclaimed mine, gandering a wildlife gamut from red grouse to red kite to retiring butterflies

NEED TO KNOW

START/FINISH: Knolls car park, Stiperstones NNR, SY5 0NL – 4.75km (3 miles) south of Stiperstones (parking free)

DISTANCE: 11.5km (7¼ miles) (circular)

TIME: 3–3½ hours

KEY SPECIES: Red grouse, red kite, greater horseshoe bat

MAP: OS Explorer 216/217

TRANSPORT: Church Stretton railway station – 11.75km (7¼ miles) southeast

WALK ACCESSIBILITY: Not wheelchair/pushchair accessible; dogs under close control and on leads Mar–Jul around Nipstone Rock

DIFFICULTY: Easy–Moderate

MORE INFORMATION: shropshirehillsaonb.co.uk, bogvisitorcentre.com and shropshiresgreatoutdoors.co.uk

Described as a 'bare upheaval of hills' by DH Lawrence, the Stiperstones NNR surrounds a glorious ridge protruding from the Shropshire Hills AONB in multiple broken, Brobdingnagian vertebrae. The ridge offers fine moorland walking, where buzzards, ravens and red kites wheel and red grouse rustle in the heather-clad slopes that provide their southernmost stronghold in Britain. But fascinatingly, another distinctive habitat has formed below the moors in former mining area The Bog. Here, nature-reclaimed spoil heaps attract grayling butterflies, manmade lakes have become crucial refuges for newts and dragonflies and an old mining tunnel houses horseshoe bats.

Choose a clear late spring day, when ridgetop views leave you speechless and early morning or late evening walkers may see bats returning to subterranean roosts. Late summer brilliantly blankets moors in heather. While you'll climb to 536masl at Manstone Rock, you start off high, so ascents are not so severe. Ridge paths are rocky; around The Bog it can get – you guessed – squelchy.

ROUTE DESCRIPTION

1) At the car park, you want the path through a gate flanked by information boards, on the left as you come in. Begin your climb onto Stiperstones ridge. The path is good: the Cross Britain Way long-distance path trundles through. Your first objective, and one of the ridge's best viewpoints, is **Cranberry Rock**, a detour left from the main path, where the panorama includes the Mid Wales mountains to the southwest. Once up on the moors, keep eyes peeled for red grouse and common lizards in the quilt of heather, gorse and rocks.

2) Take the well-defined trail northeast from Cranberry Rock to rejoin the main ridge path, after which it's 400m to ridge high point **Manstone Rock**, a quartzite crag resembling a castle from the northern side. Watch on these ridgetop stretches for red kite, buzzards and trilling skylarks. Hear a sound like two smallish rocks smacking together, and it's likely a stonechat. Continue along the well-trodden route 475m to come alongside the ridge's most striking crag, **Devil's Chair**, then on a gentle 475m descent to a cairn-marked track crossroads.

GREATER HORSESHOE BAT
One of the largest UK bats is named for its sizeable horseshoe-shaped nose-leaf, which helps give the mammal superb echolocation. The bats formerly favoured caves for their colonies: today, at The Bog, an old adit does just as well.

3) Head straight over here with the next crag, **Shepherds Rock**, ahead. After 400m and just before the rock, you hit another cairn-marked track crossroads. The ridge continues; you turn left on a grassy track. This descends and divides into minor paths after 225m: turn right, 50m later bearing left on a path which then descends steadily through a pretty, woodsy valley, upgrading into a track after reaching a lodge and holiday cottage.

4) Follow the track 750m past several houses around Green Hill's steep slopes into Stiperstones village. Turn left past **Stiperstones Inn** and, 425m later, take a path swinging up left after a house by the village entrance sign. This path immediately swings right, following the edge of Bergum Wood up a grassy field, then near the tapered field end turns left up through woods at a stile. Emerge onto the moor, swing right and keep on a path sticking close to and then along the NNR edge beside the field-moor divide. The path now becomes a track. Pass over a track crossroads after 700m. Afterwards, the way is quite clear, running over patches of moor and fields almost 1.5km to meet a metalled track before a road bend.

5) Bear right on the road, descending to **The Bog Visitor Centre**. This ex-mining area has become a wildlife bastion, and the visitor centre tells the story. Afterwards, follow the trail leading along the lane south from the visitor centre then right, beside the

Miner's Institute remains, to loop around the small nearby **reservoir** (look for newts and dragonflies). Return to the lane after 300m and turn right: 75m along on the left is the short out-and-back path to another **reservoir** and the **Somme Tunnel**, where bats roost.

6) Afterwards, back on the lane, turn left (south) for 625m. You pass patches of conifer and a campsite before **Nipstone Rock** rears up on the left: take the track left, then the right-hand out-and-back path to the rock. The area is the focus of a project to restore heathland across the Stiperstones, aiming to coax back red grouse, curlew and emperor moths. Afterwards proceed right (east) along the track 250m and keep ahead on a path that curves right and through a zone of part-felled forestry to reach a stile on the left.

7) Your path passes along two field hedges to reach a gate onto a lane, Frogs Gutter. Turn left for 875m, then turn right on a lane signposted 'The Stiperstones National Nature Reserve'. Your car park is 675m along the lane.

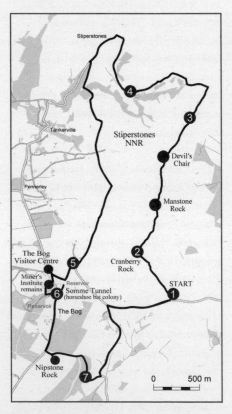

39. Caistor to Tealby on the Viking Way

Disprove generalisations about Lincolnshire's flatness with this wander into the low chalky hills of the Wolds

NEED TO KNOW

START/FINISH: Caistor town hall/Arts Centre car park by Co-op supermarket, LN7 6QU/Tealby village hall car park, LN8 3XU (parking free)

DISTANCE: 15.5km (9¾ miles) (one way)

TIME: 4½–5 hours

KEY SPECIES: Barn owl, hedgehog, red kite

MAP: OS Explorer 282

TRANSPORT: Caistor Market Place bus stop (buses to Market Rasen/Lincoln/Grimsby) – 175m south (and en route)

WALK ACCESSIBILITY: Not wheelchair/pushchair accessible; dogs allowed

DIFFICULTY: Easy–Moderate

MORE INFORMATION: lincolnshire.gov.uk and lincswolds.org.uk

Gentle the rolling Lincolnshire Wolds AONB may be but, nevertheless, here is the East of England's highest land between Kent and Yorkshire and the best locations to spot birds associated with open uplands within this 300km stretch. Because of how the wolds weave into the close-by tapestry of habitats, including woodland, farmland and villages, an interesting contingent of other wildlife shows up. Meandering through the AONB is the Viking Way, a long-distance footpath illuminating this region's Norse history. But what this stage of the trail shows much more of is East Midlands countryside at its finest.

In open grassy uplands, look for red kites, sightings of which have increased significantly in recent years, buzzards and kestrels. Lincolnshire also has one of the highest concentrations of barn owls in England and, according to a 2022 report by the British Hedgehog Preservation Society, a particularly high hedgehog density: watch the ground where you walk as well as the skies.

May, when wildflowers like common spotted orchid and cowslip colour the scene, catches this green and pleasant land at its loveliest. This is a straightforward walk of gentle ascents and descents.

ROUTE DESCRIPTION

1) A cut-through from the car park, past the public toilets and down the side of the town hall to emerge by Co-op supermarket entrance, begins the walk. Turn left on High Street, then right to reach the Market Square in **Caistor**. A one-time Roman camp (a Roman cemetery was unearthed during construction of the Co-op), its many Georgian buildings make for a pretty centre. Continue straight ahead down Plough Hill to **Caistor Arts and Heritage Centre**, right on dead-end Fountain Street, right again where it meets Westbrooke Grove and then immediately left up steps. At the top, walk left along the path hugging the churchyard's south edge, where there is a section of Roman wall. Turn left on Cromwell View, continuing to the junction with Navigation Lane. Swing left, then turn immediately right on Nettleton Road, which hits the bustling A46 in 175m. Now carefully proceed left along the road's narrow left-hand-side footway for 400m. After a clump of trees appears on the left, look for steps on the right and carefully cross the road to descend them.

2) Your route now follows often-overgrown field edges southwest to Nettleton village. Entering the eighth field with buildings ahead, swing left across the field to emerge on the driveway of The Barns. Turn left, then hang a right on the lane. At the crossroads, you turn left, following Normanby Road 450m to a tarmacked left-hand driveway by Old White Cottage. You pass Nettleton Grange on the right, cross the stream of Nettleton Beck, then turn right on a footpath.

3) Farmland-upland boundaries like this can be great for spotting barn owls, but skylarks may also hover above along with upland raptors like buzzards, kestrels and red kites. This next stretch follows beautiful, wild Nettleton Beck for 1.25km, beginning by passing one pond and ending at a track junction with another pond

HEDGEHOG

A British wildlife walk book would be remiss not to spotlight this stalwart countryside and garden species. But this cute, spiny creature is in big decline countrywide: Lincolnshire is one of few remaining English locations recording high densities. You can report hedgehog sightings at sites like ptes.org: this helps monitor the hogs and provides environmental organisations with critical information to help protect them better.

surrounded by woodland ahead. Turn left and, 150m later, right on a path through the same woodland. You'll pass the red-brick remnants of mine workings before exiting the woodland and tracing Nettleton Beck, still on your right, once more. Stay with the stream, climbing up the valley. Before the stream head Nettleton Beck's course steers directly southwest and you continue in this direction around 475m beyond the stream head to a junction with a bridleway.

4) Turn right, then presently left on Normanby Road. Continue along this pleasant country lane for 1.75km. Off left is the radar station near Lincolnshire's highest point, **Wolds Top** (also called Normanby Hill) at 168masl. You pass a signposted lane turn to Normanby le Wold and Thoresway, 275m after which you'll see a kissing gate on the left. Pass through this and head across a couple of fields to the lane near houses in Normanby le Wold. Turn left, then turn right at the next lane junction to the tiny village's St Peter's Church.

5) Your route passes right of the church on a muddy track soon becoming a grassy southbound bridleway with Claxby Wood off right. The bridleway curves left (southeast) to reach a path fork 1.4km after the church. Here, you bear right,

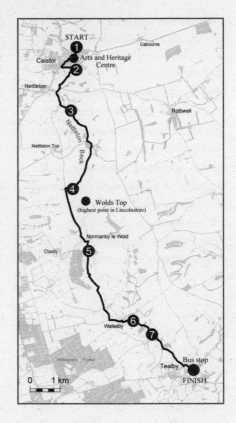

diagonally down across the field to the far right-hand corner. Then follow the hedge line down the next field and in the field after, branch diagonally left to Mill House Farm track. Turn right to reach Moor Road and bear left into Walesby village. Keep on Rasen Road to where it curves left and a tarmacked signposted track leads straight on. Proceed on this until it bends sharp right to curve around peaceful **Rambler's Church**. The newer church you walked past in the village superseded this as it was supposed

141

parishioners would be reticent to venture uphill here to services.

6) The path cuts across the churchyard southwest of the church and into the field south. Turn left, tracing the hedge along to a gate and then heading straight across the next field to a track before a copse. Go through the gate ahead and bear left through the copse to turn right along the fence line running southeast. Next, cross a stream and head across the field to emerge on a drive to the right of Risby Manor.

7) Keep straight over, looking out for the local flock of Lincoln Longwools, Britain's biggest native sheep. Hit a broad track in 250m, continuing straight through a gate, then veer diagonally up to Bedlam Plantation. Keep along the plantation edge to the corner with Castle Farm off right. Now swing diagonally left (southeast) across the field ahead. In 250m, spot another field hedge running parallel to your path off right and follow this down a slope to the field corner. Cross a bridge, then follow the path across two fields into Tealby, branching diagonally across the second field and aiming for the left of three houses ahead. A path squeezes beside this house onto the B1203 road. Turn left. The road curves right and you pass All Saints Church to your left. At the crossroads, turn right to arrive at Tealby village hall.

RETURNING TO START: Bike or car

40. Mortimer Forest on the Climbing Jack Trail

Wend through ancient forest hunting grounds in the Welsh Marches where an animal found nowhere else in the world resides

NEED TO KNOW

START/FINISH: Vinnalls FE car park, SY8 2HG – 2km (1¼ miles) northeast of Pipe Aston (parking free)

DISTANCE: 14km (9 miles) (circular)

TIME: 4–4½ hours

KEY SPECIES: Long-haired fallow deer, wood white butterfly, wall lizard

MAP: OS Explorer 203

TRANSPORT: Ludlow railway station – 5.5km (3½ miles) northeast

WALK ACCESSIBILITY: Not wheelchair/pushchair accessible; dogs allowed

DIFFICULTY: Moderate

MORE INFORMATION: forestryengland.co.uk and friends-of-mortimer-forest.org.uk

Green and gentle-looking today, the Herefordshire-Shropshire border was once the domain of the Marcher Lords: a group of rough, tough barons appointed by William the Conqueror to police the England-Wales border and protect it from incursions by the native Welsh. Hereabouts, that task fell to the Mortimers, whose vast estates included Mortimer Forest, their private hunting ground that had previously been Saxon hunting forest.

Extensive resinous ranks of 20th-century-planted evergreen plantations meld with ancient nooks of broadleaf woods and heath, enticing rare species and one utterly unique one: the long-haired fallow deer. More fantastic fauna thrives here too: not least unusual Lepidoptera family member the wood white butterfly, adders, wall lizards, birds like goshawks and three bat species.

Bluebells bewitchingly coat heaths in spring, wood white butterflies perform distinctive courtship rituals in summer and long-haired fallow deer rut deep into autumn. The Climbing Jack Trail gives the grandest possible overview of the forest, but is rocky, rooty and muddy in places. You ascend over 150m of elevation, climbing to High Vinnalls at 375masl in the walk's first half, too.

ROUTE DESCRIPTION

1) You begin on a wide forestry track forging south from the car park entrance, a field on the right. After the field end, ignore another track approaching from the left and a subsequent left-hand fork to reach a track T-junction after 225m. Turn right. This track curves gradually right (southwest) along a clearing edge then swings more pronouncedly right (west) at the next track junction after 300m. Continue 175m, then swing left on a path down the straight side of a long, narrow, J-shaped clearing. Look out for long-haired fallow deer as you enter this less-trammelled part of the forest.

2) Swing left diagonally across a clearing immediately beyond. Then curve right along the treeline ahead, either following it or staying just within it for 375m with a wide break between forest patches on the right. You then cross straight over a wider track and stream but 50m later your path swings left, bending through denser forest to brush a field corner to the right after 225m. It's then 400m along the forest edge, fields off right, to hit a forest track.

3) Turn right here, then sharp left around 150m later on the Herefordshire Trail long-distance path, rising steadily through forest to connect with a forestry track as it makes a U-shaped bend. Turn right, following the track around left. As you climb into open heath, 825m later, you reach **High Vinnalls** (375masl), a wonderful viewpoint.

4) You are now on **Climbing Jack Common**. In spring there are huge spreads of bluebells here and goshawks may be seen roving above. June is good for observing wood white butterflies' elaborate courtship, entailing antennae-waving and head-nodding. Turn right (east) off the main track at the viewpoint on a track through ferny scrub, meeting another track after 200m. Turn left, then immediately right. Your path is soon running with fields off right and forest off left. Forest then takes over either side and you reach a track junction after 450m.

5) Turn right, then left 425m later. Your way now twists through the trees 500m to turn left on a track. Next, bear left on a path before the track junction just ahead. Follow this path,

LONG-HAIRED FALLOW DEER

There are thought to be fewer than 100 of these creatures worldwide, their only known location being Mortimer Forest. Their hair grows to twice the length of normal fallow deer: the likely consequence of a gene mutation.

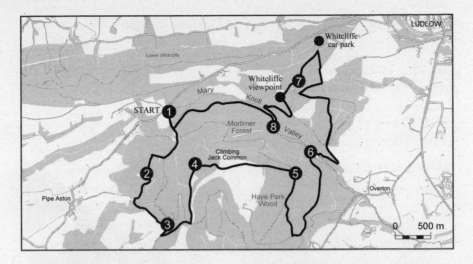

ignoring several side-turnings, for 800m to where it reaches a cross-path with open ground off right with views to deciduous woods, redstarts and wood warblers frequent. Continue straight (north), then curve left down into **Mary Knoll Valley**. Watch for rare wall lizards here.

6) At a track junction bear briefly left then swing acutely right over the stream, proceeding southeast to the forest edge then swinging northwest for 275m with fields on the right. Keep straight over at the cross-track, denser forest then flanking you either side. After 650m, turn left on a track, then after another 425m, turn sharp right on a path soon meeting the field edge again. Turn left (north) on a path hitting the main southwest-leading route from Whitcliffe car park after 450m. Turn left, and follow this track for 500m.

7) Take the right-hand (southwest) branch-off from the track to **Whitcliffe viewpoint**, swinging southeast afterwards and rejoining the track temporarily. Soon afterwards, select a right-hand path curving right and descending forest to brush open ground ahead 425m later. This then pivots left to carry on the descent for 375m and cross the stream bottom of Mary Knoll Valley.

8) On the other side of the stream, on the track, turn right (north). Over the next 1.75km you'll follow this track, which soon bears northwest, leaving conifer plantation to journey through open mixed woodland and heath and then swings west then southwest to meet your outward route at a T-junction. Turn right 250m to the car park.

41. Stanage Edge from Hathersage

Live life – and spot birdlife – on the edge for the day: the most iconic edge in the Peak District, no less

NEED TO KNOW

START/FINISH: Hathersage railway station, S32 1DT

DISTANCE: 10.25km (6½ miles) (part circular, part out-and-back)

TIME: 3–3½ hours

KEY SPECIES: Ring ouzel, red grouse, curlew

MAP: OS Explorer OL1

TRANSPORT: Hathersage railway station at start

WALK ACCESSIBILITY: Not wheelchair/pushchair accessible; dogs allowed but on leads in ring ouzel breeding season (Mar–Jul)

DIFFICULTY: Moderate

MORE INFORMATION: visitpeakdistrict.com

Ring ouzel

Up in the Peak District, edges are escarpments: grand gritstone divides between tousled moorland above and green sheep fields below. Stanage Edge is the most iconic of these. This 6km bulwark of impregnable-looking crags provides the stage for some of the NP's finest hillwalking and climbing as it curves above the wildly scenic setting for one of the most seminal British novels, Charlotte Brontë's *Jane Eyre*.

The flagship species here is the red-listed ring ouzel, nesting on or below Stanage Edge. But this important upland bird site also hosts the likes of curlew and skylark, and red grouse are such constants that grouse drinking bowls were carved on Stanage Edge rocks in the early 20th century. Common lizards and adders can often be seen warming themselves along this walk's abundant rocky surfaces too. The best time to come is early (March/April) in ring ouzel breeding season, when the birds are most in evidence.

The other beautiful thing about this route is that you can rock up on a train from Sheffield in 20 minutes and start walking: an eco-friendly, fuss-free build-up to one of the must-do Peak District walks. The climb to Stanage Edge from the station is 275m, but gradual and on well-defined, well-waymarked paths.

ROUTE DESCRIPTION

1) Out of the railway station, turn left along Station Approach, then right on Back Lane, following it to its end at the Crossland Road/A6187 road junction. Continue ahead along the pavement on the left side of the A6187 into **Hathersage** village centre, crossing to the opposite pavement when the left-hand one ends. Look for narrow right-hand turn Baulk Lane, running along the side of an Alpkit store. Pass the cricket club and allotments off left and then three houses on the right. The well-defined path then runs north-northeast through several gates, Stanage Edge already impressive ahead and Hood Brook a field's breadth across to the left. Curve northwest to the right of Brookfield Manor 850m after the previous house. Then cross the next meadow to Birley Lane.

2) Keep straight over here. Another meadow follows: at its end pass through a gate in a dry-stone wall into winsome broadleaf woodland. Presently spot a green footpath sign, before which you turn left, crossing

RING OUZEL
Stopping over between March and September along England's south and east coasts, plus a few other UK sites, this red-list species resembles a longer-tailed blackbird with males sporting distinctive white chest bands.

Hood Brook on a footbridge. Ascend the wood, presently passing straight ahead through three fields to the buildings at Green's House. At a stile and gate, turn left for a few metres through a yard between buildings, then right with a wood-fringed stream on the left. Go through a gate and then scale a stile, climbing first north-northwest then northeast, to a gap in a wall on the right. Pass through, now keeping the wall immediately left to keep climbing, swinging left (north-northwest) with conifer woodland off left up to a lane.

3) Turn left across the cattle grid to where the lane bends left at the end of the conifers. Here veer right through Dennis Knoll car park on the track up onto **Stanage Edge**. This arcing approach north, northeast and then southeast shows the edge off gloriously. Watch for curlews and skylarks on the moor and ring ouzels closer to the crags. Up on top, you'll pass a waymark at the left-hand fork to Stanage Pole; carry straight on. Shortly afterwards is the acutely angled rocky right-hand path down off the edge, 1.8km after the car park (reach a wooden gate on the ridge-top path and you've overshot). The walk takes this, the most straightforward descent, though there are other paths down. You turn acutely left shortly after the descent begins, then head southeast, traversing spreads of ferns and some mixed woodland and aiming for the road running parallel with the edge below, delineated by another band of mixed woodland.

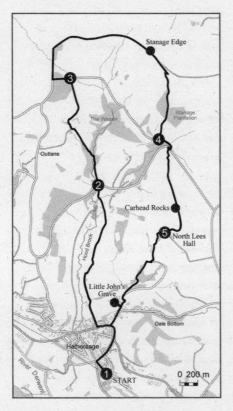

4) Turn left on the road, soon reaching a crossroads. Turn right over the cattle grid, then swing left on a path that gradually climbs south over Cattis-side Moor, passing alongside **Carhead Rocks** before swinging right (southwest) just below them on a path beside a wall. This descends to Leveret Lane at **North Lees Hall**, inspiration for Mr Rochester's Thornfield Hall in *Jane Eyre*.

5) Turn right, swinging around the hall through woods and then descending south along a treeline to Kimber Court Farm. Your way then passes Moorseats Hall, the drive swinging right then left, at which point a gate indicates a right-hand path that runs along the edge of a field with a helipad before veering left (southwest) down through more beguiling woods along a stream. About 250m down, the path veers left to cross a stream, then resumes the same direction to reach a gate and the lane at Camp Green 225m later. Turn right, then at Church Bank turn left. Immediately on the right is the short path to visit the **Little John's Grave**, trusted lieutenant of Robin Hood. Afterwards continue down Church Bank and continue straight ahead on School Lane. This meets the A6187 in 175m. Turn left, retracing your outward route to the station.

42. Kinder Scout from Edale

Tread where countryside access for all began in the realm of the mountain hare

NEED TO KNOW

START/FINISH: Edale railway station, S33 7ZN

DISTANCE: 15.5km (9¾ miles) (part circular, part out-and-back)

TIME: 5–5½ hours

KEY SPECIES: Mountain hare, merlin, short-eared owl

MAP: OS Explorer OL1

TRANSPORT: Edale railway station at start

WALK ACCESSIBILITY: Not wheelchair/pushchair accessible; dogs allowed

DIFFICULTY: Moderate–Difficult

SPECIFIC EQUIPMENT: Compass

MORE INFORMATION: visitpeakdistrict.com and nationaltrust.org.uk

Mountain hare

A hike around Kinder Scout is not just another wild Peak District day out. This, the highest point in the Midlands, is most crucially for nature lovers the scene of 1932's Kinder Scout Mass Trespass, which changed how we use the outdoors in Britain forever. Several hundred walkers, divided into three groups, converged on Kinder Scout from different directions simultaneously to protest against the public then being denied access to vast swathes of countryside. The trespass, and prison sentences given to protagonists, attracted wide-scale sympathy and became a huge contributing factor in the establishment of UK national parks, starting with the Peak District, and long-distance trails, starting with the Pennine Way.

Up on top, the streamlet-scored, rock-scattered Kinder Scout plateau more resembles Iceland than England and is an NNR that was extended in 2022 in recognition of ongoing work here researching the role peat moorland can play in combatting climate change. And there is much wildlife to celebrate. Mountain hares survive here and nowhere else in England or Wales. Scarce raptors like merlins and short-eared owls are moorland residents and ground-nesting birds like curlews are on the increase thanks to conservation efforts.

This tramp's trickiness lies not in its climbs but in the navigation necessary after Kinder Downfall waterfall across moorland where paths are faint for 3km, in stark contrast to the well-trodden trails elsewhere on the walk.

ROUTE DESCRIPTION

1) Come out of the station onto Mary's Lane and turn left into **Edale** village. You pass **Edale Visitor Centre**, a brilliant resource on the Peak District outdoors and a base for Moors for the Future, a partnership founded to promote, protect and restore moorland. Edale is the start of the Pennine Way, Britain's original long-distance footpath, and you will now be walking the first leg. The official start is **Old Nag's Head** 400m along Mary's Lane: the trail bears off left just beforehand. The route initially passes through a tree tunnel behind a campsite to reach a fork at the end.

2) Bear left (you'll return along the other fork) and follow the

MOUNTAIN HARE
Mountain hares are most recognisable for their white winter coats. These they grow in winter in place of their grey-brown fur to blend with their snowy home surroundings. They do not live in burrows, but in shallow depressions in the ground.

path southwest across fields to **Upper Booth Farm**. Here, recent surrounding peatbog restoration has significantly improved the wildlife showing by enticing back insects that ground-nesting birds like golden plover and curlew feed upon. Turn left at the gate, skirt around farm buildings on your left and then turn right on the track by the phone box.

3) You now enter remote country: there is no civilisation of any kind for 11.5km. Your route trundles along a metalled farm track, the River Noe on the left and bare hills gradually displacing the farmland ahead. You pass through Lee Farm, and the track becomes a path over the next 1km to the photogenic **Packhorse Bridge** over the river. Next, turn right to clamber up the relentless steps of **Jacob's Ladder**, after which you're on open moorland: a good place to catch merlins and short-eared owls hunting low over the heather. Proceed on the path to a fork in 500m. Turn right, the way being marked by paving slabs.

4) A large cairn marks another fork 300m later. The right-hand option is your return loop route if you do not fancy the rougher return path from Kinder Downfall waterfall taken by this walk. Both return routes converge 1.9km along this right-hand path, but this walk's route takes 5km to reach the same spot, taking in a beautiful waterfall and significantly increasing chances of wildlife sightings on a remoter part of the NNR. Sticking with this walk, fork left for the gradual climb to **Kinder Low trig point** (633masl) after 600m. The trig point is 3m lower than **Kinder Scout**'s highest point, about 800m out in the moors northeast of here. Note the bizarre shape of the trig point's rocks: Henry Moore was supposedly inspired by Kinder Scout's weather-blasted boulder formations into creating many of his sculptures.

5) The awe-inspiringly wild area you are now walking through falls within Kinder Scout NNR. As you progress along the next 2km north-northeast to Kinder Downfall, passing **Cluther Rocks** with Kinder Reservoir away out west, you were, until 2022, walking to the NNR's very edge. Now, with its extension, you are reaching its heart, so don't forget to wildlife-watch, with the aforementioned species all spottable here. **Kinder Downfall** itself is an impressive 30m-drop waterfall that blows back on itself in certain winds, creating spectacular spray clouds.

6) The next 3km bumps this walk up the difficulty ratings. You may need compass skills here. First, follow the River Kinder right, upriver away from the Pennine Way. Maps disagree which side of the River Kinder you follow, but the side you are on is best,

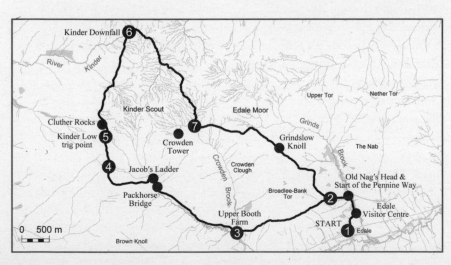

and this is not a difficult river to cross if necessary. Continue alongside the river about 950m, initially northeast then southeast or south-southeast. The route then crosses and leaves the River Kinder, heading east, then southeast along another stream. Presently, though, you'll need to take one of several minor paths zigzagging southeast: the number of them testimony to the different ways hikers have taken over time. Ultimately, you're aiming southeast to pick up the north-south-running Crowden Brook, which you should come alongside 300–700m after leaving the previous stream. Follow this south to hook up with the other return route mentioned in Point 4. Four routes and several streams converge here within the depression of a valley head below the crag of **Crowden Tower**.

7) Turn left. It's 1.1km along this path to a cairn where you turn southwest to **Grindslow Knoll**, from where it's 625m of gradual ascent to this wonderful hilltop viewpoint. From the summit (603masl) it's a steep 1.5km descent southeast back into the fields to Point 2. Retrace your outward route back to the station.

SOUTH
WALES

43. Kenfig Pool & Dunes

Be amazed by sand-blessed Kenfig Pool, dunes and beach as you search for rare flora, avians and amphibians

NEED TO KNOW

START/FINISH: Kenfig NNR car park, CF33 4PT (parking charges may apply)

DISTANCE: 6.25km (3¾ miles) (part circular, part out-and-back)

TIME: 1½–2 hours

KEY SPECIES: Bittern, great crested newt, orchids

MAP: OS Explorer 151/165

TRANSPORT: Heol Llan bus stop (buses to Porthcawl/Bridgend) – 2.25km (1½ miles) northeast

WALK ACCESSIBILITY: Mostly accessible to wheelchair/pushchair users except west shore of Kenfig Pool; dogs allowed

DIFFICULTY: Easy

SPECIFIC EQUIPMENT: Compass

MORE INFORMATION: kenfigcorporationtrust.co.uk

Who would have guessed that behind Port Talbot industrial area awaits one of Wales' wildest and finest sandy coastscapes? Resembling the frenzied excavations of a labour of giant shore-loving moles, Kenfig's colossal dune system, abutting the largest natural lake in South Wales, Kenfig Pool, is surreal and special. A medley of vast beaches, deep grass-topped dunes, mires, reedbeds and woods, this NNR- and SSSI-designated area is one of Britain's few year-round refuges for the bittern and protects numerous other nationally endangered species, like the great crested newt. Half the country's 59 known butterflies have been seen here too. Come in spring or summer, when the reserve's many orchids, including the fen orchid found in just two locations UK-wide, garland the dunes. Even in winter, terrain diversity ensures interesting bird spots like the stonechat and merlin.

Most paths are well defined, if muddy around Kenfig Pool, but myriad dune cross-paths make it easy to go off-piste. Embrace it and

embellish this walk by extending it into
the lonelier, possibly lovelier, north or
south of the reserve, where wildlife
sightings can be even better. There are
the usual dune ups and downs, but this
is a level walk overall.

ROUTE DESCRIPTION

1) Behind the Kenfig NNR Visitor
Centre (the side with the totem pole)
a connector path leads away from
the car park 40m to a path-side sign
pointing right to **Kenfig Pool**. Turn
right, following the path as it bears left
and descends across a wide grassy area
to the pool's sandy **beach**. Continue
around the shore through trees to
South Hide. Here, you can spot
waterbirds like ring-necked ducks and
grey herons, plus other scarcer birds
that stop by.

2) After passing between trees, your
path emerges into the open, bearing
right around the pool's west shore.
Pass through patches of trees and
more open grassy areas, reedbeds
to your right. The path then swings
along the north shore to reach an
elaborately carved bench with a
fish as the backrest.

> ### GREAT CRESTED NEWT
> The longest of the seven native UK
> amphibians (up to 17cm!), the great
> crested newt is black with an orange
> belly. Their black belly spots are
> unique to the individual newt, just like
> fingerprints to humans.

3) You now leave the pool for **Kenfig
Dunes**, also known as Kenfig
Burrows. Cut up to the right of the
bench, left of the treeline, to bend
left and pick up a path that runs
generally west as it threads towards
Sker Beach. The dunes host birdlife,
including short-eared owls, sandpipers
and terns, but dune paths are not
always clear. It is unlikely you'll get
lost, but if you are exploring beyond
the scope of this walk, a compass
is good back-up. Your route skirts
several small pools. It is the many
dune slacks, depressions that often
get flooded, that provide added
protection for wildlife here. Your path
runs beach-wards to reach the coast
path 1.75km after the bench.

Great crested
newt

155

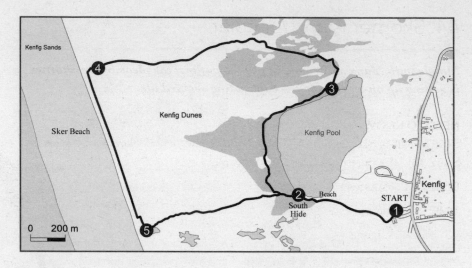

4) Here, at a waymark post, turning right takes you into the remoter northern dunes, but with no clear round-trip route. On this walk, now either follow the coast path left or continue straight, through a gap in the shoreside dunes, then left along the tawny sands of **Sker Beach**. After around 900m, leave the beach and return onto the coast path. A bridleway sign marks your return route off left through the dunes back to Kenfig Pool.

5) On the return leg, there again appear to be several paths. Try and follow the one heading east-northeast and bearing along a long, level grassy stretch. Almost 1km after the bridleway sign, you'll reach the woods surrounding Kenfig Pool, coming alongside **South Hide**. From here, retrace your outward route 650m to the car park.

44. Skomer Island Circular

Mingle with Manx shearwaters; peer at puffins: the pleasure on Skomer is getting up oh-so-close to the captivating seabird life

NEED TO KNOW

START/FINISH: Skomer ferry landing platform, Skomer (3.25km/2 miles west of SA62 3BL, the closest postcode for sat-nav purposes)

DISTANCE: 6km (3¾ miles) (circular)

TIME: 2–2½ hours

KEY SPECIES: Puffin, Manx shearwater, grey seal

MAP: OS Explorer OL36

TRANSPORT: Martin's Haven car park bus stop (buses to St Davids/Broad Haven/Solva May–Sep) – 3.25km (2 miles) east, on mainland. Then walk 300m (¼ mile) northwest to Martin's Haven ferry terminal and take ferry to start

WALK ACCESSIBILITY: Not wheelchair/pushchair accessible; no dogs

DIFFICULTY: Easy

MORE INFORMATION: welshwildlife.org

Manx
shearwater

Around half of the world's breeding population of Manx shearwaters; Southern Britain's largest Atlantic puffin colony: tiny Skomer's wildlife boasts are big indeed. Seabird breeding season here (April–August) also features razorbills, oystercatchers, kittiwakes, storm petrels and cormorants. *Springwatch* visited the area, one of the most important seabird breeding sites in Southern Britain, both in 2019 and 2022. Short-eared owls swoop along the island's North Valley, Skomer's own endemic bank vole sub-species rustles in the undergrowth, rabbits bound and burrow and the flora is dazzling: scout out for scarce fern lanceolate spleenwort and rock sea-lavender among ubiquitous pink cloaks of sea campion.

But there are two headline acts. Cross-continental travellers Manx shearwaters, 300,000 of which breed here, only show themselves in darkness for fear of the gulls that prey on them. This leaves daytime showmanship to the puffins: around 12,000 check in for the breeding season in clifftop burrows rabbits have often helped excavate. Sand eels, to judge from their over-stuffed bills, are the set menu, and pretty much every bird flunked the flight school lesson on graceful touchdown techniques.

Not permanently inhabited since 1950, NNR and SSSI Skomer is a place where wildlife has learned not to fear humans. This means you can get close, but do not abuse the privilege, and leave the creatures some space. You'll make a circuit of Skomer on this amble, undulating but grassy and easy-going after the initial climb from the landing platform.

ROUTE DESCRIPTION

1) Places aboard any day's sailings to Skomer are limited and fill fast: book tickets in advance and pay for them at **Lockley Lodge Visitor Centre** on the mainland at Martin's Haven, where there is also visitor information on Skomer and neighbouring isle Skokholm. On the island, clamber the steep steps from the landing platform to the **visitor information booth**, where the newly arrived get an introduction to the island and its wildlife from the island warden.

2) From here, take the path heading up; ignore a grassy right-hand path and meet the stony main island track in 175m. Turn right here (left is private) and a few metres along take the narrow left-hand path signposted to The Wick. Views off left here are of The Neck, a bulbous Skomer peninsula not accessible to visitors. Your path follows the coast along clockwise, crossing the base of a hammerhead-shaped peninsula to arrive at puffin metropolis **The Wick**. Here thousands of puffins go about their business seemingly unconcerned by their human onlookers nearby. There is action on both sides of the paths as puffins fly in from out at sea to burrows almost at onlookers' feet. On the more vertiginous cliff ledges, a motley crew of kittiwakes, fulmars, razorbills, guillemots, cormorants and more make their nests. You're so in among the puffins, though, that you'll want to stay for some time.

PUFFIN

With their broad, brightly hued bills, black-and-red eye markings, muttering croaks and ungainly landing strategy, puffins are the comics of the cliffs and among the world's best-loved, most easily recognised birds, their appearance registering somewhere on the spectrum between melancholy and ridiculous. They breed in big numbers at just a few UK sites.

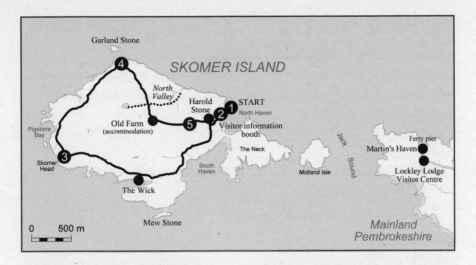

3) Continue clockwise around the island coast 950m to **Skomer Head**, a springtime spectacle of sea thrift and sea campion. The path then swings north to **Pigstone Bay**, a stretch along which grey seal sightings are likely on offshore rocks. As you turn to the northeast for the 1.25km walk along to the island's northern tip, the seal-spotting gets better yet: **Garland Stone**, off the northernmost point, is a favourite seal playground and, in autumn, pupping site.

4) There is no path on around the coast from here: instead, swing inland (southeast). The buildings of **Old Farm**, Skomer's only accommodation, are soon visible ahead but first up you cross **North Valley**, a gentle vegetated dip in which you may spy short-eared owls hunting. At Old Farm, you pick up the other end of the main island track. Turn left (east).

5) After 450m along the track, turn left on a grassy path, which curves right to a path crossroads after 250m. Just left along here is the 1.7m-high **Harold Stone**, a prehistoric monolith. Afterwards, it's the right-hand path at the crossroads you want, which reaches the track again after a few metres. Turn left, and you are on your outward route back to the landing platform.

45. Bosherston Lily Ponds, Broad Haven South, St Govan's Chapel & Elegug Stacks

Mix in head-turning company: lakes, woods, beaches, soaring cliffs, solitary grasslands and their eclectic resident creatures

NEED TO KNOW

START/FINISH: Bosherston Lily Ponds NT car park, Bosherston, SA71 5DN (parking charges may apply)

DISTANCE: 19.5km (12¼ miles) (circular)

TIME: 5–5½ hours

KEY SPECIES: White water lily, red-billed chough, guillemot

MAP: OS Explorer OL36

TRANSPORT: St Michael's Church bus stop, Bosherston (buses to Pembroke May–Sep) – 100m southwest

WALK ACCESSIBILITY: Mostly accessible to wheelchair/pushchair users; dogs allowed

DIFFICULTY: Moderate

MORE INFORMATION: nationaltrust.org and gov.uk (for firing range information)

Few places can mix so many different terrain types so beguilingly in such a short distance as Bosherston and its vicinity's enclave of woodland, wetland, beach, big weather-chiselled cliffs and grassland plateau. This is grand news for nature hereabouts, for which variety is the spice. But two singular habitats here really let wildlife flourish, both artificial. The first is Bosherston Lily Ponds, created by local landowners in the 1780s

White water lily

> **WHITE WATER LILY**
> A hallmark of country estate water features and thriving on such old ornamental ponds and lakes, as well as other slow-moving water bodies, this plant produces the UK's largest flower – reaching 20cm in diameter.

over limestone beds, encouraging stonewort to thrive that in turn improves biodiversity. The other is the Castlemartin Range, an army training zone since the 1930s and thus shut off from the vast majority of human activity detrimental to wildlife.

Around the ponds the white water lilies are in full glory during June and July, reed and sedge warblers rustle in lakeside undergrowth in summer, and the UK's most endangered bat, the greater horseshoe, musters in maternity colonies from May. Spy otters with luck year round. Rare red-billed choughs and dark green fritillary butterflies are found on the range's unspoilt grassy heathlands. And then there are the clifftop seabird shenanigans: guillemots hogging the rock stack tops, with razorbills, fulmars and some puffins also tumultuously staking out vertical tenancies from May through July.

This route is long but level, and mostly on the firm paths of national trails or lanes. The coastal stretch is wheelchair- and pushchair-accessible (park at Broad Haven South Beach):

Bosherston Lily Ponds entails steps. Check Castlemartin Range firing times before setting off: you cannot walk beyond Broad Haven South when firing is in progress.

ROUTE DESCRIPTION

1) For the first 1.5km you are walking through the Stackpole NNR, Wales-renowned for its species diversity. Descending to the lakeside from the car park there are two paths: a lower (down steps) and an upper. Take the upper one, initially brushing a grassy picnic area, descending to **Bosherston Lily Ponds**, turning left and crossing the lake's western arm on the causeway. This is a great spot for enjoying dense carpets of white water lilies. Next, follow the western arm's north shore for 400m, ascending slightly to a right-hand branch-off, which soon leads to a cleared bluff. This is a wonderful lake **viewpoint** where you can also espy green spreads of stonewort, a rare algae important for biodiversity, in the water.

2) Back on the main path, you presently descend steps to cross another causeway over the central arm. Turn right, soon meeting a wider track and bearing right again: you'll then bend left and cross the eastern arm on Grassy Bridge. Enter Stackpole Warren, emerging from foliage with open grass and dunes off left and presently, as reeds start dominating the lake's southern reaches, keep a summertime eye out for reed and sedge warblers. Watch for otters here too. Now leave the lake behind you, ignoring the eastbound coast path on the left and reaching a bench with a boardwalk onto **Broad Haven South Beach** ahead. Descend onto the beach, distinctive off-shore **Church Rock** framed beyond. After exploring the dune-backed sands, exit from the beach's far southwest corner back up onto the coast path just above.

3) The coast path skirts left of the beach car park, then cuts across a grassy field to the guard booth and gate signifying your entrance onto Castlemartin Range. This is a stunning section of the walk, through grassy, gorsey coastal heath and

atop cliffs wrought into incredible formations. The way is straightforward (keep the sea on your left) until Elegug Stacks 6km along the coast path. But there is much to see beforehand.

4) The bulky peninsula of **St Govan's Head** now rears ahead. Turn off after 875m to walk out along its far side: it's a good spot to scour the sea for dolphins and appreciate the cliff scenery looking back. Bear left on the return to connect with the coast path again, and presently make the diversion down steep steps to **St Govan's Chapel**, perched within a cliff cleft. Sixth-century Irish monk Govan supposedly founded the chapel but the building is 13th-century. A little further along the coast path is impressive **Huntsman's Leap**, a narrow, sheer-sided geo running over 150m back from the open sea.

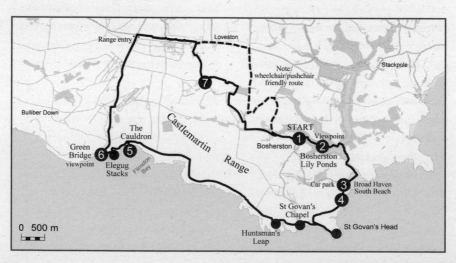

5) Another 4km, and you reach a series of spectacular coastal formations, enhanced by vast populations of chattering seabirds. First, it's **The Cauldron**, a gargantuan cliff-edged depression in the ground through which the sea swills. **Elegug Stacks**, a pair of mighty off-shore rock pillars 400m further on, are the seabirds' favourite. 'Elegug' means guillemot in Welsh and these noisy roosting tenants steal the limelight in the May–July breeding season, though other seabirds including puffins are also present. Another 250m beyond the stacks is a viewpoint from where you can look back on **Green Bridge**, a rock arch.

6) From this viewpoint, you can retrace your outward route along the coast or make a round trip by first following a grassy path leading northeast to a car park and onto Ermigate Lane. Follow this 2.5km across Castlemartin Range to the B4319 road. Turn right for 1.25km: after 325m you can use a roadside path alongside the MOD complex. Then turn right on a dead-end lane signposted 'Thorne Chapel'. The lane kinks left then right, terminating in a gate onto Castlemartin Range.

7) After the gate, turn sharp left along the path on the other side of the next hedge. Swing around three field edges to a copse, turn right, cross the MOD road and follow the right side of a field hedge to its end. Carew Farm is then passed on your left, and your path curves left to join the farm track after the next field. Turn right: the track swings left, meeting the road into Bosherston at a gate 900m later. Turn right and the car park entrance is 450m on the left.

46. Llyn y Fan Fach, Llyn y Fan Fawr, Fan Brycheiniog & Carreg yr Ogof

Enter the sacred swooping ground of the red kite, an elemental domain of elegiac lakes, escarpment and emptiness

NEED TO KNOW

START/FINISH: Llyn y Fan Fach car park, just east of Blaenau Farmyard campsite, SA19 9UN (parking free)

DISTANCE: 19.75km (12¼ miles) (part circular, part out-and-back)

TIME: 6½–7 hours

KEY SPECIES: Red kite, buzzard, raven

MAP: OS Explorer OL12

TRANSPORT: Llangadog railway station – 14km (8¾ miles) northwest

WALK ACCESSIBILITY: Not wheelchair/pushchair accessible; dogs allowed

DIFFICULTY: Moderate–Difficult

SPECIFIC EQUIPMENT: Compass

MORE INFORMATION: breconbeacons.org

An emerald patchwork of river-threaded fields and wooded valleys below and rolls of yellow-green, red-brown moor ruptured by craggy escarpment above, the Brecon Beacons NP spans half the width of Wales: a dramatic divide between the Welsh valleys to the south and Mid Wales to the north. This hike provides the perfect mix of the aforementioned terrain types, arranged around two talismanic *llyns* (lakes) theatrically ramparted by steep, fluted rockfaces and some of the NP's most solitary scenery.

Before the bird's successful reintroduction in other parts of Wales and England, this was one of the last refuges of the red kite, and it is still a key stronghold for the raptor, along with buzzards, kestrels and ravens. Streams on the lower ground, meanwhile, are magnets for pied and yellow wagtails and dippers. The Mynydd Du (Black Mountain) SSSI covers the entire walk, as does Fforest Fawr Geopark: bestowed for the rare plant life, like the dwarf willow and roseroot, clinging on to the escarpment here and standout examples of glacier-wrought geological features, such as those around Llyn y Fan Fach. Nor does the fun stop at sundown: the Brecon Beacons became Wales' first International Dark Sky Reserve in 2013.

Any time of year could scoop sightings of the above birds, but plump for a clear day. This is one lung-busting leg stretch, with steep, relentless ascents and some faint, boggy paths that require navigation skills if bad weather sweeps in.

ROUTE DESCRIPTION

1) Continue on up the solid track from the car park that curves right (southeast) over the Nant Melyn stream and climbs alongside the rushing waters of Afon Sawdde, a good bet for spotting dippers. You'll pass a trout farm in 925m and draw level with the emergency shelter and dam at **Llyn y Fan Fach** in a further 1.1km. The llyn, naturally occurring despite being dammed, is not merely a highlight of this hike, but of Welsh hiking generally. The water nestles right into a magnificent glacial cirque that rises steeply above southern and western shores, its green cliffs horizontally scored by prominent rock strata and vertically by many stream gullies. It harbours its own non-Arthurian Lady of the Lake

RED KITE
These handsome raptors with their chestnut colouring and deeply forked tails (the latter distinguishing them from buzzards, which have fan-shaped tails) are flourishing today, but almost became extinct UK-wide in the 20th century. They were saved only by one of Europe's most successful all-time wildlife conservation projects, begun in 1989, which reintroduced the birds to England and Scotland.

legend too. The great thing about the onward route is that you'll get to see the escarpment that curls northeast from here in a stunning stretch of geological showiness both from the base and from the topmost edge.

2) First: the escarpment base. Continuing east-southeast past Llyn y Fan Fach dam on your right, the path presently curves left to meet a leat right below the escarpment's face. Stay alongside this for 525m, presently curving right (northeast) to meet the Afon Sychlwch (here a narrow gully of a stream). You swing right here, Afon Sychlwch nearby on your left. Continue for 925m, coming close under the escarpment's riven sides, to where a steep path zigzags up the cliff just before your cliff-base path crosses a stream. Take note of the zigzagging cliff path: the walk shortcut returns this way.

3) The cliff-base path continues 75m east-northeast over the stream to a fork: keep right, beside the escarpment. Your route bends beside the steep ground to your right. Head northeast, north and then northeast – 1.2km in total – then veer southeast with the escarpment a further 1.1km to hit the north edge of **Llyn y Fan Fawr**. This llyn is as large and dramatically situated as Llyn y Fan Fach but is remoter and so gets fewer visitors. Skirt the eastern shore, then swing along the south shore to clamber northwest up the escarpment: an elevation gain of 120m.

4) Turn right along the escarpment top, looking out now for red kites and buzzards on the upland and ravens in the crags. Ascend gradually northwest to **Fan Brycheiniog**. At 802masl, this is the fifth-highest point in the NP and indeed anywhere in Wales or England south of Snowdonia. *Fan* is Welsh for peak but is usually associated with the Brecon Beacons' distinctive summits and their shapes resembling waves about to break.

5) From here, you're tracing the escarpment line back to Llyn y Fan Fach, only now more dramatically from the sometimes-vertiginous lip. Although you keep the sheer drops off right, the lip still negotiates big ups and downs. Head northwest to cairn-crested **Fan Foel**, thrusting out over the lower ground, from where views back to Fan Brycheiniog and on to Picws Du, the escarpment's next big protrusion, are superb. The route swerves southwest from Fan Foel 825m to the top of your return

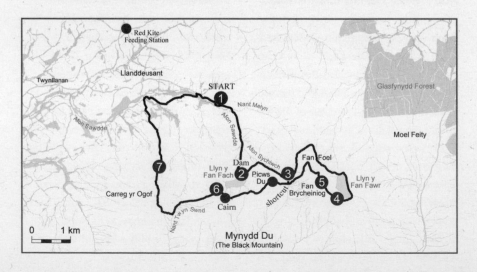

shortcut down the escarpment to map Point 3 (retrace your outward route from there). It's then 450m up to **Picws Du** and another sweeping 1.75km to where you swing left (southwest) away from the escarpment lip. The trick is knowing exactly when to turn, as the path off is indistinct. As the main path bends right as it passes Llyn y Fan Fach's southwest corner, there is a cairn above left. The turn-off is 250m further along the escarpment lip path.

6) Follow the faint path, which becomes clearer in places, for 1.1km southwest, gradually approaching Nant Twyn Swnd stream off left. Though not marked on most maps, the path continues, swinging south-southwest with the stream for 425m to meet a far-firmer path. Here, turn right. Proceed west-northwest then north to the next clear objective, **Carreg yr Ogof** (585masl) with its trig point and **cave** just north of the top. Your path heads north, skirting just east of the stone-scattered summit to then join the Beacons Way long-distance path.

7) Continue north 1km down to a rusty gate and stile indicating your exit from the moor. Moorland-farmland divides like this are known as *ffridd* in Welsh and are their own unique habitat, popular with birds like foraging wheatears in summer. A pretty path descends tree-dotted field edges, passes into woodland and becomes a track, then a lane at the far treeline. Bear right down the lane, then turn right on the metalled track in 350m. This skirts left of farm buildings in 675m to continue northeast to Gorsddu Farm and its Wildman Woods campsite in another 375m. Turn left on the farm drive. This becomes a lane swinging left over the Afon Sawdde river in 450m. Then turn right on the lane, which you will recognise as the way you accessed the walk start. Pass Blaenau Farmyard campsite off right, skirt right around the actual farm just afterwards and proceed along the track to the start car park.

47. Rhossili Bay, Worm's Head, Rhossili Downs & the Burrows

Enter avian Elysium on a sublime coastal circuit beloved by seabirds, raptors, waders and wildfowl

NEED TO KNOW

START/FINISH: Rhossili Bay NT car park, Rhossili, SA3 1PR (parking charges may apply)

DISTANCE: 29.5km (18¼ miles) or 34km (21 miles) with Worm's Head extension (circular)

TIME: Full day

KEY SPECIES: Marsh harrier, sanderling, yellow whitlow grass

MAP: OS Explorer 164

TRANSPORT: Rhossili Terminus (buses to Swansea) – 200m east

WALK ACCESSIBILITY: Not wheelchair/pushchair accessible; dogs allowed

DIFFICULTY: Difficult

SPECIFIC EQUIPMENT: Swimwear

MORE INFORMATION: nationaltrust.org.uk

One of the UK's most gobsmacking sandy beaches, Rhossili Bay's 4.75km smile of golden sand rather dominates conversations about what to do on the delightful Gower peninsula AONB's western seaboard. But there are other talking points aplenty, as this epic reconnoitre reveals.

Early stages whirl you out to Worm's Head, a tidal island named for its serpent-like shape and a seabird and grey seal haven. You'll traverse Gower Coast NNR, known for its rare flowers like early gentian and yellow whitlow grass, found only here within the UK. Progress onto glorious Rhossili Downs and you might descry skylarks, yellowhammers, red-billed choughs or cavorting brown hares. And as you reach surfing hotspot Llangennith, you are into Burrows territory: some of Britain's most extensive dunes that combine with marshes at Whiteford NNR to create a fantastic avian habitat for pintail ducks, knots, sanderlings, redshanks, snipe and golden plovers. One of Britain's rarest raptors, the marsh harrier, also hunts over the Gower's northern marshes. May is a great seabird month, but come in winter for Whiteford NNR's wildfowl and wader action.

This walk has everything: tidal islands, towering cliffs, flower-rich heath, huge dunes, coastal woods and wide-open marshes. Check tide times for accessing Worm's Head, reachable only for around 2 hours either side of low tide. Terrain is easy-going enough but the distance should not be underestimated.

ROUTE DESCRIPTION

1) From the car park, the **Worm's Head Hotel** and **Rhossili Bay** beach to the right look enticing but save them for later (this walk returns along the beach). Turn left (sea on your right) along the coast path to begin. Pass the old coastguard cottages, continuing through a gate along a broad metalled track. Off left over the dry-stone wall is **The Vile**, a medieval open field strip-farming system, NT managed with nature-

friendly methods. After 875m the surfaced track swings left: continue straight on the grassy path for increasingly dramatic views of Worm's Head ahead. This runs along grassy clifftops to the NCI station 375m later.

2) Here is the access path down to the causeway to **Worm's Head**, tide permitting (the out-and-back route adds 4.5km to the walk). You can walk to the end of this steep-sided snaking tidal island, a magnet for kittiwakes, razorbills, fulmars and grey seals. Beware of getting cut off by the tides. This misfortune once befell Welsh bard Dylan Thomas, who based *Who Do You Wish Was With Us?* on the experience. Afterwards, continue along the coast path, gorse thickets off right and a dry-stone wall soon off left. Keep the wall left until a headland with **Fall Bay** ahead. Continue around above the bay, pick up the wall off left again and stay straight ahead, close to the wall, when the coast path swings right at the bay's end. Presently, spot an iron ladder beside steps to a kissing gate. Pass through and branch right across the field through another gate. Your route now trundles through fields, heading northeast along a green lane that reaches Middleton village at Rhossili Bunkhouse.

3) Turn briefly right on the B4247 road, left on School Lane at the post

YELLOW WHITLOW GRASS

These diminutive yellow-flowered Gower pots of gold are more usually found in the Mediterranean, but within the UK they grow only on rocks and old walls along the Gower peninsula.

box for 625m, then left on a gorse-flanked track by a metal gate on the right. You now wind up onto **Rhossili Down**, following a broad, initially stony, then grassy track up through the bracken up to **The Beacon** (193masl) after 1km, from where views of western Gower, a montage of moor, beach, farmland and distant marsh, are fantastic. These downs have been significant to people for millennia and, scattered around the clear path north that eventually descends to the road to the north of Hillend Camping

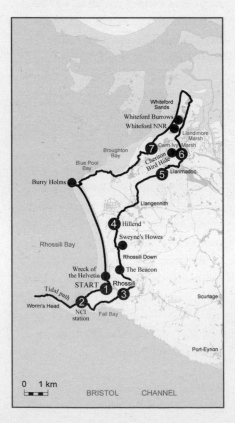

Park 2km later, is much archaeological interest. Many cairns dot the hillside and you can branch right (off-route) to see Neolithic **Sweyne's Howes** chambered cairn after 750m. This is also a stretch for spotting moor-loving yellowhammers and red-billed choughs, plus swooping peregrine falcons and kestrels.

4) Turn right along Moor Lane for 1.25km to a mini-roundabout in Llangennith village. Continue straight on a dead-end lane. This ascends to a bus stop and right-hand lane after 125m. Follow this straight up past houses onto the slopes of Llanmadoc Hill. You're now beset with many path choices, but continue straight up ahead and then left, crossing a broader track and picking up a clear path heading north then east around the hillside for 2km. Handily for orientation, Llanmadoc village slides into view, fetchingly framed by the marsh, woods, dunes and sands of Whiteford NNR, your next objective, behind you.

5) Your path comes right alongside the field edge for one field's length, after which a track bends left off the heath, left, right, then right again onto a metalled lane. Follow this down into the village, turning left on a lane in 150m, then right onto Frog Lane. Next, in 325m, turn left on a pedestrian cut-through beside a white house, curving round right between houses to meet the left-hand track onto the marsh in 125m. This bends through then along a curling finger of **Cwm Ivy Woods** to a path junction 650m later. Take the left-hand out-and-back 625m path to **Cheriton Bird Hide** here for possible spots of kingfishers, marsh harriers and other wading and wildfowl birds on **Cwm Ivy Marsh**.

6) Back at the path junction, now proceed north-northwest across the marsh to a gate before the right-hand end of some Monterey pines and a coast path sign. Turn right. You'll now skirt the wood-stippled vegetated sand dunes (burrows) of **Whiteford NNR**, bounded by vast Llandimore Marsh (east) and Whiteford Sands (west), for 5.5km. This avian paradise offers more excellent birdwatching: start by looking for species mentioned in the walk introduction. Follow the coast path north-northeast, round the northern end of the colonised dunes and swing southwest down the other side. You'll pass Whiteford Sands and eventually the other side of the same pinewoods you encountered at the beginning of Point 6. After the final patch of conifers, curve left inland.

7) Next, turn right along the coast path. The way runs along field edges, dunes and sands below. You'll pass Whiteford Bay Leisure Park and Broughton Farm Caravan Park skirting Broughton Bay, then follow the north edge of Broughton Burrows' colonised dune tops past **Blue Pool Bay**, a pretty swimming spot, to **Burry Holms** ahead. This tidal island becomes accessible 2½ hours after high tide – check tide times beforehand – and is a riot of summertime thrift and sea campion. You're now at the northern end of Rhossili Bay beach. Finish this hike with the beautiful sandy beach walk south until the path back up to the clifftop, Worm's Head Hotel and car park at a footpath sign after 4.25km.

MID &
NORTH
WALES

48. Gwenffrwd-Dinas Reserve & Twm Siôn Cati's Cave

Stroll sessile oak woods on the cusp of the Mid Wales moors

NEED TO KNOW

START/FINISH: RSPB Gwenffrwd-Dinas car park, SA20 0PG – 5.5km (3½ miles) north of Rhandirmwyn (parking free, entry charges may apply)

DISTANCE: 3.75km (2¼ miles) (part circular, part out-and-back)

TIME: 1–1½ hours

KEY SPECIES: Sessile Atlantic oak, pied flycatcher, redstart

MAP: OS Explorer 187

TRANSPORT: Llandovery railway station – 16km (10 miles) south

WALK ACCESSIBILITY: Not wheelchair/pushchair accessible; dogs on leads

DIFFICULTY: Easy

MORE INFORMATION: rspb.org.uk

England has Robin Hood; Wales has Twm Siôn Cati. While much of remote, hilly Mid Wales, far from frequented highways, would have been the domain of outlaws in past centuries, the most brigand-beleaguered part was this neck of the woods, where the fertile farmland of the River Tywi swoops up into the *mynydd* (upland). One man made this area notorious for lawlessness. Twm Siôn Cati garnered a reputation hereabouts in the late 1500s and early 1600s for robbing from the rich and relieving them of their wealth through all manner of cunning schemes (his giving to the poor was rather less well documented.) Cati roamed all the land between the Tywi and Tregaron, but his supposed lair was a cave on the wooded knoll that is today the Gwenffrwd-Dinas reserve.

Pied flycatcher

ATLANTIC OAK WOODS

These increasingly rare woodlands are found in the wet uplands of western Britain from Sutherland (Scotland) through Gwynedd (Wales) down to Cornwall. A mild, moist oceanic climate lends these usually sessile oak-dominated woods huge species diversity, from the birdlife down to the wealth of lichens and bryophytes.

It is almost as hidden away now as in Cati's era. The steep, isolated hillsides mean trees here have never been in danger of being felled for pasturage and so these gnarled spreads of oak and alder have survived centuries with little human intervention, guarded by the tumbling waters of the Tywi and Pysgotwr and with spectacularly wild moorland rearing behind.

May and June are special times to visit, when lower slopes are carpeted in bluebells and a chorus of tree pipit, redstart and wood warbler reverberates through the branches. Later summer is perfect for pied flycatchers, with the reserve one of Britain's best places for spying them. Glance skywards, and you are almost certain to see red kites. This part of Wales was instrumental in bringing the raptors back from virtual extinction in the 1960s.

This circuit of the reserve is on defined, well-marked woodland paths throughout, with a couple of sections requiring scrambling over boulders and tree roots.

ROUTE DESCRIPTION

1) Exit the car park under the arched shelter and through the gate onto the boardwalk. Follow the boardwalk through the wooded wetland for about 450m.

2) At the end of the boardwalk you meet paths leading left and right around the wooded knoll forming the bulk of the reserve. This is a great place for bluebells in spring. Take the left-hand path, initially ascending gently, winding clockwise around the lower slopes of the wood.

3) Where the path comes close to a stile and gate onto a road on the left, keep following the clear, narrow path clockwise around the wood (not entering the field ahead) for almost 1km. Towards the end of this stretch, the path climbs more steeply over rocks to reach a waymarked path junction.

4) The path bearing steeply up the wooded slope for approximately 250m is the out-and-back path to **Twm Siôn Cati's Cave**. The cave is more of a cliff fissure and is carved with traveller graffiti dating back to Victorian times.

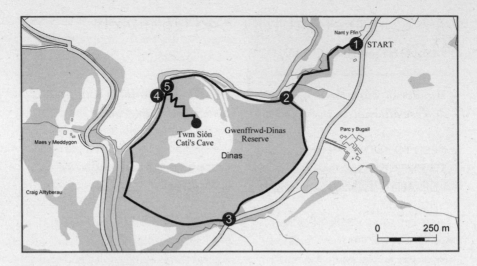

5) Back at the waymarked path junction after visiting the cave, turn right to continue on a rocky, sometimes slippery, section, soon descending alongside the Tywi. There are beautiful riverside picnicking spots here and impressive views onto the moors above where red kites can often be found wheeling. Following the riverside path a short distance returns you to the boardwalk at point 2 again, and your outward route.

49. Coed Felenrhyd, Coed Llennyrch & Ceunant Llennyrch

Wander through the dripping Welsh rainforest for a more wildlife-diverse alternative to Snowdonia's classic mountainscapes

NEED TO KNOW

START/FINISH: Lay-by 100m northeast of Maentwrog Power Station on A496, LL41 4HY – 1.25km (¾ mile) southwest of Maentwrog (parking free)

DISTANCE: 4km (2½ miles) (circular)

TIME: 1–1½ hours

KEY SPECIES: Atlantic oak, lesser horseshoe bat, otter, redstart

MAP: OS Explorer OL18

TRANSPORT: Llandecwyn railway station (request stop) – 5.25km (3¼ miles) southwest

WALK ACCESSIBILITY: Not wheelchair/pushchair accessible; dogs allowed

DIFFICULTY: Easy

MORE INFORMATION: woodlandtrust.org.uk

Welcome to the Snowdonia below the cinematic peaks. In ancient Welsh text *The Mabinogion*, Coed Felenrhyd was the final resting place of the hero Pryderi, King of Dyfed; today it comprises among the last and largest stands of Atlantic oak woods, also known as Celtic rainforest, left in Wales. This walk is a pretty preamble to a serious subject: woods like these are a particularly threatened terrain type. Together with adjacent woodland Coed Llennyrch, Coed Felenrhyd spreads in an inky band of oak, beech, rowan and birch along the steep slopes of the Afon Prysor river and its gorge Ceunant Llennyrch, the name given to the over-arching NNR. Some areas have been almost untouched by human activity since the last Ice Age.

Over 60 nationally rare species of liverworts, lichens and mosses swaddle the gorge's trees and rocks, including signal moss, found only in North Wales and Southwest Ireland. This is a sanctuary for lesser horseshoe bats, otters scout the river for fish and ravens favour the gorge's crags. Other native birds include jays and water-loving dippers, while redstarts join them in spring and summer.

The woods get dazzling springtime bluebell displays, with May a magnificent month to witness them and the birdlife at its most varied. Woodland paths do get muddy and this walk begins with a fairly steep climb.

ROUTE DESCRIPTION

1) From the lay-by, carefully head down the A496 road past Maentwrog Power Station, taking the gated track left immediately after. The way soon forks, with your return path to the left, but fork right for now and presently pass through a kissing gate up ahead to enter the fecund depths of **Coed Felenrhyd**. Coed Felenrhyd excellently exemplifies regenerating broadleaf woodland: as you ascend quite relentlessly southeast on the path you will be able to contrast this with the conifer plantations further

up the hill that started to dominate the ancient woodland in the 20th century, developed to allay fears about inadequate home-grown timber supply. The main difference for nature is the lush understorey in Atlantic oak woods that supports an abundance of life – the forest floor in conifer plantations is usually dead. There is only really one path up, passing a bench and through a gap in a dry-stone wall near the top of the climb. From here it's another 300m before the path swings up sharply right (southwest) to a kissing gate and track.

2) Turn left on the track, reaching a fork in 50m near some buildings: turn left here. This track leads past a cottage on the left and later an old barn. Veer round to the right of the wall that subsequently crosses the path to descend to another wall set with a kissing gate alongside a stream. This is the entrance to **Coed Llennyrch**, which is worth an exploration (this walk pops across for a quick look; remember however far you venture that you must return the same way). The woods feel different to Coed Felenrhyd, having never been planted with conifers and instead historically used for small-scale grazing. This has meant a more moss- and flower-rich forest floor has developed here.

REDSTART

Likely the most instantly identifiable creature in these woods with its vibrant orange-red tail and slate-grey upper parts, the redstart bears similarities to robins (behaviourally) and nightingales (in size and shape). It prefers mature oak and birch woodlands and within Britain is most prevalent in Wales.

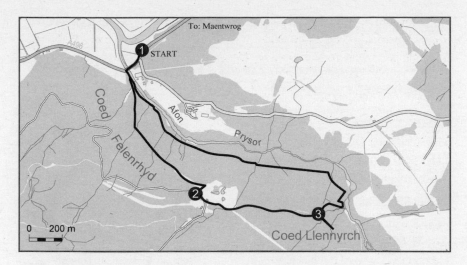

3) The onward route does not go through the gate but swerves left, with the wall on the right, descending to cross a stile. It then bends left and right to reach a viewpoint over the gorge by an impressive **waterfall**. Afterwards, this path now continues, heading west downhill and then uphill again before dropping down steps to cross a footbridge. There will be an area of boulders on the left before you descend again on more steps. You'll cross another footbridge and come down again beside the Afon Prysor. Look for otters and bank voles here before passing the aptly ivy-draped Ivy Bridge off right and continuing riverside to rejoin your outward route on the track alongside the power station, the A496 ahead.

Redstart

179

50. Newborough Forest & Ynys Llanddwyn

Wander wondrous forests, beaches and a tidal island searching for red squirrels, waders and seabirds

NEED TO KNOW

START/FINISH: Llyn Parc Mawr car park, LL61 6SU – 2km (1¼ miles) northwest of Newborough (parking free)

DISTANCE: 16km (10 miles) (circular)

TIME: 3–3½ hours

KEY SPECIES: Red squirrel, raven, Brent goose

MAP: OS Explorer 263

TRANSPORT: Newborough Forest bus stop
(buses to Newborough/Malltraeth/Menai Bridge/Bangor) – 100m southwest

WALK ACCESSIBILITY: Accessible to wheelchair/pushchair users until Traeth Llanddwyn; dogs under close control in Newborough Forest; no dogs on beach stretch May–Sep

DIFFICULTY: Moderate

MORE INFORMATION: naturalresources.wales

Red
squirrel

Spiritual Ynys Llanddwyn is a far-removed finger of land jutting into the sea off southernmost Anglesey, surrounded by some of Wales' most exquisite sandy beaches, dunes and forest. A tidal island, it was Ynys Llanddwyn to which Dwynwen, Welsh patron saint of lovers, retreated in the 5th century AD to become a hermit. Dwynwen raised a chapel, purportedly studying healing properties of local herbs and becoming widely renowned for her curative powers; the chapel site later became a major medieval pilgrimage destination. Visitors aplenty still come: holidaymakers drawn by the history and serenity of the spot, and abundant wildlife too.

Newborough Forest forms this walk's splendid approach to Ynys Llanddwyn and beguiles with its immense Corsican pines, initially planted for dune stabilisation. The large, light forest offers Wales' best red squirrel-spotting and is an important raven roosting site. The Afon Cefni estuary is a nesting and feeding area for wigeon, teal and lapwing, plus wintering migrants like Brent geese, while breeding cormorants jostle on the rocks off Ynys Llanddwyn in spring. The whole thing is an NNR of immense topographical variety.

This walk is chiefly on level, well-made all-ability paths and tracks, though dunes may challenge wheelchair/pushchair users.

ROUTE DESCRIPTION

1) From the car park, this walk begins with the circular **Llyn Parc Mawr** trail. This is an important site for red squirrels, and the forest is managed accordingly. This walk takes the clockwise route. Branch left at the fork after the picnic site on a woodland path along to a forest track, turning right along the forest track to where it bends sharp left. Leave the track, continuing straight about 100m to view the lake. Afterwards, return along the forest track a short distance to take a left-hand woodland path back to the car park.

2) At the car park's entranceway onto the A4080 road, cross it, turning right along the roadside path to Malltreath car park. Here, take the path on the car park's far side heading west towards the forest edge to pick up a firm path, the coast path. This trundles south along the boundary

between forest and dunes for 1km to meet the main forest track.

3) Turn right. Follow the track through the enchanting Corsican pine forest. After 1km, turn right to stay on the Wales Coast Path along a sandy, grassy route that continues to brush the forest-dunes boundary. There are far-reaching views of **Malltraeth Sands** and the **Afon Cefni river estuary**, where marsh, mudflats and grassy dunes forge a critical habitat for wading birds. Here, this walk takes the dune-side path; you could

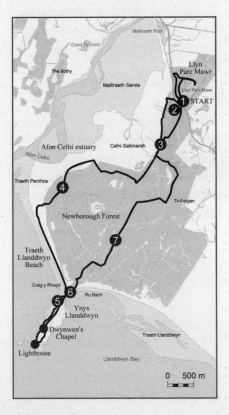

also take another path just within the forest confines that bends in a similar direction. Both dune-side and forest paths presently swing southwest, intersecting with a gravelled forest track at a bend.

4) Turn right on this track. Fork right again after 250m on a minor grassier track that wriggles out of the forest and through dunes onto glorious **Traeth Llanddwyn** beach. Turn left (southeast). Stroll along the beach, as stunning views of Llanddwyn Bay and Newborough Warren, beaches hosting some of Britain's finest sand dunes, stretch into the distance. Ynys Llanddwyn draws nearer ahead.

5) Follow the main path on to **Ynys Llanddwyn** from its east side. On this peaceful grassy promontory, you will see the remains of the medieval **chapel**, built over Dwynwen's, two turn-of-the-20th-century **crosses**, a **lighthouse** and, returning via the less-busy northwest shore path, **Dwynwen's well**, the original place

of pilgrimage. Returning to where Ynys Llanddwyn meets the beach, turn right, walking along the arcing sands with the forest on your left.

6) Pass some large rocky outcrops in the sand and, a short distance beyond, some lower outcrops at the back of the beach. The path away from the beach is discernable at a tree break beyond. The path skirts the edge of a forest clearing, meeting a forest track at a vehicular access barrier. Turn right. This track curves left at a path junction, right at another path junction after 375m and then, at a junction by a blue- and black-marked horse-riding signpost, turns left. At the junction soon afterwards, stay straight ahead on the main track. Then 500m later, at a broader intersection of forest tracks, turn left, then immediately right.

7) This track heads northeast for 800m, swings right (east-northeast), crosses another major forest track, curves northeast to pass another right-hand track 600m later, and soon swings northwest to meet your outward route. Turn right on this forest track, following it 1km to meet the A4080 opposite Llyn Parc Mawr car park entrance.

RED SQUIRREL

Red squirrels are declining UK-wide but on Anglesey grey squirrels, the reds' nemeses, have been eradicated, leading to a steady red squirrel increase. Red-brown with creamy-white chests, they have an average life expectancy of three years.

51. South Stack & Holyhead Mountain

Feast your eyes on seabirds, seals, peregrine falcons and red-billed choughs across ragged Anglesey seaboard and craggy moor

NEED TO KNOW

START/FINISH: RSPB South Stack lower car park opposite Tŷ Mawr Hut Circles, LL65 1YH – 4.5km (2¾ miles) southwest of Holyhead (parking and entry charges may apply)

DISTANCE: 11km (6¾ miles) (part figure of eight, part out-and-back)

TIME: 3½–4 hours

KEY SPECIES: Puffin, razorbill, spatulate fleawort

MAP: OS Explorer 262

TRANSPORT: Maes y Mynydd bus stop, Llaingoch (buses to central Holyhead) – 2.75km (1¾ miles) northeast of start but only 525m (¼ mile) southeast of Point 8 on walk

WALK ACCESSIBILITY: Not wheelchair/pushchair accessible; dogs under close control

DIFFICULTY: Moderate

SPECIFIC EQUIPMENT: Compass

MORE INFORMATION: rspb.org.uk and visitanglesey.co.uk

Holyhead, it might surprise many to learn, is much more than the main ferry port linking Great Britain to Ireland. Anglesey's western extremity (in fact a road-linked separate island, Holy Island) is an assemblage of sheer serrated cliffs, stacks, reefs and rocky outcrops and a nature reserve representing Wales' best chance to observe seabirds without boarding a boat. Puffins, razorbills and guillemots headline this ragged seaboard's biggest annual show each May to July. Behind, Holyhead Mountain's rock-studded moor helps create a great habitat for peregrine falcons and red-billed choughs. There is the chance of seeing spatulate fleawort, a yellow spring-flowering fleawort sub-species found nowhere else on Earth, and you could also descry harbour porpoises and dolphins off shore, most likely in late autumn or winter. Grey seals, meanwhile, relish the rocky surrounds of North Stack. There is much of historical and geological interest hereabouts too.

It's starkly wild at times on Holyhead Mountain, with some steep rocky paths. The way is always well-defined, but up high when the cloud comes down a compass is handy for orientation.

RAZORBILL
Perhaps the scarcest inhabitants of Britain's epic seabird colonies, the black-and-white razorbill spends most of its life at sea, only heading landwards to breed on craggy North Atlantic coasts in late spring through to July. It is similar to the commoner guillemot, best identified by its thicker bill.

ROUTE DESCRIPTION

1) This walk begins at the first (lower) of the two RSPB car parks. First, cross South Stack Road, taking the 400m out-and-back path to **Tŷ Mawr Hut Circles**, the remains of some 20 round stone houses dating from around 4000 years ago, and one of Wales' best-preserved such groups. Back at the car park, take the slightly rougher path from the far end leading towards the clifftops, which are reached 175m later.

2) Turn right, with your next objective, **Ellin's Tower**, a castellated Victorian tower, prominent along the cliffs ahead. Reach the building, now an information centre on the local birdlife, in 375m. From here you'll spot South Stack Lighthouse ahead. If you want to go to it (the approach is thrilling and some key seabird action happens on the cliffs around), as this walk does, first visit **RSPB South Stack Visitor Centre**, the white building visible up the hill inland. Besides vending lighthouse tickets and having a café/shop, the centre rents binoculars and arranges guided nature walks. Back down at Ellin's Tower, ascend the clifftop path to the road at a small car park and turn left (or walk up the road from the visitor centre). It's 150m to the road end where, with a lighthouse ticket, you can descend the steep, stepped walkway corkscrewing down the cliffs to the bridge onto **South Stack** and **South Stack Lighthouse**. Thousands of breeding seabirds favour the precipitous rockfaces here for their nesting sites.

3) Back at the road end, take the stony clifftop path past the information board. This climbs to an old look-out, levelling and revealing imposing views of Holyhead Mountain ahead, and 650m later over the heathery clifftop heath, reaching a wide metalled track. Continue straight across.

4) This wide path divides just afterwards at a 3-way junction: bear left here on the coast path. You aim initially for the very middle of Holyhead Mountain's west-facing rockface on this well-defined route, on which you climb up the mountain to its left-hand side and reach the right-hand branch-off to the summit 600m later. Climb to **Holyhead Mountain**'s craggy top (220masl) for spectacular views and the nearby remnants of **Caer y Twr** Iron Age hill fort.

5) Back on the main path, the mountain slopes now above right, continue to soon follow a north-northwest trajectory, waymark posts guiding you on. Views of Holyhead Breakwater open up off northeast; look up and you may see peregrine falcons wheeling. Descend off the mountain;

you'll soon spot the track to **North Stack lighthouse** below. Your path eventually meets the track: turn left to zigzag down to the lighthouse, around where grey seals are often sighted.

6) Next, take the path around the northern clifftops towards **Breakwater Country Park**. You rejoin the lighthouse track just beforehand. Turn left on the track with the old quarry faces on your right. Follow the track, soon with a lake on the right. This becomes metalled before a road junction where you turn right. The road soon swings left and reaches a metal gate on the left, an old brickworks chimney looming ahead.

7) Turn left on the metalled path then immediately right. Your path winds around crags off right to reach

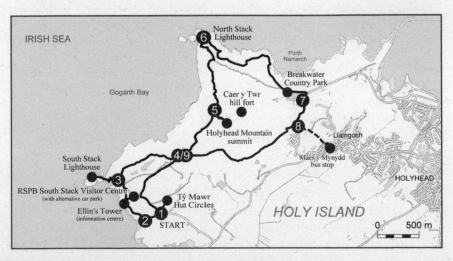

185

a metalled house drive and, shortly afterwards, a lane end. Follow the lane 100m to a grey house.

8) You now turn up right on a dead-end lane. The path from Llaingoch's Maes y Mynydd bus stop will join the route here. As the lane becomes a track and kinks sharp left, bear straight ahead on a stony path. With the mountain on your right, you now proceed through heathland where you can spot red-billed choughs, rock and meadow pipits, essentially skirting around the mountain and keeping it close on your right for the next 1.25km, and eventually curving right (northwest) around the west-facing rockface. At a fork your path then branches left, away from the mountain, heading southwest and reaching the waymarked 3-way junction you passed earlier (marked Point 4 and 9 on the map).

9) Your outward route leads left and right from this point but you take the path not yet taken, the only other distinct left-hand turn. This path continues straight onto a wider track 175m later and, in another 175m, reaches a 4-way track junction. Bear slightly left on a stony path descending to South Stack Road opposite the visitor centre car park. Turn left for 300m to the lower car park.

52. New Quay to Aberporth via Llangrannog

Observe Britain's biggest dolphin population, seabirds and seals over cliff and along cove

NEED TO KNOW

START/FINISH: Rock Street car park, New Quay, SA45 9NR/Aberporth Heol y Graig car park, SA43 2HA (parking charges may apply)

DISTANCE: 21.75km (13½ miles) (one way)

TIME: 6½–7 hours

KEY SPECIES: Bottlenose dolphin, grey seal, guillemot

MAP: OS Explorer 198

TRANSPORT: Mason's Square bus shelter, New Quay – 275m (¼ mile) southwest

WALK ACCESSIBILITY: Not wheelchair/pushchair accessible; dogs allowed

DIFFICULTY: Moderate–Difficult

SPECIFIC EQUIPMENT: Swimwear

MORE INFORMATION: walescoastpath.gov.uk and nationaltrust.org.uk

This romp across elemental clifftops, beside sandy bays and through dinky coastal villages is the longest stage of the Ceredigion Coast Path, looking out over waters where Europe's largest resident bottlenose dolphin population cavort. Spy them, along with grey seals and huge quantities of guillemots, razorbills, kittiwakes, fulmars, shags and more.

April through November are the best dolphin-spotting months, while September and October see seals pupping along rocky shores like Cwmtydu. The hike is no walk in the park, though: expect several steep climbs, plus muddy and surprisingly remote sections.

ROUTE DESCRIPTION

1) Follow Rock Street in **New Quay** along to a turning circle by a fish factory: here, your path swings up left, clambering over shale slopes to twist to another turning circle at the end of Marine Terrace. Before the first of the Marine Terrace buildings, climb right up steps behind houses onto

Lewis Terrace. Turn right, up past the last house and road end to a Wales Coast Path sign.

2) A level stretch of coast path follows, passing several fields before skirting coast-side of a campsite and reaching **Cardigan Bay Lookout**, a good spot to scour the sea for signs of dolphins. Here too you will see (and hear) **Bird Rock**, one of mainland Wales' largest seabird colonies. About 725m later, the path corkscrews down a steep slope to negotiate Nant y Grogal stream and traverse Craig yr Adar Nature Reserve. Ascend again and soon come above lonely **Cwm Silo Beach**. Drop down to the beach and cross a footbridge.

3) Climb again, reaching **Castell Bach hillfort** and, just beyond, **Castell Bach Bay**. You next round

Craig Caerllan headland, zigzagging down around the land-slipped cliffs into **Cwmtydu Cove**, passing onto the lane through a gate near a car park. Grey seals often grace rocks around the cove.

4) Turn right. Follow the lane around and south, upstream and through pretty Cwmtydu hamlet. Turn right at a small car park and cross a footbridge beside a toilet block. Your path swings right, through a kissing gate, then left to climb a slope into woods. About 350m later, at a kissing gate and path junction near the houses at Pen y Parc, turn acutely right, climbing out of the woods to meet a gap in a wall, where the route starts swinging left, then a signpost where you swing left again to head southwest.

5) The next 3.75km section whisks you up and down along thrilling,

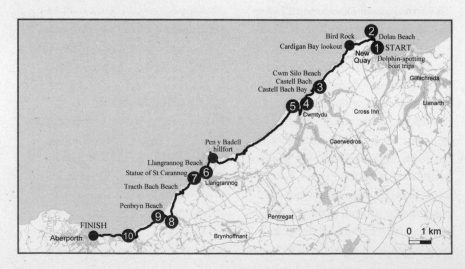

rugged cliffs. You eventually reach a sign at a kissing gate pointing left uphill to continue towards the Urdd Gobaith Cymru activity centre. A sign before the centre indicates the way right alongside a dry ski slope. Beyond rears snaking headland **Ynys Lochtyn**, part island at high tide. Your path skirts right of **Pen y Badell**. You can explore Ynys Lochtyn by branching right here. Afterwards, your path curves left around the hillfort, going through a gate. Fork immediately right, following the coast path down towards **Llangrannog**: it twists and turns, descending via steps to **Llangrannog Beach** after 850m.

6) Walk along the beachfront past the Pentre Arms pub. Where the road runs briefly inland, follow it round a sharp right-hand bend to climb to the **Statue of St Carannog**, founder of a 6th-century church here, at the next bend.

7) The next stage whisks you up around the cliffs, passing several mighty rock outcrops, each here known as *carreg* (castle). You soon come down steep steps to a dip, footbridge and side path to enticing **Traeth Bach Beach**, where you'll need to scramble to reach the sand. Head up steep steps again and pass through two gates as you climb the heath into a long field. Ascend this, aiming right of a mast ahead, then skirt around the field edges and pick up an ancient track descending into Penbryn.

8) Your route bends right along the lane with the **Plwmp Tart Café** off left, temporarily leaving the coast path to descend to **Penbryn Beach**. Here, cross the Hoffnant stream on a footbridge, then climb above its banks through woods to a sharp right-hand turn after 100m that again ascends through woods into the open and rejoins the coast path.

9) This section sees another significant climb before a steepening descent down a wooded slope to cross a metal footbridge into **Tresaith**. Turn right up to a road junction and walk straight over, just right of a bus shelter, down steps and a paved path. Turn left at the bottom, passing in front of a toilet block along the sandy beach top.

10) Your short final leg runs on a well-surfaced path past two caravan parks, then crosses grassy clifftops to reach a fork on the eastern edge of Aberporth. Here, the coast path branches right, but continuing left, you pass between houses on a path meeting Heol y Graig street at a bend. Turn right to immediately reach the car park and walk end.

RETURNING TO START: Bus T5, car or bike

53. Cwm Idwal & the Glyderau from Llyn Ogwen

Encounter traces of the last Ice Age in this exquisite hanging valley backed by charismatic peaks

NEED TO KNOW

START/FINISH: Ogwen car park at west end of Llyn Ogwen, LL57 3LZ – 8.5km (5¼ miles) northwest of Capel Curig (parking charges may apply)

DISTANCE: 10.75km (6¾ miles) (circular)

TIME: 4–4½ hours

KEY SPECIES: Snowdon lily, merlin, ring ouzel

MAP: OS Explorer OL17

TRANSPORT: Pen y Benglog bus stop (buses to Bangor/Corwen) – 75m east

WALK ACCESSIBILITY: Not wheelchair/pushchair accessible; dogs allowed

DIFFICULTY: Moderate–Difficult

SPECIFIC EQUIPMENT: Compass

MORE INFORMATION: nationaltrust.org.uk

The glaciers that gouged out the cirque of Cwm Idwal 10,000 years back left one of Britain's best examples of a hanging valley: a lower valley separated from a tributary valley by a semi-circle of sheer rock, dramatically ramparting the lake of Llyn Idwal below. This terrain was studied by Charles Darwin who, principally a geologist, furthered his understanding of how the planet's rocks were formed after visiting here. It subsequently became Wales' first NNR: not solely for sporting Snowdonia's craziest-looking rockscape both around the lake and on the peaks behind, but also for the vestiges of Arctic-Alpine flora surviving here since the last Ice Age.

Extremely rare plants like the Snowdon lily, with Snowdonia its only known UK location, prettify these rocky ledges in June, which is the best time to stop by. Late spring and summer see ring ouzels frequent the crags and merlins scouting for small upland-loving birds like wheatears.

This walk traverses the NNR, also tackling one of the biggest climbs

(700m of up) in this book to bag you Snowdonia's 5th- and 6th-highest summits (the Glyderau of the walk title). Paths are often rocky and a compass is advised in poor visibility, but this is a well-trodden route.

ROUTE DESCRIPTION

1) Facing the snack bar/shop building from the car park, begin by taking the path to the building's immediate left. This path swings left at the building's far end: stick on the crazy-paved path (do not take the right-hand turn). You'll presently pass through a gate and cross a footbridge over the rushing Afon Idwal river. After 225m, this path bends right with a narrower path branching left. The left-hand path is your return route: now continue on the wider crazy-paved path.

2) Ascend gradually to **Llyn Idwal** in 600m. This route goes anticlockwise around the shore. Skirt round the north lakeshore after re-crossing Afon Idwal and pass through gates in two dry-stone walls, the second intersecting with the lake after a beach.

MERLIN

This small, handsome falcon generally breeds further north in places like Iceland but a small breeding population frequents high rocky ground across Britain: only in winter are the birds seen at lower elevations.

3) Soon, the crags press in gloriously and the mountain panorama is already among Wales' best: headed up by the prominent pointy rock of **The Devil's Chimney** (Devil's Kitchen on some maps) on the cwm ahead. Look for wheatears and ring ouzels in spring and summer here. The path leaves the lakeshore, rising above it. Passing the lake's southern end below you hit the 400masl contour, then continue 350m, climbing stone steps to the right of the moraine to curve left along the top of it on the distinct path with steeper slopes off right. You're now at 500masl. Descend about 125m, keeping Llyn Idwal's southern end below left. You'll reach a curved line of deliberately piled stones. This marks where you leave the lake loop path, turning right to climb the steep rockfaces heading the cwm.

4) Once on the route up the cwm, it's a straightforward if tough climb. Watch for Arctic-Alpine plants Snowdon lilies and purple saxifrage in the rocks. After the steep climb, it's a gentle descent southwest to come above **Llyn y Cwn**'s northeast corner, where you turn left. The path now climbs high above this lake on the rocky route up **Glyder Fawr** (1001masl), heading south, then swinging southeast and finally northeast to reach the summit just over 1km later.

5) Here you join the Cambrian Way. Head east from the summit 350m over stones on a cairn-marked section onto the ridge linking to Glyder Fach. Continue east along a grassier section of ridge onto the pass of Bwlch y Ddwy Glyder: then as you descend off the ridge, still on grassy ground, turn right at the path fork. This path avoids the jagged **Castle of the Wind** rocks standing between you and Glyder Fach, and skirts it to the south to reach **Glyder Fach** (994masl) summit, best approached from the east on a brief scramble. Another 100m east you'll find the **Cantilever Stone**, a precariously balanced rock slab upon which hikers like to stand.

6) From here, head east-northeast from the summit for 250m, then begin your descent. Avoid the hairier scramble heading north-northeast and continue briefly east, southeast 250m, briefly east-northeast, southeast about 200m and then east 100m, descending to join the Miner's Track. You'll swing north here down towards Bwlch Tryfan but first, at the small cairn, continue on the 800m out-and-back path east to **Llyn Caseg-fraith** for some unforgettable views of other Glyderau range member Tryfan.

7) Back at the cairn, descend briefly north, then briefly west, then northwest for 700m to cross the dry-stone wall at Bwlch Tryfan. Afterwards, it's a clearer 975m descent to the northern end of **Llyn Bochlwyd** at its outflow of Nant Bochlwyd. After crossing the stream, the route leads straightforwardly down 875m north then north-northwest to reach Point 2 on the map. Bear right to retrace your outward route.

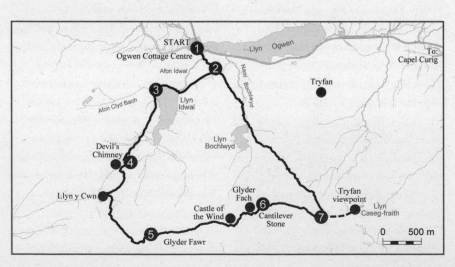

54. Llanbedr Dyffryn Clwyd to Loggerheads Country Park via Moel Famau, Moel Arthur & the River Alyn

Get rugged ridge top, ravishing riverside and everything from black grouse to water voles in the drama-charged Clwydian Range

NEED TO KNOW

START/FINISH: Llanbedr DC village hall, LL15 1UP (parking free)/Loggerheads Country Park, CH7 5LH – 5km (3 miles) west of Mold (parking charges may apply)

DISTANCE: 20.25km (12½ miles) (one way)

TIME: 6½–7 hours

KEY SPECIES: Water vole, grizzled skipper butterfly, black grouse

MAP: OS Explorer 265

TRANSPORT: Griffin Hotel bus stop, Llanbedr DC (buses to Mold/Ruthin/Denbigh) – 250m south

WALK ACCESSIBILITY: Not wheelchair/pushchair accessible; dogs allowed

DIFFICULTY: Moderate–Difficult

SPECIFIC EQUIPMENT: Compass

MORE INFORMATION: clwydianrangeanddeevalleyaonb.org.uk

This is a walk of two halves. First off, the billboard tramp is along one of Wales' finest lesser-known ridges, the Clwydian Range, heathery moor sculpted into a sequence of dramatic hillforts without compare in the UK. The second part delves through secretive ash woods along the River Alyn, one of the increasingly few bastions of the water vole.

It is devastatingly gorgeous hillwalking to begin, encompassing the range's high point, Moel Famau, a double act of hillforts and sensational views of North Wales and Northwest England along long-distance trail the Offa's Dyke Path. Notable fauna spots up high could include the declining black grouse. But the finale along the Alyn might wind

WATER VOLE

Similar to brown rats, but with small ears and furry tails, these are Britain's biggest vole species. But they are severely threatened due to the loss of the soggy habitats they love. A good indication they are nearby is riverbank burrows, often with nibbled grass around the entrance.

up delighting you most, not just for Devil's Gorge's craggy thrill, but for the seclusion and the wildlife seclusion attracts. Watch for the water vole, which the Clwydian Range and Dee Valley AONB is working hard to conserve. The wooded glades and lime-rich grasslands produce wild strawberries, feeding grizzled skipper butterflies, absent from most of Wales. Otters have made a return too, and when water levels lower, kingfishers sometimes fish. Great avian entertainers like the dipper and grey wagtail are also present.

Come in May for pleasant weather up top and to see woodlands come alive with flowers and birds. There are several steep climbs that, together with the length, raise the ramble up in the difficulty rankings.

ROUTE DESCRIPTION

1) From Llanbedr DC village hall, turn right on the B5429 road through the village for 225m, then right along the drive of the old Llanbedr Hall Estate for 700m. This curls around wood-dotted grounds to houses on the former hall site, then branches left (northeast) on a solid track, climbing into Coed Ceunant wood. Cut east-northeast through the wood, veering left of a house, then continuing northeast to a small lake on the wood edge. Next, climb east-northeast, following a stream. The path briefly joins a wider grassy trackway as it enters a left-hand hairpin curve, then branches right to proceed northeast indistinctly for 225m to a clearer track near the Bwlch Penbarras road. Turn right on the track then left on the road to Moel Famau car park on the left.

2) The route now joins the well-worn Offa's Dyke Path (ODP), a long-distance trail along the approximate course of the 8th-century earthwork raised by King Offa to protect his English realm Mercia from the rival realms in what would become Wales.

Water vole

The dyke itself is less in evidence here, but ancient fortifications there are aplenty. East of the road rears **Foel Fenlli**, an Iron Age hillfort and the second-highest summit in the Clwydian Range (you can walk up on a short out-and-back detour). Your route, however, now visits the range's highest point, Moel Famau, followed by a still more impressive hillfort (Moel Arthur). From the car park, head northwest, swing northeast and finally north on the ODP for 2.5km to **Moel Famau** (554masl).

3) There are stunning views from this summit. Castle-crowned Denbigh is the town to the west, but clear skies reveal Wales west across to Snowdonia and north to the Irish Sea, with England's Chester and Liverpool visible too. Attracting as much attention are the remnants of **Jubilee Tower**, built in 1810 for King George III's golden jubilee: clamber up for some added elevation. Afterwards, descend west-northwest on the ODP for 1km, next bearing north up to the subsequent summit, Moel Dywyll. Off left is **Moel Famau Country Park**. Curlews (spring) and stonechats (year round) can be descried here and in the surrounding moorland. After Moel Dywyll, continue with a descent northwest, then negotiate a few more moorland ups and downs as you swing north and ascend your next objective, **Moel Llys-y-coed**, 2.3km after Moel Dywyll. The vista ahead to Moel Arthur hillfort from here is superb and a stone wall immediately on your right for all of this section helps you stay on track.

4) From Moel Llys-y-coed, steeply descend to Moel Arthur car park. The 1.5km detour up to **Moel Arthur** and back is steep too, but worth it to wander about this well-preserved Iron Age hillfort. After you return, leave the ODP and turn left (northeast) along the lane 200m to a forest track on the right, passing through a gate and along the forest edge for 800m. Afterwards, the southeast-running track becomes a lane in 1.2km, coming down past Cilcain car park to a T-junction where you turn right to reach the church in Cilcain village.

5) Keep left of the church but then, by the White Horse Inn, turn right. This lane soon departs Cilcain, heading downhill to a left-hand track just shy of a house. Pass a lake below right then bear left, through the wood then along the top of it, to bend past houses onto a lane corner in 900m. Follow the lane down to cross the **River Alyn**, then in 200m swing right on the path along its banks – the Leete Path.

6) You follow this path, with the river on its right, for 3.25km: a beguiling stretch of ash, hazel and alder woodland and one of the best places in the AONB for spotting the species listed in the introduction. The notable feature is the deep fissure of **Devil's Gorge** after 1km, crossed over by the path. The path passes into **Loggerheads Country Park** and turns right over a bridge to reach the park's **AONB information centre**, **café** and restored mill 1.2km after crossing a lane. Continue straight on, re-crossing the river to the A494 road, to the **We Three Loggerheads pub** and the bus stop back.

RETURNING TO START: Bus X1, car or bike

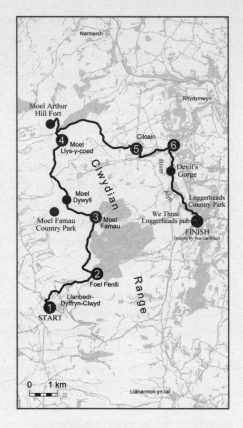

YORKSHIRE

55. Gordale Scar & Malham Cove from Malham

Amble in awe by chasms, peregrine falcon-frequented crags, crashing waterfalls and a curious tarn

NEED TO KNOW

START/FINISH: Malham car park behind National Park Visitor Centre, Malham, BD23 4DA (parking charges may apply)

DISTANCE: 11.75km (7¼ miles) (circular)

TIME: 3–3½ hours

KEY SPECIES: Peregrine falcon, great crested grebe, redshank

MAP: OS Explorer OL2

TRANSPORT: Buck Inn bus stop, Malham (buses to Skipton) – 75m east

WALK ACCESSIBILITY: Not wheelchair/pushchair accessible; dogs allowed

DIFFICULTY: Easy–Moderate

MORE INFORMATION: malhamdale.com and nationaltrust.org.uk

'Like the age-tinted wall of a prodigious castle,' was how priest-cum-author Thomas West, a pioneer of guidebook writing, described Malham Cove's amphitheatre-like rockface in 1778. The description – for this and gobsmacking gorge Gordale Scar on the other side of Malham village – is still apt. These craggy limestone phenomena seemingly erupt from nowhere, but this classic walk, visiting both sites, holds further surprises: not least the wildlife congregating at Malham Tarn, Britain's highest limestone lake.

Peregrine falcons are a massive attraction at Malham Cove, nesting there since 1983, with chicks born in May and June. Meanwhile, great crested grebes, teals and breeding waders like redshank and oystercatcher revel in Malham Tarn NNR's wetlands, while woodland bluebells near Janet's Foss bewitch all-comers in spring.

This route captures immense drama despite being easy to follow and easy going, save for some brief scrambling at Gordale Scar.

ROUTE DESCRIPTION

1) Take the pedestrian-only route from the car park's east side to Malham **National Park Visitor Centre**, handy for discovering more about the area's walking routes, geology and wildlife, including Malham Cove's peregrine falcons. Afterwards, turn left on Chapel Gate, walking into **Malham Village** as far as Malham Smithy.

2) Here, a right-hand path crosses the footbridge over Malham Beck. Afterwards, turn right: your route, here the Pennine Way long-distance path, follows the stream awhile, then veers away to a signpost at a wall corner 375m later. Turn left. Now proceed on the well-waymarked footpath bound for Janet's Foss. Pass through three gates, joining Gordale Beck. Now keep this stream on your right, passing five fields on the left. Staying streamside, the route swings north, passes a barn and heads through two gates to enter Little Gordale and Stone Bank woods. At the end of this glorious stretch of ancient broadleaf, eventually tapering almost to a gorge, is **Janet's Foss** waterfall. Janet, queen of the faeries according to legend, lived behind the falls at this enchanting spot.

3) You now climb beside the waterfall to a gate onto Gordale Lane. Turn right, passing a lay-by with refreshments. After the lane corners, turn left on a broad path ushering you 675m along Gordale Beck to the foot of **Gordale Scar**. One of the Yorkshire Dales' finest sights, this chasm was carved by Ice Age meltwater. A beck tumbles between these mighty limestone walls and while it looks from a distance like a dead end, from the bottom of the beck's waterfall the path up is detected. The slight scramble now necessary delivers you up left and soon away from the stream's sheer sides over grass-and-rock slopes. Enjoy grand crag-sided valley views while ascending to a dry-stone wall and stepped stile. Beyond, the route briefly sticks near the crags, then swings northwest to hit Tarn Road at another stepped stile.

Great crested grebe

4) Immediately branch right on a dry-stone wall-hugging track. This meets a tarmacked track in 325m: continue straight along this track, north then north-northwest, for 675m to a wall by a small plantation. Turn left for 625m, following this boundary then skirting left of another plantation to a track. Turn right, then acute left on a path cutting across grass to a protruding, dry-stone wall-enclosed group of trees.

5) The path now curves close to **Malham Tarn** (377masl). One of only a few upland alkaline lakes in Europe, and with a mix of wet woodland, raised bog and pasture, this is a special place for wildlife and a bastion of the great crested grebe. Protests against 19th-century use of this bird's plumage in clothing led to the founding of the RSPB. Leaving the tarn's southern corner, the path reaches Watersinks car park. See how the car park gets its name by turning right on the road and then left on the path after the dry-stone wall: on the left, Malham Water mysteriously disappears into the ground at **Water Sinks**.

6) At the nearby signpost and path fork bear left, coming alongside a dry-stone wall before descending into the dry, dramatically cliff-flanked **Watlowes Valley**,

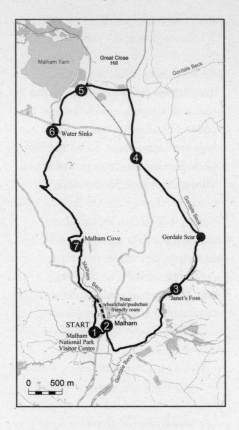

negotiating steep contours via sharp right and later still-sharper left turns. Emerge from the valley 800m later, cross a stile and arrive on top of the walk highlight: **Malham Cove**. This colossal, 70m-high, 300m-long arcing limestone cliff, a visitor attraction for centuries, is a refuge for peregrine falcons. Birds nest in March–April and raise chicks from May–June among the crags here. Take care turning right along the top of the cove, then left at its end to descend down the stone steps on an especially pretty stretch into the woods at the bottom.

7) At the foot of the steps are choices. Turning left, as this walk does, is for a closer, worthwhile exploration of the cove on an out-and-back path. Right is your onward route. Keep Malham Beck on your left, cross two fields through two gates, come alongside Cove Road and join it at a campsite entrance. Turn left along the road 100m, then right on a track signed to Hilltop Farm Bunkbarn. After 550m this emerges on a road with your starting point car park immediately left.

PEREGRINE FALCON
These large, graceful falcons with their blue-grey backs and white-and-black 'barred' breasts faced extinction in the 1960s but can once again boast a healthy population. The avian athletes are the world's fastest living things, achieving 300km/h+ in flight.

56. Muker Meadows & Upper Swaledale

Rejoice in Britain's best-preserved upland hay meadows and a profusion of waterfalls

NEED TO KNOW

START/FINISH: Muker village car park, DL11 6QG (parking charges may apply)

DISTANCE: 8.25km (5¼ miles) (circular)

TIME: 2½–3 hours

KEY SPECIES: Wildflower meadows, curlew, brown hare

MAP: OS Explorer OL30

TRANSPORT: Kirkby Stephen railway station – 22km (14 miles) northwest

WALK ACCESSIBILITY: Muker Meadows accessible to wheelchair/pushchair users, full walk is not; dogs under close control

DIFFICULTY: Moderate

MORE INFORMATION: ydmt.org and yorkshiredales.org.uk

The upland hay meadows outside comely Muker are precious: 97 per cent of this habitat has been lost in the UK since World War II, but here land is farmed fertiliser-free, creating pristine tracts of meadowland ablaze with wildflowers during late spring and summer.

This walk presents one of Britain's best opportunities to see undisturbed wildflower meadows, along with the insects, birds and brown hares that they attract. It also serves a scenic slice of Upper Swaledale, one of the loveliest Yorkshire Dales. Becks (streams) and fosses (waterfalls) crash through woodsy gorges, centuries-old stone barns pepper riversides and abandoned mines guard the hills above.

May and June are the grandest months, when wood cranesbill, melancholy thistle and lady's mantle splash meadows in purple and yellow, swallows dart and curlews forage in the long grasses.

ROUTE DESCRIPTION

1) Turn left from the car park onto the B6270 road, then left again on the bridge over the River Swale, following the B6270 to the first right-hand turn

at the Muker Literary Institute. This
lane winds through **Muker** village:
follow the lane at a wooden walker's
signpost to take the right-hand turn at
the post box.

2) The route becomes a paved path
through **Muker Meadows SSSI**.
The flower-rich riverside meadows,
divided by dry-stone walls and
squeezed by the green flanks of
the Dales rising either side, form a
quintessential time-lost Yorkshire
scene. In the seventh meadow, a
wooden gate leads you down steps to
the riverbank. Turn sharp right along
the river to cross via Ramps Holme
footbridge, visible ahead.

3) Turn left after the footbridge,
following the stony riverside track for
2km. Watch out after 600m for **Arn
Gill**, within a wooded ravine on the
right, where the tumbling beck waters
form impressive waterfalls. Around
the 2km mark, the main track climbs
away from the River Swale, bending
right alongside **Swinner Gill** to cross

the beck's footbridge. **Catrake Force**,
a flight of several stepped waterfalls,
and a ruined lead-smelting mill lie to
the right.

4) Go through a gate, climbing the
hillside on the track to a junction.
The acute right-hand track leads
to ruined farmhouse **Crackpot
Hall**. Continue along the slopes
of Beldi Hill, once a major lead-
mining area, and soon take the stony
track curving left around a ruined
building. This proceeds above the
River Swale's steeply wooded banks,
descending to a footbridge over
East Gill Force waterfalls.

Brown
hare

203

5) Turn left after the bridge, descending on a metalled track, part of the Pennine Way, to cross another footbridge over the River Swale. Bear right, climbing steps to a track. The right-hand route heads to **Keld** village; the left-hand returns you towards Muker.

6) Bearing left, and left again at the first fork, you soon pass a rough, signposted path on the left running the short distance to **Kisdon Upper Force**, two further fabulous

cascades on the River Swale. Shortly afterwards, another junction sees the high-level return route to Muker, following the Pennine Way, fork right, while this walk forks left on the low-level return route.

7) The track traverses Ruskin Wood, emerging in the meadows on the River Swale's western side that you likely glimpsed on your outward route. Sticking within the meadows, you pass by several historic farm buildings over the next 2km.

8) You eventually reach a stone building at the end of a long finger of woodland, with Ramps Holme footbridge visible again across the meadows ahead. Here, bear right, gently uphill on a track passing patchy woodland to emerge at the bend of another track just above Muker. Continuing ahead here brings you back into Muker and thus to the walk start.

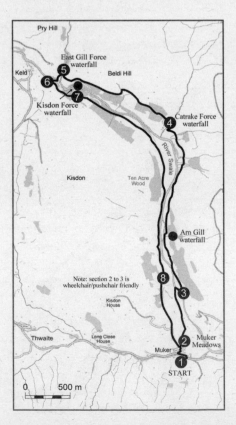

57. The Farndale Daffodil Walk, returning via Farndale Moor

Amble among gold through Britain's daffodil capital, then switch scenery to moody maroon for moorland bird-spotting

NEED TO KNOW

START/FINISH: Low Mill car park, YO62 7UY (parking free)

DISTANCE: 17km (10½ miles) (circular)

TIME: 5–5½ hours

KEY SPECIES: Wild daffodil, lapwing, plover

MAP: OS Explorer OL26

TRANSPORT: Kirkbymoorside Market Place bus stop (buses to Helmsley/Pickering/ Scarborough) – 10.5km (6½ miles) south

Wild daffodils

WALK ACCESSIBILITY: Daffodil Walk accessible to wheelchair/pushchair users, rest of walk not; dogs under close control

DIFFICULTY: Moderate

SPECIFIC EQUIPMENT: Compass

MORE INFORMATION: northyorkmoors.org.uk

Bringing bright early spring cheer to Northern England, Farndale, or 'Daffodil Dale' as it is dubbed, has probably Britain's optimum wild daffodil-growing conditions. And sure enough, the damp woods and meadows along the adorable River Dove here are gilded in unsurpassed spreads of pale-gold narcissi from mid-March to late April.

The Daffodil Walk deservedly numbers among the North York Moors NP's most popular. This route follows it one way, then swerves spectacularly off-piste. You'll evade valley-bottom crowds climbing onto Farndale Moor, one of England's highest, most extensive moors, ripe for sightings of lapwings, golden plovers and red grouse – plus some memorable panoramas.

A clear late March day would perfectly suit this walk, which starts easy before ascending over 200m onto the moor. Well-defined paths are followed throughout the route.

ROUTE DESCRIPTION

1) North York Moors NP runs an information booth at Low Mill car park during daffodil season. Follow the green sign marked 'Public Path to High Mill' from the car park entrance on a well-surfaced path crossing grass to the river, passing through two gates. Turn left along the **River Dove**. For the next 2.25km this melange of broadleaf woods and moist meadows is a riot of daffodils during spring. A little later, the bluebells are lovely too. Keeping on this riverbank, you pass through several gates en route to High Mill. Here the route passes between some buildings including aptly named **Daffy Caffy**, a lovely refreshment stop.

2) You continue onto Mill Lane, following it to the junction at Cross Houses. Bear right to reach **The Feversham Arms** pub, then turn left onto Daleside Road. Keep on this dead-end lane up Farndale, the River Dove meandering off left, for almost 3.25km. You'll pass Lendersfield House off right, Esk House off left, then on the next bend branch right on a path alongside a small stream.

3) This path climbs steadily northeast. Soon the tendrils of woodland flanking Oak Beck advance from the

> **WILD DAFFODIL**
> It is wild daffodils carpeting Farndale: smaller and more fragile than the domestics found in many gardens. How to differentiate? The wild ones' pale yellow petals surround a darker trumpet; garden daffs are more single-tone.

right: this path comes alongside them just before a field boundary. Pass through a gate, cross Oak Beck, swing north-northeast and 250m later pass through another gate in the final field boundary before open moor. The next section of path is distinct enough but a compass is handy back-up in poor visibility. It's another steady climb, for the first 150m or so northwest and then swinging north-northeast for around 325m, to reach the course of the old **Rosedale iron ore railway**. This is today among the North York Moors' best high-level paths, providing great opportunities to relax from way-finding and watch wildlife.

4) Turn right on the path. This surprisingly level little-trammelled route hugs the 360masl contour as you follow its curves across Farndale Moor. With luck you might spot many birds here. At scrub level are some healthy red grouse populations, while golden plovers favour this open ground, where they can see predators approaching, for spring and summertime nest-making. Look for lapwing courtship rituals in spring too. A 3.25km trundle along the railway's course and you'll reach the 1.1km out-and-back detour to 16th-century **Lion Inn**, England's fourth highest-elevation pub: a pronounced left-hand grassy path leads 400m to the main road, where you turn right to the inn.

5) Back on the old railway path, continue left. Hit the lane on Blakey Bank near a road junction on Blakey Ridge after 1.1km; turn right. Descend

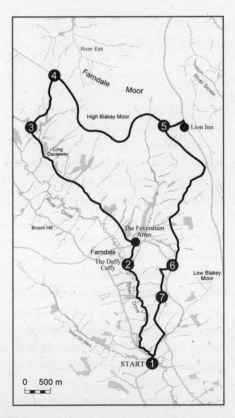

on this lane for 1.25km. Fine views of Daffodil Dale now open up again and, among charming dry-stone-walled fields again, you turn left at a signpost. This lane in turn reaches a lane junction in 925m.

6) Turn left, then immediately branch right, where a footpath sign indicates your way right down a dry-stone-walled drive. Proceed towards the house, turning left before it on a track. Next, after a wall on the right, take the path bearing right (south) across a field to pass in front of Bitchagreen Farm. After the farm buildings keep straight on a path as the farm drive curves left. The route passes to the right end of a treeline after the next field, then behind two more sets of houses and their outbuildings.

7) Ignoring a right-hand path, you then gradually descend south-southwest along one field edge, cut across a second field and at the far boundary veer left (southeast) to arrive at High Wold House. Before reaching the lane, take the path leading right (southwest) between buildings. This follows one field edge and passes through a hedge to cross a Dove River tributary. One field now separates you from the tree-lined River Dove below. Through the riverside gate, you pick up your outward route, re-crossing the river with the car park steps ahead.

58. Captain Cook's Monument & Roseberry Topping

Roam around this iconic North York Moors beauty spot yielding some of Yorkshire's best views and wrapped by woods where bluebells bewitch

NEED TO KNOW

START/FINISH: Great Ayton railway station, TS9 6HR

DISTANCE: 11km (6¾ miles) (circular)

TIME: 3–3½ hours

KEY SPECIES: Bluebell, purple hairstreak butterfly, green woodpecker

MAP: OS Explorer OL26

TRANSPORT: Great Ayton railway station at start

WALK ACCESSIBILITY: Not wheelchair/pushchair accessible; dogs allowed

DIFFICULTY: Moderate

MORE INFORMATION: nationaltrust.org.uk and northyorkmoors.org.uk

Eminent 18th-century explorer James Cook spent his childhood on a farm near Great Ayton, and clambered up Roseberry Topping to unwind. Even back then, this distinctive buckled conical summit was a well-established beauty spot and the dazzling views it commands, across the patchwork-quilt plain of North Yorkshire framed by bracken-clad hills, have not diminished over the centuries.

This route is almost theatrical in how it builds up the approach to Roseberry Topping, coaxing you on with increasingly impressive vistas. Some of the finest wildlife sightings lie beneath, however. The woods draping these hillsides are festooned by some of the country's most radiant bluebell displays in May and migrant birds like blackcaps and chiffchaffs join garden warblers, tree pipits and green

BLUEBELLS

Ancient bluebell-carpeted woodlands are among the British countryside's loveliest scenes. The native flowers providing such springtime joy thrive in sun-dappled woodland understorey, distinguished from Spanish bluebells by their sweet scent and droopier heads.

woodpeckers to make a melodious soundtrack. In summer, the woods welcome uncommon butterflies like the speckled wood and purple hairstreak. You might catch fleeting glimpses of roe deer at any time.

Paths are generally well defined but wooded sections get muddy, and there are three significant climbs.

ROUTE DESCRIPTION

1) From Great Ayton railway station's approach road, turn right on Station Road to cross the railway bridge, then continue another 300m on Dikes Lane to a crossroads at two white houses.

2) Turn right on the minor lane. This soon reaches a lane junction; keeping straight on, the lane becomes a bridleway at a red-brick house. The bridleway brushes the southwest edge of some woodland as it climbs the hillside and, 350m after leaving the woods, meets a path fork on a bracken- and gorse-dotted slope at a field corner, with more woodland above.

3) Turn left along a wall, ascending into **Ayton Banks Wood**. The path soon meets a grassy cross-path; turn right then immediately left, climbing through the wood onto Easby Moor. As you emerge onto open ground, you will see Captain Cook's Monument to the right (southeast); head for the monument on the clear path.

4) Captain Cook's Monument was erected in 1827 in memory of the local lad who became one of the world's best-known explorers. At the monument, your route joins the Cleveland Way long-distance trail. Follow this route north away from Captain Cook's Monument on a flagstone-studded path descending into forest, meeting a forestry track. You hit Dikes Lane again at a gate on the forest edge, 900m below the monument.

5) Turn right on the lane, then almost immediately left on the Cleveland Way as it climbs onto the moor. Your route traces a dry-stone wall, with open moor on the right, curving gradually left (northwest) as splendid views of Roseberry Topping reveal themselves. The track meets a grassy path crossroads 2km after leaving Dikes Lane, squeezing through a gate in a dry-stone wall. Your route ahead, dipping down then steeply ascending across moorland to Roseberry Topping's prominent hilltop, is clearly visible.

6) From the broken stony summit of **Roseberry Topping**, once you have marvelled at the views and, with luck, observed the wall butterflies sometimes basking on the rocks, descend north on a slim grassy path. Ignoring several faint side paths, you meet the ancient trackway of Brant Gate. Turn

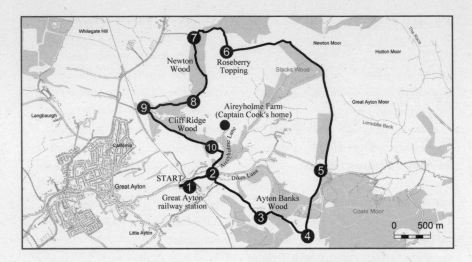

left. Brant Gate threads down into Newton Wood to meet the top end of Roseberry Lane.

7) Pass through a gate to take the bridleway ascending through **Newton Wood**. This is one of Yorkshire's loveliest vestiges of semi-natural oak woods: springtime spreads of bluebells are enchanting, while the purple hairstreak butterfly is seen here in summer. You reach the moor edge at a path junction and bridle gate. Continue along the top of the wood another 300m to a clearing.

8) At the path fork, turn right, down through the trees to meet another path snaking along the foot of the wood. Turn left along the wood bottom; this path intersects with a wider track at the wood's end.

9) Turn left on the track running towards the old Cliff Rigg Quarry. After 50m, and before the quarry, fork left again where a National Trust sign points the way on a path through **Cliff Ridge Wood**, also blanketed by bluebells in late spring. Take the right fork at a path junction soon afterwards. This path threads along the bottom of the wood, with fields to the right (south), crossing an outlying triangle of woodland to reach a kissing gate onto a field after 1km.

10) Your path heads straight across the field on the right side of the fence to Aireyholme Lane. Left up the lane is **Aireyholme Farm**, where Captain Cook lived and worked with his family from 1736 to 1745. Your route turns right down Aireyholme Lane, however, reaching Dikes Lane. Turn right on your outward route back to the railway station.

59. Bempton Cliffs & Flamborough Head

Check out England's seabird capital as you reconnoitre ragged chalk cliffs

NEED TO KNOW

START/FINISH: RSPB Bempton Cliffs, YO15 1JF – 2km (1¼ miles) north of Bempton (entrance charge to Bempton Cliffs reserve may apply)

DISTANCE: 22.75km (14 miles) (circular)

TIME: 6–6½ hours

KEY SPECIES: Shag, puffin, gannet

MAP: OS Explorer 301

TRANSPORT: Bempton railway station – 2.25km (1½ miles) south

WALK ACCESSIBILITY: Mostly accessible to wheelchair/pushchair users; dogs under close control

DIFFICULTY: Moderate

SPECIFIC EQUIPMENT: Swimwear

MORE INFORMATION: rspb.org.uk and ywt.org.uk

Dubbed 'Nou Camp of the bird world' by Chris Packham, the gargantuan chalk cliffs near Bempton are England's seabird central, and were the site of the 2015 *Springwatch* Easter special: some half a million gannets, guillemots, kittiwakes, razorbills, fulmars, shags and herring gulls breed here between March and October, and a series of viewing points means you will get as close as humanly possible to this clamouring, vertiginous avian metropolis. There is seabird action all along the chalky coast to Flamborough Head, and this walk tracks it, continuing around to South Landing before looping back on country roads and tracks. The grasslands behind the cliffs also support barn owls, wintering short-eared owls, skylarks, corn buntings and a rare colony of tree sparrows.

May to July is the height of seabird shenanigans, when the colony is established and embellished by those clifftop comedians – puffins. The route is on easy, level paths manageable by wheelchairs and pushchairs with just three minor detours.

ROUTE DESCRIPTION

1) This is not a walk that believes in saving the best until last. Having looked around the **visitor centre** beside the car park, which informs about the area's birdlife, make for the cliffs (via the longer, northwest-running path) to watch phenomenal seabird antics. Note that your admission fee is for the centre and its facilities and does not give you exclusive right to the cliffs: the clifftop path is a public right of way freely accessible from other places including North Landing (southeast, on this walk). The path from the centre hits the cliffs then runs left to **Mosey Downgate seabird viewpoint**. Vast numbers of seabirds arrive on the cliffs here to nest during spring and summer – so many that they are distinguishable from satellite – with puffins performing April through July only and gannets last to depart in October. The cliffs, rearing to 100masl, are gobsmacking too.

2) Now turn and walk along the cliffs with the North Sea to your left. Pass **Grandstand seabird viewpoint**, then a wooden signpost pointing along grassy clifftops to Flamborough. You next pass **New Roll-Up** and **Staple Newk** seabird viewpoints, the latter especially impressive as jutting cliffs give a great perspective on one of Britain's few mainland gannetries. After Staple Newk, the cliff fence

SHAG
Scrawny, green-black and with ruffled head crests, shags are the somewhat 'ugly ducklings' of seabird cities, but spare them some love: they breed in significant numbers at just a handful of sites UK-wide.

ends and you proceed along open but nevertheless striking cliffs for almost 4km to come above **Thornwick Bay**. Just before the bay, the main route makes a V-shaped inland detour to skirt the rugged slopes of the stream feeding enchanting **Little Thornwick Bay**. You can choose to visit the bay on steep, stepped paths: both routes rejoin at **Thornwick Bay Café**. Next, head down the track 350m to a broad left-hand track.

3) The wheelchair/pushchair-friendly path continues southeast on the main track to Marine Road here, turning left and rejoining the main route at North Landing car park. This walk visits sand-and-shingle **Thornwick Bay** with its **rock arch**, then on the return ascent climbs steps on the left to rejoin the clifftop path. Cliffs are now far lower than at the walk start. Curve around the next headland to North Landing car park after 850m, a stretch including a shimmy down and up flights of steps to negotiate the valley of **Holmes Gut** just beforehand. Here, uncommon wildflowers like pyramidal orchids and pink thrift thrive and the chalky grasslands are especially butterfly-rich.

4) After the car park, turn left along North Marine Road briefly, passing Caravel Bar. You can optionally visit **North Landing Beach** ahead or bear right to continue the clifftop route towards Flamborough Head. Next of note is the impressive rock stack **Queen's Rock** after 1km, while 200m beyond there is a short out-and-back path to a **hide** for observing birds like short-eared owls and whinchats.

5) Back at the beginning of the hide path, it's a 1.5km run along the cliffs down to a path junction above multi-coved, shingle **Hidden Beach**, where the cliffs hang thrillingly overhead. Left, your onward route reaches the beach while right meets

the road, 250m inland along, which brings you to **Old Flamborough Lighthouse**, one of Britain's oldest completed lighthouses (1674). Up from Hidden Beach, the path meets the **Flamborough Head Lighthouse** and car park. Turn left along the track to the signal station and explore the paths around **Flamborough Head**.

6) Here, the wheelchair/pushchair-friendly path runs back past the lighthouse(s), west along Lighthouse Road (the B1259), rejoining the walk at Bempton Lane in Flamborough. You can also retrace your steps along the cliffs to the start point. This walk, however, makes a round trip, proceeding along the clifftops. You soon pass **The Drinking Dinosaur**, a protruding rock formation with a rock arch. After this it's 3.5km along grassland-backed cliffs to **South**

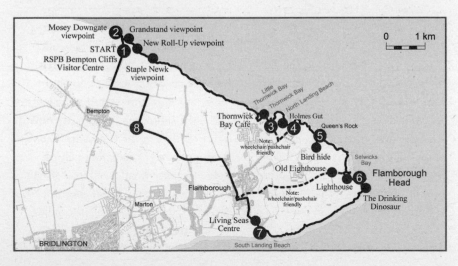

Landing Beach: an opportunity to turn eyes away from seabirds to grassland birdwatching, which includes barn owls and skylarks. Pass an impressive down-and-up set of stairs and a lighthouse sculpture along the way.

7) From the beach, follow Sea Road 250m inland to **Living Seas Centre**. This fantastic resource, informing visitors on all aspects of Yorkshire's marine life, is currently only open for arranged-in-advance bookings, although drop-in visitors are welcome at its café. Continue 750m along Sea Road into Flamborough village, turning left on Lily Lane then right on West Street to a triangular grass junction. Head straight across, onto Bempton Lane, the B1229 road. This leads alongside a churchyard and eventually out of Flamborough for 3.5km.

8) Just before reaching **Bempton**, turn right on the dead-end Stonepit Lane for 875m. This terminates in Blakehowe Lane, a track. Turn left for 975m, then turn right on Cliff Lane for 1km to the car park.

NORTHEAST ENGLAND

60. The River Tyne to Jesmond Dene through Gateshead & Newcastle-upon-Tyne

Find out why nature should be up there with the arts and football as a reason to visit metropolitan Tyneside

NEED TO KNOW

START/FINISH: Baltic Centre for Contemporary Art car park, Gateshead, NE8 3BA (parking charges may apply)

DISTANCE: 6.5km (4 miles) (one way)

TIME: 1½–2 hours

KEY SPECIES: Kittiwake, kingfisher, otter, dipper

MAP: OS Explorer 316

TRANSPORT: Baltic Square bus stop (buses to Newcastle Central railway station) opposite Millennium Bridge near start

WALK ACCESSIBILITY: Tyneside/Jesmond Dene stretches wheelchair/pushchair accessible; dogs allowed

DIFFICULTY: Easy

MORE INFORMATION: newcastlegateshead.com, tynekittiwakes.org.uk and jesmonddene.org.uk

Big cities attract a colourful mix of fauna just like they do people, throwing together a menagerie you'd normally need to travel to many separate locations to clock. This walk connects the two sources of Newcastle-upon-Tyne's unusually abundant nature: the River Tyne and the wooded valley of Jesmond Dene.

In the city centre's Tyne riverside, a kittiwake colony has come further inland than any other known on Earth to breed between February and August above an arts centre rather than the usual sea cliffs. Jesmond Dene, meanwhile, has recorded four bat species, including Daubenton's and noctules, the largest British-based bats. Otters have bred here in recent years, dippers perform waterside antics and tawny owls and great spotted woodpeckers are seen and heard in the centuries-old woodland. A blue flash along Ouse Burn might be a kingfisher; a russet flicker in the branches could be a red squirrel.

This amble is also an interesting study in how wildlife can adapt to flourish in the most unlikely manmade environments and in how, happily, countryside can penetrate the very heart of our bustling metropolitan centres.

> **DIPPER**
>
> A great gauge of Jesmond Dene's clean water is the dipper, normally associated with remoter upland rivers. The small bird is a big entertainer: on dry land it does considerable bobbing and tail-cocking, and it is unique in the way it walks into and then underwater to find food.

ROUTE DESCRIPTION

1) Your walk begins at the **Baltic Centre for Contemporary Art**, the site of great kittiwake activity between February and August. The Newcastle-Gateshead Quayside area hosts over 1000 of the seabirds, and the Baltic alone around 200. Some birds were displaced by the arts centre's modernisation, and the **Kittiwake Tower** was built further downriver to provide these with a new home. It's a 2km out-and-back walk from the walk start to the tower (not included in the walk distance) if you want to see them at closer quarters than is usually possible at the Baltic Centre. Having ogled the kittiwakes, cross **Millennium Bridge** from **Gateshead** across the Tyne into **Newcastle-upon-Tyne**. Turn right, continuing along the northern riverbank until the mouth of **Ouse Burn** in 750m.

2) Join the road behind the brick building near the Tyneside path's end. Turn right, crossing Ouse Burn, then turn left to then immediately pass left of the Tyne Bar. Head under the large red-brick bridge and come alongside Ouse Burn's east bank. Follow the burn under Byker Bank, another red-brick bridge carrying the A193 and two railway bridges. You then ascend steps to a path, turn briefly right, then left, negotiating more steps to reach the City Stadium and park. It's then a pleasant walk ahead along the park's east side to the exit at Newington Road near where a set of bollards prevents vehicular access. Turn left, crossing Warwick Street and continuing along a far-busier section of Newington Road to Stratford Grove West. Turn right, then left on a path swinging right alongside Ouse Burn again.

3) Proceed with the burn on your right. Your path hits the road again at Jesmond Vale in 200m. Head straight over Springbank Road. Jesmond Vale becomes Fore Street ahead which, before kinking left, has your path branching right off it just shy of a tower block. This path runs close to Ouse Burn with allotments off right, later ignoring a bridge on the right, to meet the road again at Benton Bank in 625m, right where it passes beneath the A1058 road. Turn left under the bridge. You'll presently spy some steps on the right; take these and turn right to cross **Armstrong Bridge**, built in 1878 to a design by industrialist William Armstrong, who donated Jesmond Dene to Newcastle's citizens upon his death in 1883. Swing left after this into **Jesmond Dene** at the park entrance.

4) The remotest reaches of the UK outdoors would do well to boast Jesmond Dene's number of species. The woodland – native oak, ash and cherry, with exotic Victorian additions like silver lime and black walnut – is impressive in itself. You follow the main path, Red Walk, through this pretty city park. After passing **Millfield House Visitor Centre & Café**, with records of wildlife locally spotted, on the right, continue on this path beside Ouse Burn for 900m (other paths fork off should you wish to explore further) to a bridge. Turn left across this, then turn right along the edge of a grassy picnic area. You'll reach the short out-and-back path to **Jesmond Dene Falls** in 175m. This picturesque spot beside **Old Mill**, a

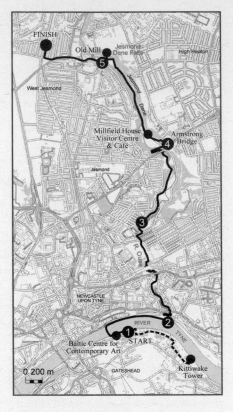

ruined watermill built in 1739, is a fitting finale to your stroll.

5) The path then continues around the picnic area, cutting through to Jesmond Dene Road. Turn right to come into the city's West Jesmond district, bearing right on Moorfield in 600m then right on Albany Road to reach the access to Ilford Road metro, where the walk ends.

RETURNING TO START: Ilford Road metro to Gateshead metro, then walk 1km northeast to start

61. Kielder Water's Bull Crag Peninsula

Learn about ospreys and look for red squirrels at this stunning sweep of forest and lakeside in England's far north

NEED TO KNOW

START/FINISH: Kielder Waterside holiday park, car park by pier, NE48 1BT – 9.25km (5¾ miles) west of Falstone (parking charges may apply)

DISTANCE: 10.5km (6½ miles) (part circular, part out-and-back)

TIME: 2½–3 hours

KEY SPECIES: Red squirrel, osprey, pine marten

MAP: OS Explorer OL42

TRANSPORT: Bellingham Bridge bus stop (buses to Hexham) - 21.75km (13½ miles) southeast

WALK ACCESSIBILITY: Accessible to wheelchair/pushchair users; dogs allowed

DIFFICULTY: Easy

MORE INFORMATION: visitkielder.com and kielderbopc.com

Northern Europe's largest man-made lake, Kielder Water, is encircled by England's biggest forest, Kielder Forest – it is no surprise that nature lovers flock to this mighty outdoor playground, a raptor swoop shy of the Scottish border. This walk zones in on a benign, bewitching limb of land, which protrudes into Kielder Water to offer the finest possible lake views.

Kielder Forest hosts around half of England's red squirrel population, and there is an observation hide in the beech forest early on the route. Spring is a fine time to see them scampering around. Ospreys have also been breeding hereabouts for many years and one of their favoured haunts is the Bull Crag Peninsula. March through September is best for spying the birds hunting over the water. You can learn more about ospreys in Kielder Water Bird of Prey Centre near the start point. Water vole and pine marten populations are also on the up, alongside healthy numbers of roe deer and otters. Make a night of it and star-gaze some of England's inkiest heavens afterwards.

This walk runs on well-defined, fairly level all-ability paths and tracks throughout.

ROUTE DESCRIPTION

1) Park in the car park by the pier in the Kielder Waterside complex. Views over Kielder Water are already superb. Among the maze of roads and trackways here, your route skirts past The Forest Bar & Kitchen and then some holiday park lodges on the left on a road then curving left past a large play area on the right. After the play area, bear left, following the road into a shore-hugging patch of woodland. After 100m, as the road curves right, pick up the good all-ability path on the left that twists around to reach a three-way path junction on the woodland edge.

2) Now take the path signposted 'Squirrel Hide & Shadow' (not the unsigned forest path nor the path onto open grass shore-side). This is the Beeches Walk, which cuts across the bulbous headland you now find yourself upon, and earns its moniker from the gnarled beech trees it passes beside. Continue on the path via the **Red Squirrel Hide** to reach the headland's other side after 400m.

3) Turn right along the shore on the Lakeside Way, a 42km route circumnavigating Kielder Water's shores, which you will follow for most of this walk. Pass Kielder Wakeboard & Water Ski Club, then join the wide all-ability path that bears left onto Bull Crag Peninsula. You soon reach **Freya's Cabin**, one of many sculptures dotting Kielder Water.

4) Proceed on the path along the peninsula's northern edge. You pass through the more open Jubilee Plantation and past **Otterstone Viewpoint**, from where views of the north and west of Kielder Water are exquisite and perfect for spotting the ospreys that sometimes swoop over the water. The path then enters delightful conifer forest at the peninsula tip, swinging south to reach a forest track end.

5) Continue zigzagging around the peninsula's eastern edge, skirting a small inlet and soon swinging west along the peninsula's southern edge, sticking close to the shore the whole while.

PINE MARTENS

Following population recovery in neighbouring Southern Scotland, pine martens are making more showings around Kielder Water (Scotland remains the best place to see them). Britain's rarest mammal, a mustelid like the weasel, pine martens are thought to help red squirrel populations by preying on easier-to-catch greys.

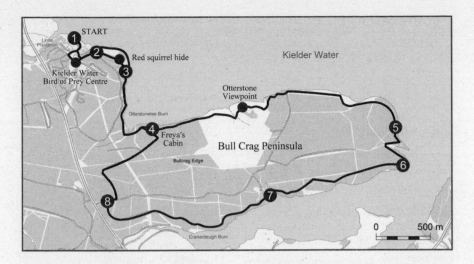

6) From the point the path swings west, you can select either the path closer to the shore or the forest track just behind to convey you along to another Kielder sculpture, **Kielder Keepsake**, after about 1.25km.

7) Carrying on along the southern shore, your path soon joins a wider forest track. This meanders through the trees for 1.5km, soon winding gradually away from the water then bending abruptly right (north) to reach a track junction.

8) Turn right. Then, after 75m, turn left on a track soon met by another track from the right before it swings right, back to reach the north shore at Freya's Cabin. Now retrace your outward route back to the car

park. This walk varies the return leg by continuing straight at the turn-off to the Beeches Trail to curve around the headland on the grassy shoreside path, maximising chances of osprey sightings (it meets your outward route at Point 2). After this, it circles around the other side of the holiday park play area to visit **Kielder Water Bird of Prey Centre**, where you can learn more about raptors and their ecological role.

Pine marten

221

62. Craster to Seahouses via Dunstanburgh Castle

Ramble a ravishing sandy shoreline rich in beaches, dunes and birdlife

NEED TO KNOW

START/FINISH: Craster Quarry car park, NE66 3TW/ Seafield car park, Seahouses, NE68 7RQ (parking charges may apply)

DISTANCE: 16km (10 miles) (one way)

TIME: 4–4½ hours

KEY SPECIES: Arctic and little terns, sandpiper, curlew

Arctic tern

MAP: OS Explorer 332/340

TRANSPORT: Bus stop immediately north of Craster Quarry car park (buses to Alnwick/Seahouses/Berwick)

WALK ACCESSIBILITY: Mostly accessible to wheelchair/pushchair users in dry weather except some stretches along the dunes/beach

DIFFICULTY: Moderate

SPECIFIC EQUIPMENT: Swimwear

MORE INFORMATION: northumberlandcoastpath.org, nationaltrust.org.uk and nwt.org.uk

Some of England's longest, loveliest sandy beaches welcome you with big, broad smiles to this fantastic tract of Northumberland seaboard. Much of the shore is fringed with dunes, creating important breeding and feeding grounds for warblers, sandpipers, terns and curlews. The big draw is the breeding Arctic and little terns at the Long Nanny reserve, but spring and autumn catch migrant birds at Newton Pools, while swallows roost within the moodily magnificent ruins of Dunstanburgh Castle near this walk's start.

And the end of the walk, for wild-lovers, is just the beginning: from Seahouses you can travel by boat to the Farne Islands, Sir David Attenborough's favourite nature spot in the UK and a nationally important sanctuary for seals, puffins and other seabirds.

This well-defined, level, grassy section of the Northumberland Coast Path is step-free.

ROUTE DESCRIPTION

1) Turn right out of the car park on the road, soon reaching Craster harbour front. Turn left on Dunstanburgh Road, signposted to Dunstanburgh Castle. The road runs alongside the harbour and ends at a double gate onto the coast path, the castle ruins already visible ahead. Keep on the broad path running levelly through grassy fields just back from the shore for 1.75km to reach a double gate in the boundary fence of **Dunstanburgh Castle**. The 14th-century fortress was built by Edward II's arch enemy, Earl Thomas of Lancaster, witnessing much fighting during the Wars of the Roses.

2) Trace the boundary fence around the castle's inland side, coming alongside the boulder-scattered beach to its north. At the castle end of the beach are the oddly shaped buckled strata of **Greymare Rock**. Kittiwakes and fulmars breed here from April to August.

3) The path then traces the edge of a golf course around the magnificent long sandy curve of **Embleton Bay**.

ARCTIC TERNS

These birds earned the nickname 'sea swallows' for their long tail streamers and body shape. White, black-capped and agile, Arctic terns have the longest migration period of any bird in the world.

You can choose to walk along the beach, watching for seals on offshore rocks, all the way to Low Newton-by-the-Sea. However, the coast path runs slightly back from the beach, skirting the road end at Dunston Steads, negotiating a footbridge over Embleton Burn and behind some beach houses to **Newton Pool nature reserve**, visited by spring and autumn migratory birds, including several sorts of warbler and sandpiper. At the north end of the reserve, the path becomes a stony driveway that reaches Low Newton-by-the-Sea at a gate by some boats.

4) Follow the narrow road beyond between Low Newton-by-the-Sea's pretty stone houses as it turns sharp right then sharp left before the beach. Your route branches right before a bungalow through a gate at a coast path sign. The path crosses several fields, heading straight over the metalled track to Newton Point, to draw alongside tussocky dunes behind Football Hole Beach. The route then swings away from the beach near its northern end, bearing northwest to reach Newton Steads car park.

5) The vast dune-backed beach now opening up is Beadnell Bay, curving all the way along to Beadnell. Again, you can choose to walk along the beach for stretches, but the coast path follows the high tide route behind the beach, crossing Newton Links and skirting **Long Nanny bird reserve**, a breeding site for Arctic and little terns. It's a 2.4km walk from Newton Steads car park to Beadnell Links Caravan Park, through which a now

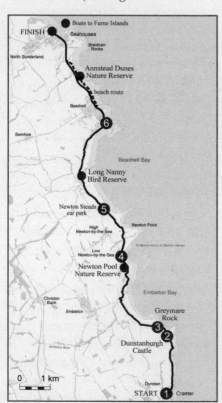

metalled track progresses to the road at Beadnell village. Follow the road through a housing estate until it curves left at a junction by the beach on Harbour Road.

6) The coast path officially continues on Harbour Road through Beadnell, forking right at the village green to meet the B1340 road after 1km. It then turns right to reach the edge of Seahouses village after a further 2.25km and the car park where this walk ends after 3km. In practice, you can mostly walk there on the beautiful sandy beach and dunes. Access them from Harbour Road in Beadnell at a wooden footpath sign on the right, where a grassy path leads past benches to the beach, or through another gate just after turning onto the B1340. You can then stroll through **Annstead Dunes nature reserve**. This mature dune system is a place to spot curlews and redshanks, plants like Northumberland's county flower, bloody cranesbill, and moths like the cinnabar. Come back onto the road at a gate before a river and golf course. From here, it's 700m along the B1340/King Street to a roundabout. Turn right, then immediately spy the cut-through passageway to Seahouses car park beside Cubby's newsagents.

RETURNING TO START: Car, bike or buses X18/418

63. Housesteads, Sycamore Gap, Steel Rigg & Greenlee Lough through Hadrian's Wall Country

Roam where Romans once established the empire's furthest frontier and where waders now stake out soggy overwintering grounds

NEED TO KNOW

START/FINISH: Housesteads Visitor Centre EH car park, NE47 6NN (parking charges may apply)

DISTANCE: 15.25km (9½ miles) (part circular, part out-and-back)

TIME: 4½–5 hours

KEY SPECIES: Large heath butterfly, curlew, white-clawed crayfish

MAP: OS Explorer OL43

TRANSPORT: Housesteads Roman Fort bus stop (buses to Hexham) at start

WALK ACCESSIBILITY: Not wheelchair/pushchair accessible; dogs allowed but on leads in Housesteads Roman Fort

DIFFICULTY: Moderate

MORE INFORMATION: nationaltrust.org.uk, english-heritage.org.uk, nwt.org.uk and hadrianswallcountry.co.uk

Hadrian's Wall has many claims to fame: it is Great Britain's biggest Roman ruin, Northern Europe's best-preserved Roman fortification, the northernmost extent of the Roman Empire and Unesco World Heritage-listed too. It marches over 117km of Northern England from Wallsend near Newcastle-upon-Tyne to Bowness-on-Solway (location of another wading bird-rich walk 64 in this book)

through mighty lonesome countryside, including over 5km on this walk. Yet while books have been filled on the wall's historical significance, less is said about its wildlife. And Hadrian's Wall Country has a great deal.

The exposed country around the wall is the domain of skylarks and meadow pipits, plus upland waders like curlew come summer. The large heath butterfly is a Northumberland speciality, inhabiting boggy sites across the region, including the mires on this walk, and only a handful of other locations in England. The return loops around Greenlee Lough, a major birding lake graced by overwintering goldeneye, whooper swans and greylag geese. It's also a haunt of the scarce white-clawed crayfish, Britain's only native freshwater crayfish.

If you can, make a clear winter's day visit when wall-top views will be far-reaching and the waders in cacophonous action on the lake. The route traverses some rough moor and marsh, but on decent paths that never vary more than 100m in altitude.

ROUTE DESCRIPTION

1) This walk begins by visiting the paid attraction combining **Housesteads Visitor Centre** with its **museum** containing Roman archaeological finds and **exhibition** on Roman military life and, up by the wall 675m away via the well-defined all-ability path,

Housesteads Roman Fort. The latter was an auxiliary fort, built in 124 AD, but nevertheless once housed 800 soldiers and is an impressive, albeit much-ruined, site. If you do not wish to pay to see all this, take the alternative route from the start marked on the map (turn right along the B6318 road briefly, then right through the gate to skirt the visitor centre and link up with the main route). This way, you still get to glimpse the fort from the walk route that brushes the site's left-hand side before hitting **Hadrian's Wall**. Started in 122 AD, this great barrier between the Roman Empire and the unconquered lands to the north is one of the UK's defining sights and took some 15,000 men around 6 years to build.

2) Now, follow the Hadrian's Wall Path along the wall for 4km. You actually walk on top of the wall here for the only time on the entire long-distance trail through a strip of broadleaf woodland, then presently rounding **Milecastle 37** out in the open again. Milecastles were built at intervals of one Roman mile along the wall, acting as additional defences to the forts and as points to levy tolls on traffic passing through. This open grassy moor is ideal for spying skylarks and meadow pipits. Upland waders, like curlews and redshanks, join the show in summer.

CURLEW

Curlews are Europe's largest wading birds and are distinctive with their long down-curving beaks and piercing two-note whistle. Despite being great adapters (they thrive on uplands in summer and make wintertime homes in lower-altitude wetlands), they are still a much-threatened, red-list species.

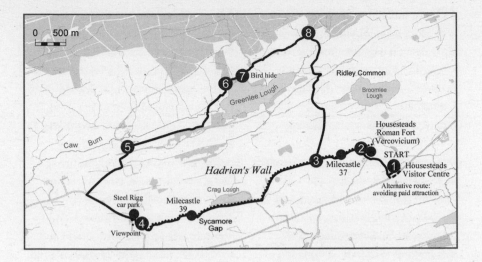

3) Another 400m after the milecastle, mark the ladder stile on the right after you cross a dry-stone wall: the Pennine Way branching right here is the path that you return upon. Continue along the wall now though: first up steep stone steps to the walk's highest point (around 325masl) before descending to pass along a treeline with **Crag Lough** lake off right below. As the lake ends, the path becomes ramparted by prominent crags on the right and drops to pass through the wall at photogenic **Sycamore Gap**. The lone sycamore is several centuries old. With the wall on your right, round **Milecastle 39** in 150m and proceed to where the wall curves left to a gate in 700m, which you pass through to behold the sudden, dramatic dip and the path to a very fine **viewpoint** in 225m. From

here the fortification looks formidable, climbing behind a sheer cragface with Crag Lough and its surrounding flatlands prostrate below.

4) After the viewpoint, follow the tarmacked path, shortly leaving Hadrian's Wall and swinging right to **Steel Rigg car park**. Turn left, through the car park, onto the lane. Then turn right. In 575m, at a sign to Gibbs Hill, branch right on a lane that reaches a wooden kissing gate and footpath sign on the right in 1.1km, shortly before a sheep pen.

5) Head straight across two fields, really fenced-in quadrants of moor, aiming for a line of trees cresting a knoll in the distance along the telegraph pole line. Reach the left-hand edge of the treeline at a gate

775m later. Next, walk along the woodland edge, briefly dipping into it, then swing left across the field along a boardwalk protecting the fragile wetland habitat around **Greenlee Lough** lake. This crosses Caw Burn, continuing to Point 6 on the map.

6) Continue straight to a gate through a dry-stone wall, then straight for another 200m with woodland and the lake beyond on your right until an out-and-back right-hand path to a lakeside bird hide. This is the best point for appreciating waders in wintertime and the summertime spectacles of great crested grebes and shelducks. It is Northumberland's largest natural lake, too, and pristine enough for the clean water-loving stonewort to grow.

7) After birdwatching, trace the dry-stone wall edge northeast to a copse, passing this on a broad enclosed path, then scale a ladder stile to pick up another wall edge on your right. Follow this to skirt the house at West Stonefolds. A metalled track then continues past a copse and then buildings at East Stonefolds, swinging right on the Pennine Way 225m later.

8) The route now negotiates boggy ground east of Greenlee Lough, over Haughtongreen Burn and tracking Pennine Way marker posts towards the higher and noticeably darker-coloured moor ahead south. This miry zone is popular with large heath butterflies. Look for a stile and footpath sign before a track running along the moor's bottom edge by a dry-stone wall: cross ahead onto the moor here. Your path follows the Pennine Way, meandering up over this rather stark section for 1.5km with Bromlee Lough off left to reach Point 3 on Hadrian's Wall again. Turn left, retracing your outward route 1.6km to Housesteads Visitor Centre.

NORTHWEST ENGLAND

64. The Solway Coast & Marshes around Bowness-on-Solway

Discover how Cumbria's northern flatlands soar higher than the Lake District when it comes to birds

NEED TO KNOW

START/FINISH: Port Carlisle Bowling Club car park, CA7 5BU (parking free)

DISTANCE: 15km (9¼ miles) (circular)

TIME: 4½–5 hours

KEY SPECIES: Pink-footed goose, barnacle goose, skua

MAP: OS Explorer 314

TRANSPORT: Hope and Anchor bus stop (buses to Carlisle) opposite walk start

WALK ACCESSIBILITY: Partly accessible to wheelchair/pushchair users; dogs allowed but under close control in nature reserves

DIFFICULTY: Easy

MORE INFORMATION: solwaycoastaonb.org.uk, rspb.org.uk and cumbriawildlifetrust.org.uk

Perhaps Bowness-on-Solway should rename itself birds-nests-on-Solway. While this amicable village on the Solway Firth shore is the end of the Hadrian's Wall Path, it is the beginning of the adventure for birdwatchers. Lovers of the close-by Lake District might dismiss this pancake-flat mosaic of coastal marsh and raised bog, but for avian action it ranks among England's best sites. Part of Solway Coast AONB and additionally protected by a reserve network including the trio seen on this walk, this is a habitat accommodating some special winged visitors. Expect a barnacle geese influx from northern Scandinavia come autumn, pink-footed geese populations that peak in February and many breeding waders wowing with springtime courtship rituals at Campfield Marsh Reserve. Bowness Gravel Pits Reserve is renowned for butterflies and Glasson Moss Reserve sports myriad bog-loving sphagnum species. Skuas are also spotted along the coast.

This is a walk with no climbs but prevalent sogginess on its many marshy sections. It's wheelchair/pushchair-accessible along the road to Campfield Marsh and as far as the reserve's bird hide.

PINK-FOOTED GOOSE
Converging from Greenland, Iceland and Svalbard to Campfield Marsh and a few other UK sites for overwintering, this is a showy, aesthetically pleasing medium-sized goose. It has pink feet, legs and beak and a high-pitched honk.

ROUTE DESCRIPTION

1) Turn right from the bowling club along the road to where it swings left at an acute right-hand side-turning. You can continue 1.75km on the road to Bowness-on-Solway (and must, at high tide) but otherwise, consider the adventurous diversion walking over the marsh to your right, best accessed here. The reason? Fascinating plants like sea lavender, samphire and wasabi-flavoured scurvy grass thrive here. There are views across to Scotland over the channel-scored sandy mudflats of the **Solway Firth**. Stick to the grass back from the gooey, sandy mud. You'll need to jump over rivulets and return onto the road at a lay-by after 800m. Now keep straight ahead into pretty **Bowness-on-Solway** along the road.

2) Business names like 'garrison' and 'wallsend' indicate Bowness-on-Solway's status as the finish of the Hadrian's Wall Path, and a right-hand signposted turn onto **The Banks** reveals a charming community garden and birdwatching viewpoint at the official

trail end (or beginning!) No trace of the wall remains hereabouts, though field hedges still follow its course. Continue through the village to the Kings Arms pub, on the site of a Roman fort, then straight on along the road. After 1km you reach a truncated viaduct, still jutting enough into the firth to make a good **skua-watching viewpoint** around high tides in April and May.

3) Another 900m on the road brings you to **Bowness Gravel Pits Reserve**, the gated entrance

Barnacle goose

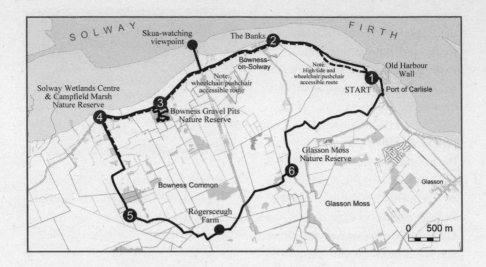

halfway along a wooded stretch after West Mead cottage. Waymarked paths wind around this lake-dotted woodland, summertime hangout of 20 butterfly species and Britain's largest dragonfly, the emperor, while barn owls, fieldfares and redwings are glimpsed in winter. Afterwards, turn left along the road to **Campfield Marsh Reserve** entrance.

4) The saltmarsh off right here provides wintertime lairs for oystercatchers. Head left up the track to first reach the site's **Solway Wetlands Centre**, presenting an overview of flora and fauna encountered here. This includes barnacle geese (autumn), pink-footed geese (February/March) and a springtime spectacle of displaying lapwings and redshanks.

Next, keep straight along the track passing two lakes, watching for the above wildlife and more. Turn right at the field boundary after the second lake, left alongside the next field boundary and head alongside woods onto the raised bog part of the reserve, where snipe and curlews breed in late spring. At a 3-way path split, branch left.

5) Keep in this direction for 275m. You're now crossing a mix of raised bog and fields, boardwalks helping out on boggier sections. Next, swing left (east-northeast) before presently curving gradually right (southeast). Pass two copses beside small lakes, then hit a track near Rogersceugh Farm. Turn left, skirting right of the farm. After the track bends right (south-southeast) you branch northeast on a footpath delivering you across a field and back over the bog. Cross a footbridge, continuing northeast, then swing right in about 350m to reach a woodland-bounded field edge 400m later. Follow the field along its wooded edge ahead then around left, swinging right across the field to the road before the next hedge.

6) Turn left for 600m, then right on Brackenrigg Farm drive. Off right is **Glasson Moss Nature Reserve**, a raised peatbog supporting flora like sundew and birds such as sedge warblers. Pass the farmhouse off left, bearing left just afterwards before some barns along a treeline for 125m. The path dog-legs right then left and, passing three intersecting field hedges on the right, bends right along the fourth in 650m. After 150m, turn left on a hedged track. This proceeds 400m to the road by a converted chapel. Turn right. Then very soon take the left-hand turn through a gate onto Hadrian's Wall Path. Turn left on the path, wide-open Solway Firth views fanning out beyond the **Port of Carlisle's old harbour wall** off right. After 250m, skirt right of a house and after passing a second house, turn left beside the bowling club to the car park.

65. Formby, Ainsdale Sand Dunes, Cabin Hill & Ravenmeols Sandhills

Delight in an epic dune system with protected natterjack toads, red squirrels and waders

NEED TO KNOW

START/FINISH: Victoria Road NT car park, Formby (650m/½ mile west of L37 1LJ, the closest postcode for sat-nav purposes) (parking charges may apply)

DISTANCE: 21.5km (13¼ miles) (part circular, part out-and-back)

TIME: 6–6½ hours

KEY SPECIES: Natterjack toad, red squirrel, northern dune tiger beetle

MAP: OS Explorer 285

TRANSPORT: Freshfield railway station – 1.75km (1 mile) east

WALK ACCESSIBILITY: Not wheelchair/pushchair accessible; dogs under close control

DIFFICULTY: Moderate

SPECIFIC EQUIPMENT: Swimwear

MORE INFORMATION: nationaltrust.org.uk, merseyforest.org.uk and gov.uk

Merseyside meets the sea here in a superlative sequence of sand dunes and pine forest of critical wildlife importance country-wide, and in some instances continent-wide. The really special habitat is not the dunes themselves but the slacks – depressions whittled by wind erosion down to water table level. The Sefton Coast stretching from here to Southport (north) and Crosby (south) supports a whopping 40 per cent share of this terrain type within England. This makes happy homes for rare natterjack toads, which breed in the slacks, while also-rare sand lizards appreciate the dunescape's array of bare sand and grass cover. Just as unusual a find are northern dune tiger beetles, one of the world's speediest six-legged things. The pines pin-cushioning the dunes are red squirrel territory. Ainsdale Sand Dunes stand out for their unusual plant life and Cabin Hill lures several overwintering wader species, most notably the bar-tailed godwit.

April to July is good for natterjacks and sand lizards; November through February perfect for wader-watching.

The titular quartet of destinations this walk visits are all nature reserves, with Ainsdale Sand Dunes and Cabin Hill NNRs. Dune walking is sometimes a case of two steps forward, one step back, but it's none too challenging and the sea's presence prevents you getting lost. Myriad dune paths mean this walk's distance is easily tweaked or divided into two days out if desired.

ROUTE DESCRIPTION

1) From the car park, begin by heading north through a green barrier with a 'Keep Clear' sign along the track towards Freshfield Caravan Park. As this bends right in 275m, take the path left (parallel to the sea on your left) through the dunes, here known as the **Formby Hills**. There is a big area of bare sand dunes perfect for spying northern dune tiger beetles and sand lizards along here. Choose any route you like initially (dune or beach): the main dune path enters an outlying flank of pine forest and on the far side picks up a broad path wriggling away from the coast northeast.

2) This is the walk's one stage where there are few alternative route options as you twist northeast through thicker pine forest 800m to a T-junction.

NATTERJACK TOAD

It's the call of these protected amphibians you'll notice first: the males' rasping from the dune slacks to attract mates, audible over 1km away during breeding season. This springtime chorus attracts not only female natterjacks but also a colourful variety of local names for the toads, like 'Bootle organ.'

Turn right on the Fisherman's Path, doubling here as Sefton Coastal Path. This leads east-southeast, dividing Formby Hills from Ainsdale Sand Dunes NNR on your left and traversing more pine forest. Turn left in 850m on a track cutting through forest, brushing the corner of a clearing to its right-hand side and bearing left again in 375m.

3) Your way now becomes a more pronounced track through the forest of **Ainsdale Sand Dunes NNR**. Trees are largely Corsican pine and a refuge for red squirrels. This route bears you along the track soon coming close to the railway line off right. Stick with the track a while longer before making a left-hand turn into the forest. It doesn't much matter which you take: you're ultimately aiming to forge through the trees and then the vegetated back-dunes west to the beach. This route continues along the track 1km after coming parallel to the railway line, branching off near a sign on the right inscribed 'Woodland Path'. You walk west-northwest, then west-southwest to the forest edge, then pick up one of umpteen paths corkscrewing through the dunes to the beach. This route turns right at the forest edge, heading north almost 1km before swinging left (west) to the beach. The dune grasslands, protected since 1965, harbour numerous intriguing flowers, including nationally scarce field gentians: June is best for seeing these four-petalled purple wonders.

4) Turn left (southwest) along some exquisite sandy beach, first **Ainsdale Beach**, then **Formby Beach**. This route heads all the way to the walk's southernmost extent on the beach, beyond the start car park and eventually swinging southeast to reach a left-hand path leading inland by a red flag demarcating Altcar Rifle Range: 8km all told. Follow this path to **Cabin Hill NNR**, circling the two lakes forming the reserve's centre anticlockwise. Fellow waders grey plovers and knots join bar-tailed godwits here in wintertime. Heading southwest on the return path to the beach, branch briefly off right to view the especially impressive dune slack of **Devil's Hole**.

5) Back on the beach, you're 3.5km south of your start point. Vary the return route by climbing into the dunes

again after 1.5km (this walk takes the right-hand turning after Lifeboat Road, marked by a colourful collection of signs at shore level but again, it doesn't overly matter which path you select). Returning through the dunes takes you to the heart of two more nature reserves: **Ravenmeols Sandhills** and then **Formby Nature Reserve**. Both exhibit slacks where you can watch for natterjacks and great crested newts. It's something of a choose-your-own-adventure weaving your way along dune paths back to the walk start.

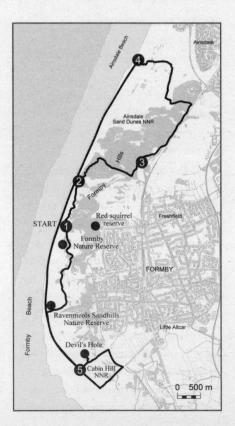

66. Buttermere & Hay Stacks

Wander one of the prettiest Lake District lakes, fabled for its fantastic trees and picturesque fells

NEED TO KNOW

START/FINISH: Car park immediately west of Buttermere Court Hotel, Buttermere, CA13 9XA (parking charges may apply)

DISTANCE: 13.75km (8½ miles) (circular)

TIME: 4½–5 hours

KEY SPECIES: Scots pine, Arctic charr, sandpiper

MAP: OS Explorer OL4

TRANSPORT: Buttermere Court Hotel bus stop (buses to Keswick Apr–Sep) – 50m east

WALK ACCESSIBILITY: Not wheelchair/pushchair accessible; dogs allowed

DIFFICULTY: Moderate

SPECIFIC EQUIPMENT: Compass

MORE INFORMATION: nationaltrust.org.uk

Sandpiper

Buttermere village could be the best of the lesser-known Lake District hiking hubs: from here you can mosey off on trails to the region's highest waterfall, Scale Force, and its most bedazzling bluebell displays at Rannerdale Knotts. But step for step, this walk is the winner: a lap of one of the national park's most aesthetically pleasing lakes, factoring in the fierce fell-side beauty of Hay Stacks summit too. Esteemed fell

hiker and guidebook writer Alfred Wainwright certainly revered this scenery, requesting his ashes be scattered on this route's ethereal Innominate Tarn 'where the water gently laps the gravelly shore and the heather blooms.'

Buttermere lake is surrounded by some of the Lake District's most entrancing trees and, with the Buttermere Pines, a stand of Scots pines on the southeast shore, some of the most photographed. The waters hide one of the country's rarest fish, the Arctic charr, while sandpipers nest on lakeshore shingle. Also watch for pied flycatchers and woodpeckers in lakeside woods. Otters, making a comeback, are also occasionally glimpsed.

Visit in July or August, when visibility in the fells is likely better, the sandpipers have finished nesting and the lakeside woods still reverberate with birdsong. Lakeside walking is gentle but the ascent to Hay Stacks is gruelling, over rocky terrain where bad weather can abruptly descend: come with your compass skills for this bit.

ROUTE DESCRIPTION

1) From the car park, head back along the lane past Buttermere Court Hotel to the B5289 road at the Bridge Hotel. Turn right, then right again into the yard at Syke Farm Tea Room. Pass between buildings on the tarmacked drive; at the end of the farm buildings, a gate leads onto a field-edge path to the left of a treeline. Views are astounding from the off:

SCOTS PINE
The UK's only native species of pine, this scaly-barked tree can live to a venerable 700 years and grow 35m high.

across the lake to a smorgasbord of summits including Fleetwith Pike, Hay Stacks, High Crag and High Stile. A broad path bears diagonally right across a second field, then swings right (southwest) along the far hedge. Turn left at a copse ahead through a gate, skirting the next field edge with a dry-stone wall on the left to a gate. Pass through the following field, a treeline to your right, to **Buttermere** lakeshore.

2) This is widely regarded as one of the prettiest Lake District lakes, flanked by the iconic Buttermere Pines at the far end. Sandpipers nest here between April and June, when the northern lakeshore immediately to your right should be avoided. Continue straight along the northeast lakeshore, passing several gates and, under **Hassness Crag Wood**, a tunnel, for 2km to the B5289. Bear right along the road.

3) After 150m, the road swings left away from the lake, the **Buttermere Pines** shore-side ahead (although photographing them from further away, encompassing the view behind, is best). The road presently reaches Gatesgarth car park: proceed past a white cottage and, after a dry-stone wall ends on the right, take the stony path right.

4) You now enter the valley of Warnscale Bottom, Hay Stacks towering off right. After 1.25km, branch right to cross Warnscale Beck stream and begin the tough climb up beside the beck to Green Crag. The exquisite panoramas back over Buttermere make your effort worthwhile! The route begins southwest, swinging west to ascend past **Warnscale Bothy**, a slate-built shelter almost completely camouflaged into the slope behind with its window framing a lovely lake-and-mountain view. An especially steep, rocky section then squeezes between two sets of crags, eventually swinging you around **Green Crag** as you join a path from the left to bear right, southwest and up.

5) You continue past Green Crag along a less-steep, cairn-studded path, precipitous drops and fantastic views off right, winding through a craggy wilderness. You'll pass the beautiful **Blackbeck Tarn** and **Innominate Tarn** and reach **Hay Stacks** (597masl), after which the path zigzags down to **Scarth Gap** (445masl) and descends Scarth Gap pass. Pick up Scarth Burn temporarily, pass between the crags of High Wax Knott and Low Wax Knott and come down to a conifer plantation near the lake. Skirt around this, keeping the trees on your right and swinging sharp right down to a dry-stone wall.

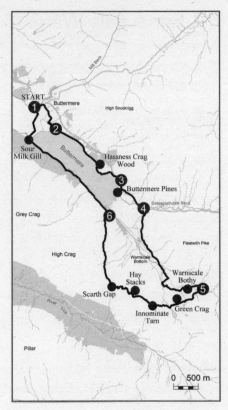

6) Do not go through the gate but follow the broad, stony path left along the southwest lakeshore for 2.25km, passing through Burtness Wood to the lake end. Here, cross the lower bridge over the churning **Sour Milk Gill** stream, curving right to cross another stream bridge over Buttermere Dubs. Now continue straight along a field edge back from the lake, turning left on a metalled track after 150m. After 550m, this bends alongside Buttermere Court Hotel near your car park in Buttermere.

67. Ennerdale Water

Relish a seminal rewilding scheme with a rosy future at the quietest, least-developed Lake District lake

NEED TO KNOW

START/FINISH: Bleach Green car park, Ennerdale Water, CA23 3AS – 2km (1¼ miles) east of Ennerdale Bridge (parking free)

DISTANCE: 11.75km (7¼ miles) (circular)

TIME: 3½–4 hours

KEY SPECIES: Marsh fritillary butterfly, red squirrel, roe deer

MAP: OS Explorer OL4

TRANSPORT: Corkickle railway station – 13.75km (8½ miles) west

WALK ACCESSIBILITY: Not wheelchair/pushchair accessible; dogs allowed

DIFFICULTY: Moderate

MORE INFORMATION: wildennerdale.co.uk, nationaltrust.org.uk, rewildingeurope.com and visitlakedistrict.com

Marsh fritillary butterfly

Westernmost of the Lake District's large bodies of water, Ennerdale Water is different from the other NP lakes. It has no roads along its shores, so your experience of the countryside will be far purer. Conservationists have had greater success at preserving Ennerdale's environs; public outcry at Forestry Commission planting of conifer forest here in the 1920s was so forceful that authorities agreed to leave 775km² of the regional lake and mountain terrain to nature. In 1980, proposals to tamper with lake water levels to increase water supply to close-by coast generated equally vehement protests, and consequently Ennerdale was never developed in the way other NP lakes were. One of the UK's biggest partnerships to preserve and restore wild countryside, Wild Ennerdale, manages the area and has brought about huge triumphs for local fauna and flora.

Probably Britain's healthiest marsh fritillary butterfly population now thrives here following a reintroduction, as does the devil's-bit scabious they favour. The red squirrel population has been protected from the greys that threatened them. Mire and heathland restoration has happened, and heavy grazers Black Galloway cattle open up more scrub, letting plant life develop. Wild Ennerdale also gained super-NNR status in November 2022, protecting these achievements in a 30km² zone and paving the way for future plans to bring beavers and pine martens back lakeside.

May or early June, when you can see talismanic local wildlife success story the marsh fritillary, is the loveliest time. The walk straightforwardly follows Ennerdale Water's lakeshore, with the one scramble of a climb coming as the path negotiates Anglers Crag near the end.

MARSH FRITILLARY BUTTERFLY
Once widespread in Great Britain, marsh fritillaries have suffered severe decline to become rather rare butterflies here. It's a lepidopterist's treasure, with brighter wing patterns than other fritillaries. It is reintroduction schemes such as that in Ennerdale that will be pivotal for its long-term prospects.

ROUTE DESCRIPTION

1) Before you begin, it's worth clocking community-operated **The Gather**, an information centre-cum-café-cum-shop in Ennerdale Bridge, where the turn-off road to the walk-start car park is. Turn left out of the car park, continuing along the lane from Ennerdale Bridge, past a right-hand driveway and onto a 7-bar gate. Follow the track beyond to the **Ennerdale Water** shore. You'll circuit the lake clockwise, beginning by turning left across the bridge over the mouth of the River Ehen and following the track just back from the shore along the lake's western edge. Views from here are picture-book Lake District. Looking down the lake, Bowness Knott

on the left and Anglers Crag on the right craggily guard the near shoreline, while at the far end Pillar (893masl) is the loftiest of the peaks visible.

2) Curving onto the lake's northern side, the track veers marginally away from the shore, but you presently take the right-hand path cutting back onto it. Follow the lakeshore path around another 1.8km, switching farmland for wood-dotted heath as you come below **Bowness Knott**. You reach the edge of the aforementioned conifer plantations as you meet the track from Bowness Knott car park.

3) The lake's appeal for wildlife, aside from the factors already mentioned, is that several distinct habitats brush its shoreline. At this point you have two of them: heath and conifer forest. The heath might yield signs of skylarks or meadow pipits. The conifers contain plenty of life too: sparrowhawks, song thrushes and wrens, plus red

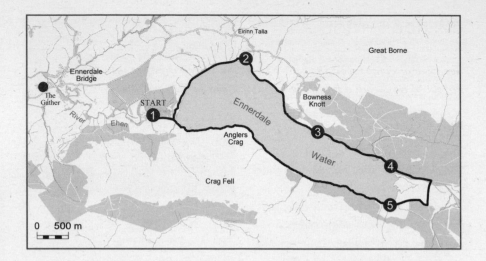

squirrels, especially in the trees east of Ennerdale Water. As you continue the 1.5km to the lake's eastern end along the forest edge, notice how the conifers are now also mixed with broadleaves like silver birch, creating an altogether healthier forest ecosystem.

4) Proceed on the track east away from the lake, passing moist meadow-land off right where marsh fritillaries may be seen. Cross the first footbridge on the right. The meadows separate two bands of conifer forest: walk over the meadows to the forest edge on the southern side, then turn right. Pass through a gate, a field, a gate and a long swathe of meadow to reach the lakeshore again.

5) The woodland here, on the south shore, is particularly beautiful broadleaf, where oak and other

trees shelter wood warblers, green woodpeckers, nuthatches and roe deer. You will see the rough slopes of Crag Fell and Anglers Crag tumbling steeply down to the shore behind the woods and this open moor might grab you sightings of wheatear, raven, stonechat and buzzard. It's about 2.75km along the south shore to where some light scrambling is needed as the path climbs over the foot of **Anglers Crag**, affording special views of Ennerdale Water framed by its mountains. After this, the path continues tight to the shore with an impressive wall mountainside on your left, but ahead you'll see the pocket of grassy farmland indicating your circuit is almost complete. Pass through a gate in a dry-stone wall, then across a field to reach the bridge in Point 1. Turning left, retrace your outward route to the car park.

68. Roeburndale

See how ancient riverside woods and lonesome moors make the Forest of Bowland a happy hunting ground for upland birds

NEED TO KNOW

START/FINISH: Bridge House Farm Tearooms, Wray, LA2 8QP (parking free)

DISTANCE: 15.5km (9¾ miles) (circular)

TIME: 5–5½ hours

KEY SPECIES: Sessile oak, hen harrier, short-eared owl

MAP: OS Explorer OL41

TRANSPORT: Proctors Farm bus stop, Wray (buses to Lancaster/Kirkby/Lonsdale/Skipton) – 475m (¼ mile) northwest

WALK ACCESSIBILITY: Not wheelchair/pushchair accessible; dogs allowed

DIFFICULTY: Moderate–Difficult

SPECIFIC EQUIPMENT: Compass

MORE INFORMATION: forestofbowland.com

The Forest of Bowland, an AONB, is renowned for its rugged heathery uplands, both for hiking and for birdwatching, with some areas getting SPA status for their excellent upland birdlife, like hen harriers and ring ouzels. But the steeply wooded valleys are important too, with Roeburndale harbouring Lancashire's most significant spread of ancient semi-natural oak woodland. The fields remain rambling meadows filled with the likes of harebell and yellow rattle.

The year's second quarter is most stunning. Bluebells fashion dusky quilts in the trees as badgers begin to emerge from setts with cubs, orange-

HEN HARRIER

This raptor is the AONB's symbol, highlighting that the Forest of Bowland is England's most important site for the birds (2022 was their most successful nesting year in some time). While numbers of the birds have declined massively in recent years, conservation projects are underway to prevent the amount of pairs from dwindling further.

tip butterflies brighten the woodland periphery and June is the best month for spotting hen harriers on open ground. Autumn is the likeliest time to spot roe deer, while winter is good for watching short-eared owls. Ups, downs, muddy sections and the fact that many woodland paths are permissive and thus not OS map-marked make this a fairly demanding route.

ROUTE DESCRIPTION

1) Take the pedestrian gate out of the pretty tearooms onto Main Street in Wray village. Ignore the lane ahead with a 'No Through Road' sign and walk a few metres left, turning right up the steep lane of Helks Brow. Continue for 725m past houses at Above Beck to a right-hand hedged track. Follow this down through Pike Gill Wood and over **Hunt's Gill Beck** to arrive opposite Alcocks Farm. Turn left on the lane for 500m to a gated footpath on the right.

2) The footpath immediately forks. Take the left-hand path, bearing diagonally across the field to a stile in the hedge (the other path, through the gate ahead down towards Outhwaite Wood, is your return path). You now follow the hedge line on your right across two fields, cross Outhwaite Farm track, and keep on the path alongside dry-stone walls to edge Wray Wood Moor. Alongside the aforementioned upland birds,

also look for skylarks and curlews. After the moorside stretch, you'll be heading southwest across several soggy fields to a barn.

3) In the next field is another fork: keep on the track straight ahead, with the field boundary on your left. As the track curves right away from the field edge, swing left aiming for the left (east) side of Harterbeck Farm. From the farmyard, the path leads south, crosses a stream and bends down around a finger of woodland to cross the footbridge over Goodber Beck near a **waterfall**.

4) In the next field, keep the field boundary on your left. In the following field, cut diagonally across it to the track running along the far boundary, and a stile in the corner. The next objective is High Salter Farm, which you reach at a lane end in four fields' time. Skirt the left-hand edge of the farm, then immediately curve left on a track that brushes the southern edge of some trees. A path then swings down southwest to reach a farm track in 300m. Turn left, crossing **River Roeburn** and skirting the right-hand (northern) edge of buildings at Mallowdale at the track's end. A path weaves down east into Melling Wood, swinging north to cross Mallow Gill and cut up through the woods into a field at a stile. Bear right (northwest) to follow the field-woodland edge, then swing left (southwest) away from the woods in the next field to meet a broad metalled track running north from the far side of Haylot Farm.

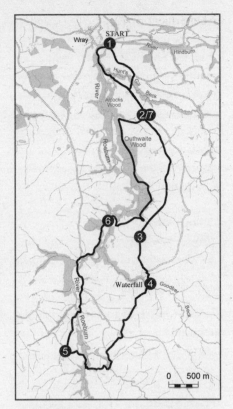

5) This passes along Wilson Wood to the right, re-crosses the River Roeburn and reaches the lane near Lower Salter. Turn left, passing Lower Salter's Methodist chapel, crossing the river again and reaching a ladder stile by the treeline. Turn right to stay close to the River Roeburn's left-hand (northwestern) woodsy bank, following the right-hand edge of two fields and then the left-hand edge of a third for 900m to a footbridge.

6) Briefly follow the right-hand riverbank north then east around the meander but then ignore the second footbridge ahead. Instead, swing right uphill on the signed path back into fields. In the first field, initially bear straight (south-southwest) across it to swing left around a protrusion of woodland and cross a stream. Then bear northeast across three fields, parallel to the treeline around 50m to your left, skirt right around another outlying finger of woodland, then turn left back into the woods. Your path twists through **Outhwaite Wood** for 1.9km. There are several paths to follow: both in the upper woods close

to the field edge and riverside (this route takes the upper paths). Either way, do not cross the river. All paths meet a broader track on which you bear right up out of the woods. Back in open pasture, follow a stream on the left initially as you ascend southeast for 275m, then northeast for 200m back to the lane at Point 2.

7) To vary the return route, turn left then continue on the lane for 1.6km, past Alcocks Farm along the river to arrive opposite Bridge House Farm Tearooms.

69. Helvellyn via Striding & Swirral Edges from Glenridding

Tackle the Lake District's most famously thrilling traverse, flying high with peregrine falcons and peering deep to spy rare fish

NEED TO KNOW

START/FINISH: Beckside car park, Glenridding, CA11 0PD (parking charges may apply)

DISTANCE: 13km (8 miles) (figure-of-eight)

TIME: 5½–6 hours

KEY SPECIES: Schelly, peregrine falcon, mountain ringlet butterfly

MAP: OS Explorer OL5

TRANSPORT: Greenside Road bus stop, Glenridding (buses to Penrith) – east of start

WALK ACCESSIBILITY: Not wheelchair/pushchair accessible; dogs allowed

DIFFICULTY: Difficult

MORE INFORMATION: visitlakedistrict.com

After Scafell Pike and Scafell, Helvellyn is England's next-loftiest peak at 950masl, but the drama of the summit approach and return, along knife-edge ridges Striding Edge and Swirral Edge, is unmatched elsewhere in the country.

Mountains here exhibit Arctic-Alpine habitat characteristics in high-altitude flowers like delicate white Alpine saxifrage, flowering up high in June. Britain's only Alpine butterfly, the mountain ringlet, is another summertime regular. Peregrine falcons and ravens are the big birds in the skies, wheatears and the rare ring ouzel breed across these uplands in summer and snow buntings frequent topmost crags during winter. A surprising resident of stunningly ridge-ramparted Red Tarn is the endemic, endangered schelly fish.

This serious hike entails occasional scrambling. Nevertheless, most relatively experienced walkers successfully complete Striding Edge, the trickiest part, despite it looking daunting from afar.

ROUTE DESCRIPTION

1) On the car park's south side, **Ullswater Information Centre** has information on local hiking routes and guided walks. Afterwards, turn right on the A592 road, following this out of Glenridding. Pass the southwestern end of **Ullswater**, the Lake District's second-biggest lake, and on to cross Grisedale Bridge at the entrance to Patterdale village. Most of this distance (950m) is along set-back roadside paths or pavements. Turn right along the lane beside wooded Grisedale Beck and, ignoring side-turns, proceed 925m to a gate across the lane.

2) Turn right, cross the beck, pass through a band of woods, continue straight at a gate and along a field to another gate. Beyond, the way forks: yours is the right-hand path climbing steadily up the side of Grisedale, as spectacular views unravel of the dale squeezed to its head by surrounding crags. Keep climbing for a relentless 2.25km to arrive at Hole-in-the-Wall, scouring the surroundings for the upland avian presence hereabouts: wheatears and ravens could be spotted.

3) Intriguingly named **Hole-in-the-Wall** now reveals itself as a humble stile in a dry-stone wall. However, the gap exquisitely frames the dale views

> ### SCHELLY
> The UK has few more obscure living things than salmon family member the schelly, inhabiting only four locations worldwide: all in the Lake District and two, Ullswater and Red Tarn, on this walk.

below. The route beyond gets wilder, through a rock-studded wilderness, ground falling away either side and tapering into the striking **Striding Edge** ridge. Negotiating this should be undertaken with care, and not attempted in high winds or poor visibility, though the path is less hairy than it first appears. Views get truly magnificent after you negotiate the rocky mound of Striding Edge's highest point, **High Spying How** (863masl).

4) Striding Edge rollercoasters on. The most difficult part is at the Helvellyn end, scrambling several metres down **The Chimney**, a rocky tower. After this, you're off Striding Edge, switching direction northwest for the final steep, rough haul up to **Helvellyn**. Panoramas from the 950masl summit both north the way you climbed and southwest to iconic fells like Scafell Pike and Coniston Old Man make this the Lake District's best viewpoint: look for swooping peregrine falcons too.

5) Keep ahead along the summit plateau's curving edge for 250m to a cairn where you descend steeply right along **Swirral Edge**, outstanding if less dramatic than Striding Edge. The path sticks on or just right of the ridge, dropping off right after about 500m towards the northeast corner of **Red Tarn**, which you can visit on a short detour to watch for schelly fish.

6) Cross Red Tarn's outflow 50m northeast of the tarn. Pick up a path running east-southeast and then east about 925m to the dry-stone wall just north of Hole-in-the-Wall. Turn left along your side of the wall. Views down to Ullswater get glorious as you bend right with the wall still on the right in 750m. Another 625m later, the path splits. The left-hand main fork also reaches Glenridding, but your route stays wall-side. Keep the wall close for just over 1km, then descend to a gate in the wall and turn right through it. The path divides immediately: bear left and descend 250m to a wider path running left to picturesque, wood-fringed **Lanty's Tarn**.

7) Pass the tarn on your right, emerging from the trees at a gate. Trace the stony downhill path bearing left (northwest, west then northwest again) to approach a dry-stone wall and gate. Just beforehand, turn right, descending to go through another gate and enter woods again. After the woodland, pass through another gate onto a track. Turn right. This comes back down into Glenridding, on the other side of Glenridding Beck from where you started the walk, reaching the road in 450m. Follow your outward route back.

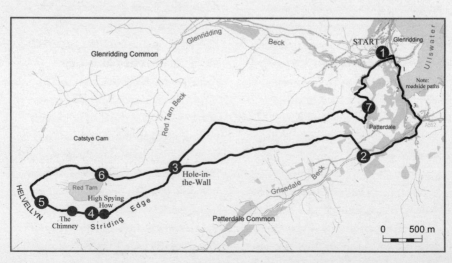

EDINBURGH, SOUTHERN & CENTRAL SCOTLAND

70. Holyrood Park & Duddingston Loch

Ascend above Edinburgh for a really wild show

NEED TO KNOW

START/FINISH: Car park south of Holyrood Abbey on Queen's Drive, EH8 8AZ (parking charges may apply)

DISTANCE: 8.25km (5 miles) (circular)

TIME: 2½–3 hours

KEY SPECIES: Pipistrelle bat, hedgehog, heron

MAP: OS Explorer 350

TRANSPORT: Scottish Parliament bus stop (buses to Edinburgh Old Town/Leith) – 475m (¼ mile) northwest

WALK ACCESSIBILITY: Mostly accessible to wheelchair/pushchair users; dogs under close control

DIFFICULTY: Easy

MORE INFORMATION: historicenvironment.scot and scottishwildlifetrust.org.uk

Embedded in Edinburgh's heart, Holyrood Park is no manicured metropolitan green space but surprisingly wild, like a chunk of Scottish Highlands juxtaposed on the city. Equally surprisingly, perhaps, it is a wildlife haven. The park and bird reserve Duddingston Loch sport sparrowhawks, geese, herons and sedge warblers among their avian inhabitants, plus pipistrelle bats and hedgehogs. Even otters, featuring on *Winterwatch* in 2020 and 2023, have at times taken up residence in the park. This is a wonderful place year round in good visibility: come outside of August, when Edinburgh is crowded.

Paths are generally manageable by pushchairs and wheelchairs but sections such as up Arthur's Seat are too rocky or narrow: with so many park paths, though, some of these suggested can be substituted for others. The walk has three notable climbs.

ROUTE DESCRIPTION

1) From the car park, with **Salisbury Crags**, the dramatic escarpment facing the city, in front, turn left along

PIPISTRELLE BAT
Evening walks may yield sightings of Britain's most common bat. These golden-brown furred mammals nest in tree holes and even roof spaces, emerging at night to eat up to 3,000 insects. They normally hibernate from November to March.

Queen's Drive for 625m. You come alongside **St Margaret's Loch**, a sanctuary for ducks, swans and geese, turning right around the loch's north shore to follow its eastern edge awhile. The pleasingly wild path forks halfway along: take the upper path, ruined **St Anthony's Chapel** visible above. Climb steps, soon with a rockface immediately left, to reach the chapel.

2) Next, keep the crags on your left to bear left (south), joining the main path south towards the park's high point, **Arthur's Seat** (250masl), which protrudes ahead and is reached 825m later. Along the way, keep right (up) at a fork and afterwards turn left on the wider path yours joins. The views at the top from this extinct volcano and SSSI are stunning: across Edinburgh, north all along the Firth of Forth and south out to the Lammermuir Hills. Descend south off the craggy top, then swing northeast and then, below the crag's eastern end, bear east on a broad grassy path gently descending with Dunsapie Loch gleaming below.

3) You reach Queen's Drive again south of the loch at the loch car park. Enter the car park, taking the path heading southeast from the southeast corner. Aim for the edge of a line of trees then follow a stone wall down on an improving path to come down to Duddingston Lodge near a car park. At a path junction the onward route turns left, on a tarmacked path through black gates. However, a short out-and-back path turns right, leading down to the road, crosses it, then descends broad steps to **Duddingston Loch**. This well-known birding sight hosts Canada geese, sedge warblers, reed buntings, hedgehogs and water voles. Afterwards, return to pass through the black gates on the tarmacked path to **Sheep Heid Inn**, purportedly Scotland's oldest tavern, at the corner of The Causeway.

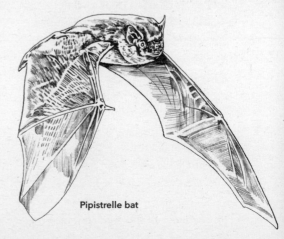

Pipistrelle bat

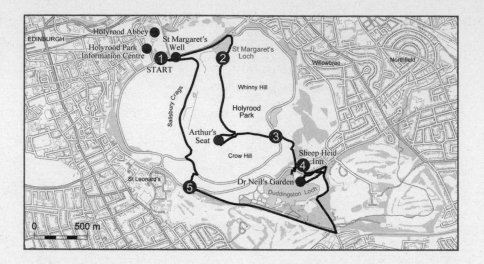

4) Turn right, then left on Old Church Lane and sharp right upon meeting Duddingston Road West. Just right along here is interesting **Dr Neil's Garden** (admission free), showcasing beautiful flowers and the Physic Garden with its many plants associated with healing. After exploring, turn right and continue along Duddingston Road West 700m to traffic lights, where you branch right on the Innocent Railway, a tarmacked path shooting across the southern side of Duddingston Loch. Meet Duddingston Low Road after 1.5km.

5) Head straight across up the grassy hill, gorse and crags to the right. Hit Queen's Drive after 150m and turn left. After a bend, turn right on a cut-through path 175m later to join the main north-south path across Holyrood Park. This is known as Volunteer's Walk: follow it 1.25km along the dip between Arthur's Seat and Salisbury Crags to eventually curve around left past **St Margaret's Well** down to the car park.

71. St Abb's Head

See how craggy cliffs and a loch combine to create a seabird and waterbird paradise on the coast south of Edinburgh

NEED TO KNOW

START/FINISH: St Abb's Head NTS car park, TD14 5QF – 500m (¼ mile) west of St Abbs (parking charges may apply)

DISTANCE: 7.25km (4½ miles) (circular)

TIME: 1½–2 hours

KEY SPECIES: Guillemot, kittiwake, puffin, fulmar

MAP: OS Explorer 346

TRANSPORT: Northfield Farm bus stop (buses to Berwick-upon-Tweed) – 50m south

WALK ACCESSIBILITY: Accessible to wheelchair/pushchair users, except section around Mire Loch; dogs under close control

DIFFICULTY: Easy

MORE INFORMATION: nts.org.uk

The beautiful, broken headland of St Abb's Head is a pile-up of hard volcanic rock flanked by softer sedimentary rock on either side, which the sea has eroded at very different rates, creating exceptionally riven formations that would render this coastline breathtaking enough alone. Add in one of the biggest, most accessible seabird colonies in mainland Scotland and you have one of the country's best coastal walks.

Huge numbers of guillemots, kittiwakes and razorbills, plus fulmars, shags and herring gulls, hog the cliffs

Guillemot

near the lighthouse, where gannets have also nested in recent years. In a grassy, tree-lined dip back from the craggy shore, snaking Mire Loch lures its own eclectic avian assortment, from herons to mute swans, reed buntings and little grebes. May to July gets the

253

key seabird action, when cliff tops resonate with a cacophony of nesting seabirds, including puffins.

This route is on distinct paths or lanes. Gradients are mostly gentle and step-free throughout.

ROUTE DESCRIPTION

1) A paved path, parallel with the main road, leads from the car park alongside **St Abb's Head Visitor Centre**, café and picnic area, crosses a farmyard and continues, divided from the road by a wall, to a patch of woods by the 30mph speed limit sign into **St Abbs.** This pretty harbour village can be visited on a short out-and-back detour: simply continue along the road for a few hundred metres.

2) By the 30mph sign, a sign on a stone wall indicates your path left to St Abb's Head. Take this path, following the wall through woods then beside a field to a gate near the wall's end.

3) The grass-flanked path gently ascends above and around Starney Bay. The coastline is immediately craggy and dotted by fascinating rock formations. Following the path over the headland, descend alongside rocky Horsecastle Bay.

4) After Horsecastle Bay, the path follows a field fence, then kinks right through a gate. Your route presently

climbs onto higher cliffs as **St Abb's Head Lighthouse** appears. The lighthouse, dating from 1862, was built by David and Thomas Stevenson, the latter being father to renowned writer Robert Louis. Aim for the left-hand edge of the lighthouse buildings' white-painted boundary wall, which your path reaches almost 1km after the gate. Continue with the lighthouse buildings' boundary on your right to the approach road and a car park. The cliffs of **St Abb's Head** around the lighthouse are prime seabird-watching territory.

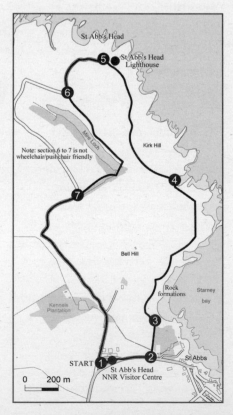

5) Turn left along the road, picking up a gully on the left where the road bends sharp right. Long, thin **Mire Loch** is ahead. The loch is a wildlife haven for freshwater birds, frogs, toads, butterflies and damselflies.

6) This gully becomes a faint tussocky path descending southeast down gorse-clad hillside to join the lochside path close to the loch's southeastern end near some wind-buckled trees. Follow the lochside path clockwise. It becomes a track at the loch's southeast corner, ascending to the road again. Wheelchair/pushchair users can continue to this point (7) on the road from the lighthouse, which skirts the loch anticlockwise to arrive here.

FULMARS
Fulmars nest higher up the cliffs than many seabirds, selecting grassy ledges and crevices for the job and spitting stinking fish oil to deter intruders! With grey-and-white colouring, they are related to those larger seafarers, albatrosses.

7) Turn left on the road, following it 1.1km back to the car park.

72. Abbotsford, Rhymer's Glen & Cauldshiels Loch

Stroll through the handsome former estate of 19th-century novelist Sir Walter Scott, an early champion of native reforestation

NEED TO KNOW

START/FINISH: Abbotsford car park, TD6 9BQ – 4km (2½ miles) west of Melrose (parking charges may apply)

DISTANCE: 10km (6¼ miles) (circular)

TIME: 3–3½ hours

KEY SPECIES: Native woodland (oak/Scots pine/ash/beech), red squirrel, otter

MAP: OS Explorer 338

TRANSPORT: Galafoot Bridge bus stop (buses to Galashiels/Tweedbank railway station/Melrose/Berwick-upon-Tweed) – 400m (¼ mile) north (and 125m northeast of Point 6 on walk)

WALK ACCESSIBILITY: Partly accessible to wheelchair/pushchair users; dogs allowed

DIFFICULTY: Easy–Moderate

MORE INFORMATION: scottsabbotsford.com

Sir Walter Scott was the early 19th century's best-selling British writer, but his paramount passion was planting trees. He was tree-planting even before taking full possession of Abbotsford, his long-term home near Melrose, in 1811. And with money soon pouring in from popular romantic historical novels such as *The Lady of the Lake* (the setting for which is the location of Walk 77 in this book), he set about expanding his estate and re-establishing native forest on his lands, gradually turning his grounds into the sort of pastoral idyll his books were full of. Much of Scott's arboreal vision, in the magnificent expanses of oak, beech, sycamore, ash and Scots pine he created, remains at Abbotsford: a trailblazing example of native reforestation. This legacy continues to be honoured by the property's subsequent custodians, with horse chestnut and lime, plus more of the same species, embellishing the tree cover.

This walk mostly explores land within Scott's former estate. Its chief joy is in wandering through the novelist's old woodlands and up Rhymer's Glen, one of his favourite walks. Along the way, it may well reveal traces of the creatures drawn to the tree-carpeted terrain: red squirrels, nuthatches, goldfinches, great spotted woodpeckers and tawny owls. Meanwhile, Cauldshiels Loch draws the feathered likes of tufted ducks and goosanders.

Come in spring as broadleaf trees green or autumn as they turn orange and gold. You'll pass quintessential borders scenery – a meander of tranquil riverbank here, a rise of ruddy moor there – as you amble.

ROUTE DESCRIPTION

1) This walk begins in Abbotsford's car park and basks in the glory of its wider estate (free for the public to roam). But it does not focus on **Abbotsford house and garden** (a paid-for but fascinating attraction). Scott lived here for 21 years until his death in 1832 and both house and gardens are shaped by a writer's lively imagination: check the garden's 'Rapunzel Tower' and greenhouse designed to resemble a medieval jousting tourney tent. The walk kicks off by continuing through the car park towards

> ### SYCAMORE
> Sycamore is not strictly a native British tree – the Romans or the Tudors (stories differ) introduced this fine-looking species. It has become part of our established broadleaf fabric, as evidenced by Scott choosing to plant it at Abbotsford, and a big attraction to aphids and honeybees. It colonises quickly, though, sometimes to the detriment of true native woodland.

the house. Reaching the path running in front of the Visitor Centre, you're on the Borders Abbeys Way (BAW) long-distance path, connecting the great ruined Borders abbeys at Melrose, Jedburgh, Kelso and Dryburgh. To enter the visitor centre, house and formal gardens, carry on ahead – otherwise, turn left on this path to the B6360 road.

Sycamore

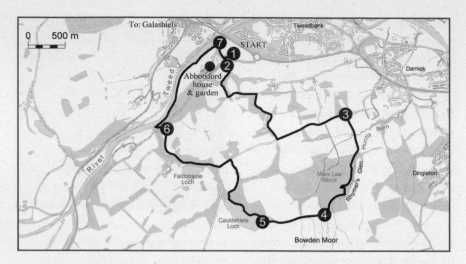

2) Cross with care, continuing straight onto a narrow lane. Follow this up as it bends through pretty woods, swinging hard left at a barn along to a lane junction. Turn right. This lane twists along another lovely stretch of tree-dappled fields and patchy woodland and in 775m meets a lane T-junction. Turn left, reaching the right-hand gravel track and turning into Rhymer's Glen in 1km.

3) The track passes a house and runs along **Huntly Burn**: 500m after leaving the lane, bear right near a pylon in the field off left on the grassy track into **Mars Lee Wood**. This is now conifer plantation, but in Scott's day this was **Rhymer's Glen**, likely just scattered with a few native trees and otherwise open land. It was one of the novelist's favourite walks. Still, there is plenty of beauty within the evergreens. Red squirrels scamper in the branches, great spotted woodpeckers drum the trunks and badgers scuffle on the woodland floor. Watch for roe deer too. Stick to the main track up: the Huntly Burn remains close on your left, except for a kink after 500m where you swing right and then back left to cross another burn. At the top of the wood, the path emerges by earthworks and strikes across the open ground ahead (southwest) to a gate in the wall.

4) Turning right along the wall's other side, your path now follows the edge of Bowden Moor. Keep by the wall for 850m, coming beside the mixed woodland bounding **Cauldshiels Loch** ahead. The loch features in local folklore as home to a bogle, a supernatural being in the shape of a water bull, but the main action you'll likely observe are great crested grebes and coots breeding here in springtime and the tufted ducks and goosanders in winter.

5) Turn right through a gate to walk between loch (left) and woodland (right). At the loch's far (northern) end, you veer right away from the water on a path presently rejoining the BAW, on which you turn right, following it to a lane. Turn left to buildings at Upper Faldonside. Next, branch right on a track that soon enters woodland with **Faldonside Loch**, an SSSI also attracting overwintering wildfowl, off left. In 500m bear right along a track to enter a large grassy field. Winsome views await as you follow the field's left-hand edge for 300m, then cut straight down across the field to a 7-bar gate and kissing gate onto the B6360.

6) Turn right for 50m to where signposted footpaths lead left and right through the woods. Turning left here, your path soon meets another: turn left again. This brings you to the path beside the **River Tweed**. Now swing right, following the path downriver towards Abbotsford. This is an enchanting stage of the walk: you pass many deciduous trees planted by Scott. You then come onto open ground, a blaze of wildflowers in spring with a fine prospect of Abbotsford House off right: keep along the riverside path for 950m and then curve right through woodland to meet the BAW once more.

7) Turn right here and follow the BAW back up to the visitor centre, with the car park then on the left.

73. Lang Craigs

Let charming Clyde-side forest, moor and crag scenery unfold alongside sightings of unusual birds, varied trees, foxes and field voles

NEED TO KNOW

START/FINISH: Lang Craigs Woodland Trust car park, just southeast of Overtoun House, G82 2SH – 4.75km (3 miles) northeast of Dumbarton (parking free)

DISTANCE: 8.75km (5½ miles) (circular)

TIME: 2½–3 hours

KEY SPECIES: Black grouse, peregrine falcon, fox

MAP: OS Explorer OL38

TRANSPORT: Dumbarton East railway station – 3km (2 miles) southwest

WALK ACCESSIBILITY: Not wheelchair/pushchair accessible; dogs allowed

DIFFICULTY: Easy–Moderate

MORE INFORMATION: woodlandtrust.org.uk

You're nearing Loch Lomond & The Trossachs NP, known as 'Scotland in Miniature' for its montage of forest, moor and lake, by the time you reach Dumbarton. But who would have guessed that in an unheralded locale within walking distance of the town and close to Glasgow's urban sprawl, you would find terrain of similar calibre? Lang Craigs is just lovely. It's your introduction to the wider, wilder expanse of the Kilpatrick Hills beyond, beginning with a rambling 19th-century country estate that ushers you up beside burn, through forest and over moor to the dark, dominant crag of Lang Craigs itself, carving out

Fox

260

a curving wall of rock high above the River Clyde flowing below.

Pretty views are matched by compelling wildlife. Woods can resound with woodpeckers, cuckoos, treecreepers and goldfinch, while foxes and field voles skulk through the vegetation, roe deer graze, black grouse hide up in the moors and raptors like peregrine falcons coast the thermals. Arboreal diversity is huge too, with Scots pine, sycamore and sessile oak all present.

FOX
Top of the woodland food chain, this gingery creature is Britain's only member of the wild dog family and is equally at home in town or country. Its varied diet has certainly helped its long-term survival: anything from wild berries to small mammals goes down well.

ROUTE DESCRIPTION

1) From the car park, continue up the approach drive to **Overtoun House**, ignoring the right-hand track signposted 'Crags Circular Path'. Pass in front of the rambling 1860s-built mansion with its grand tearoom, crossing ornate **Overtoun Bridge**. As the drive beyond curves left, turn right on a path gently climbing the left side of Overtoun Burn through woods. Otters have been seen here and you might hear great spotted and green woodpeckers and willow warblers. Scan the water for frogs and toads. After 150m, branch right over a footbridge and cut northeast then east across the grassland beyond to the track you previously ignored.

2) Turn left. The track forks 175m ahead before a pyramidal stone monument. Bear left, still following a solid, albeit soon grassy, track. The next stretch is part of the Woodland Trust's plan to return native forest to these slopes, with plantations framing fine views of Lang Craigs off right. Your way swings northeast, passing three cross-tracks: the third at an old stone boundary. Continue on in the same direction. The climb is now through open, occasionally tree-dotted grassland (much of it felled forestry) around and eventually over the **Lang Craigs** on the right, with special views of the River Clyde opening behind. Higher up, the path swings south to a path junction. Turn right to reach the **crag-top viewpoint** on a short out-and-back journey along a wider forestry track. Enjoy wild, far-reaching vistas down to Dumbarton and the Clyde, plus the possibilities of buzzards, sparrowhawks and peregrine falcons. The grassy moor also hides the threatened black grouse.

3) Next, follow the forestry track 650m southeast to **Black Linn Reservoir**,

screened to the south by conifers.
Turn right (south) upon reaching the
reservoir access track, following this
south and branching right at a fork.
Gradually swing southwest as you pass
G. Brown Hill on the left, followed
by another reservoir off right and
then a third off left. You pass much
still-standing conifer forest but, after
reservoir three, the trees end. Then
it's 350m, passing through a couple
of gates en route, down to a path
branching sharp right before the track
reaches a landfill site and quarry.

4) Take this path, which follows the
field edge northwest then southwest,
revealing more impressive views of
Lang Craigs. You then brush forestry
on the descent to the quarry approach
road. Turn right here, then in 825m
turn sharp right again on Milton Brae,
the tarmacked lane leading back up to
Overtoun House. Reach the car park
after 1.25km.

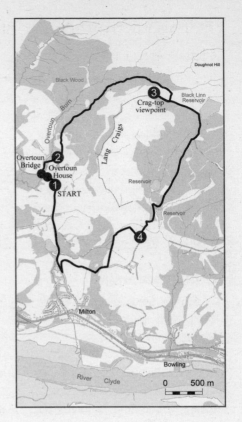

74. The Hermitage, Loch of the Lowes & Dunkeld from Birnam

Watch ospreys, behold beavers and walk beside monumental trees

NEED TO KNOW

START/FINISH: Dunkeld & Birnam railway station, Birnam, PH8 0DP

DISTANCE: 15km (9¼ miles) (part circular, part out-and-back)

TIME: 4½–5 hours

KEY SPECIES: Osprey, beaver, Douglas fir

MAP: OS Explorer 379

TRANSPORT: Dunkeld & Birnam railway station at start

WALK ACCESSIBILITY: Not wheelchair/pushchair accessible; dogs not allowed in Loch of the Lowes reserve

DIFFICULTY: Easy–Moderate

MORE INFORMATION: nts.org.uk and scottishwildlifetrust.org

On these two stunning circuits from woodsy Highland Perthshire village Birnam, doable as one memorable wildlife odyssey or two separate trips out, you'll step among some shining stars of British nature. This region is christened 'Big Tree Country' and

OSPREY

Flying an average of 260km daily on their journeys south to overwinter, ospreys return to Britain between March and September. The birds lay their eggs in April, with fledglings hatching about 37 days later. They bear similarities to eagles but are a separate species.

the walk delivers the goods, visiting a vestige of the Birnam Wood that featured in Shakespeare's *Macbeth* and an enchanting forest turned into a pleasure ground by the Dukes of Atholl, guarded by some of Britain's tallest trees.

The River Tay is one of Scotland's two places where beavers have been released into the wild (the other, Knapdale Forest, is the location of walk 75 in this book) and sightings are regular, while the Loch of the Lowes offers superb osprey-viewing. Red squirrels do tree-branch dances, pine martens sneak between woods and water and otters have been loch residents since the 1990s.

Stop by in late April, May or June as greenery colours the woodlands again, bluebells spread their violet carpets and ospreys return to breed.

ROUTE INFORMATION

1) Turn left from the railway station entrance, across the car park down steps into Birnam Glen, a quiet lane alongside Inchewan Burn. Turn right, under the A9 road, continuing to Perth Road in Birnam. Turn right, left on St Mary's Road and left again on Oak Road. After 300m, near the River Tay, you'll find **Birnam Oak**. Shakespeare's *Macbeth* is informed his ill-gotten kingship will continue until Birnam Wood comes to Dunsinane, his castle. Woods cannot move, so Macbeth assumes he is safe, but then his enemies sneak up camouflaged by

Birnam Wood tree branches. This oak is supposedly the sole survivor of that original wood. Next, turn left along the wooded riverbank path, watching for beavers. Pass under the A923 road after 600m.

2) Next, 300m later, meet Tay tributary the **River Braan**, swinging left along tree-lined banks then passing under the A9. Straight afterwards, turn right over a footbridge and follow the path along the Braan's north bank and around a forestry depot, turning right on a lane by a caravan park. You then take the pedestrian cut-through onto the A9 250m later and follow a barricaded pavement to The Hermitage turn-off.

3) Transformed by the 2nd and 3rd Dukes of Atholl with the establishing of Scots pine, Douglas fir, oak,

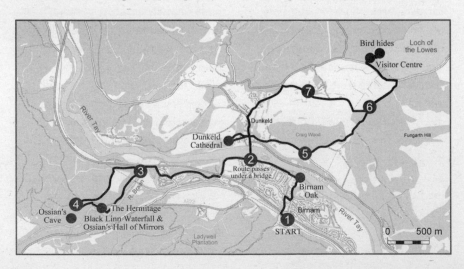

rowan, larch and sycamore forest, **The Hermitage**, the NTS-managed arboreal wonderland you now walk through along the River Braan, numbers among Britain's prettiest. Head under the railway bridge on the main path, then branch left after 350m to come still closer to the riverside, passing some of Britain's tallest Douglas firs. You'll see **Ossian's Hall of Mirrors**, a 1780s-built temple-like viewing point, restored with a mirror-lined interior entrancingly reflecting **Black Linn Waterfall** nearby. You can explore this lovely locale for longer, watching for red squirrels, herons and dippers. This walk returns to the main path, turning left for 225m to pass a totem pole then curving right to meet the Old Military Road.

Osprey

4) Turn right along this by-way for 1km through Craigvinean Forest to a car park, after which you are back at the Hermitage entrance. Retrace your outer route to Point 2. Here, as the woodsy River Tay path comes under the A923, climb steps onto the bridge and cross the river into **Dunkeld**. Take the second right on Brae Street and leave town (you will see it again later!). This forest-fringed lane meets a left-hand track, signposted to Loch of the Lowes, after 725m.

5) Bear left at a track fork in 275m. Continue for 350m, having ignored left-hand paths off through the woods and, after a short open section and before a sharp right-hand bend, turn left onto a glorious old wooded section. You'll meet another path after 350m.

6) At the path junction, bear right, alongside a golf course, to a wooded lane at a gate. Cross this, turning left on another delightful path along **Loch of the Lowes**. Reach a car park 450m later, bearing right to **Loch of the Lowes Visitor Centre**. Short trails lead to **hides** where you can view ospreys via telescope – it's arguably Britain's best spot to do so.

There is also a live osprey webcam. Otters, pine martens, great crested grebes and reed buntings might also be spotted. Afterwards, retrace your route to the beginning of Point 6, where, at the path junction, you now keep right. Your track keeps curving right, passing a cottage and becoming metalled. Where the metalled track swerves right, pass through a gate ahead, crossing a grassy field to the golf club car park.

7) Follow the golf club drive 300m to a minor road branching left just before the A923. This becomes Spoutwell as it gently descends into **Dunkeld**. Turn left upon reaching the A923 at a car park. Then, at the point you previously turned onto Brae Street, turn right on The Cross for an out-and-back reconnoitre of **Dunkeld Cathedral**, 200m along this road through black-iron gates. This magnificent grey sandstone building, dating to the 14th century, stands on one of Scotland's most important early Christian sites. Afterwards, follow the A923 back across the river into Birnam, heading down the steps onto the riverside path and retracing your outward route to the railway station.

75. Loch Barnluasgan, Loch Coille-Bharr & the Faery Isles

See beavers on this foray into Knapdale's forests, their first reintroduction site in Britain

NEED TO KNOW

START/FINISH: Barnluasgan car park (2km/1¼ miles north of PA31 8PS, the closest postcode for sat-nav purposes) – 2.5km (1½ miles) southwest of Bellanoch (parking free)

DISTANCE: 9.75km (6 miles) (part circular, part & out-and-back)

TIME: 3–3½ hours

KEY SPECIES: Beaver, Atlantic oak, red squirrel

MAP: OS Explorer 358

TRANSPORT: Lochnell Street bus stop, Lochgilphead (buses to Glasgow/ Tarbert/Campbeltown) – 10.75km (6¾ miles) northeast

WALK ACCESSIBILITY: Not wheelchair/pushchair accessible; dogs allowed

DIFFICULTY: Easy–Moderate

SPECIFIC EQUIPMENT: Insect repellent, swimwear

MORE INFORMATION: forestryandland.gov.scot

This well-wooded part of Knapdale, above the Mull of Kintyre, has been at the vanguard of Scotland's rewilding movement since it became the first location in Britain to successfully reintroduce beavers. Beavers are busy creatures, felling trees and causing micro-flooding that results in a more-or-less constantly changing landscape here. But at least the change is natural and native, and the precious wetland habitats beavers create are returning.

Visiting the shores of three bewitching lochs and a fair few tracts of the encompassing forest, scrub and bog that beavers like to call home, the walk is skewed in favour of showing you these super-cute rodents and the traces they leave. In between the conifer forestry are pockets of Atlantic oakwood – magical temperate rainforest draped with bryophytes and lichens. Red squirrels dance through treetops, and ospreys and eagles may be seen overhead. The environs are all protected as one of Scotland's 40 NSAs.

The walk is level, mostly on firm tracks but with several boggier, rougher sections south of Loch Coille-Bharr. Pick a low tide for the Loch Sween end of the walk: dawn or dusk are best for spying beavers.

BEAVER

This furry, water-loving, highly skilled lumberjack was once widespread in Britain, but hunted to extinction in the 16th century for its fur and scent glands. In a happy turnaround, the first beavers to inhabit Britain in over 400 years were released in 2009 in the area this walk traverses. They have flourished here ever since.

ROUTE DESCRIPTION

1) Barnluasgan Information Centre (unstaffed) at the car park harbours useful information on wildlife spotted hereabouts. The main fauna focus is undoubtedly the beavers, well-gnawed signs of which are prevalent around the shores throughout this walk. The route begins with an anticlockwise circuit of **Loch Barnluasgan**. Take the well-surfaced path from the back of the car park at the opposite end to the information centre to complete the 1.4km loop, visiting the **hide** on the northeast shore, a handy beaver-watching spot, and passing patches of beautiful Atlantic oak woods before returning to the car park entrance along the roadside path.

2) Back at the car park entrance, turn right along the road a short distance towards the war memorial and B8025 road turning to Tayvallich. Beforehand, on the left, is a gate: pass through onto a path curving left, initially following the line of the B8025 before continuing ahead alongside the northernmost appendage of **Loch Coille-Bharr**. Keep the loch on the left at first before bearing right into woodland at a gate. The path then curves 150m west and southwest to reach Loch Coille-Bharr car park.

3) Your track now runs south-southwest from the information board at the car park's southern end, red waymark posts pointing the way, reaching deserted village **Kilmory Oib** in a clearing after 350m. A right-hand path leads around the houses, a tranquil grassy area with an upright **carved stone** at the far end etched with a sun, moon and pair of birds. Returning to the main track, turn right. Another 500m on you pass ruined **Coille-Bharr mill** and about 150m later the way divides.

4) Continue your onward route around Loch Coille-Bharr on the left fork later: for now, bear along the right track fork on the out-and-back diversion to the Faery Isles. This is an enchanting section in parts, stippled with hazel, holly and oak trees. You come onto more scrubby open ground, arriving at another track fork 575m later. Forking right here brings you to great views of Loch Sween, but this walk sticks with the left-hand fork. In 700m this often-boggy track starts bending around a lonesome woodsy arm of Loch Sween. Keep the water on your right, winding along the loch

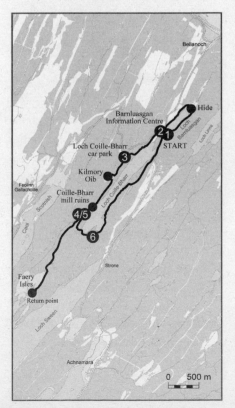

shore. The track becomes a path that soon reaches the most northeastern of the **Faery Isles**, which is accessible at low tide. This enchanting section is populated with hazel, holly and oak trees. Watch for beaver tell-tale traces: trees felled to well-honed stumps and shavings of bark deposited nearby. Afterwards, retrace your route to Point 4/5 on the map.

5) Turn right on the track, proceeding with the Loch Coille-Bharr circuit. In 275m the path bends left to head across the loch's southern end, with a viewpoint and picnic tables. Contrasting bands of broadleaf and conifer forest winsomely flank the shores here. After 350m of winding along the southern shore, turn left on the track bearing along the northeast shore.

6) Following the northeast shore, the track presently reverts to path status, 650m later squeezing between the main loch and diminutive **Dubh Loch** off right, its surrounds now fashioned into a wetland by beavers. The path then leaves the loch, swinging across the north end of Dubh Loch by a boardwalk, and you continue northeast on a track. After 550m pass through a gate and reach the steps to a small jetty. Shortly afterwards, you reach a road; turn left for the 400m walk to the car park entrance.

76. Grey Mare's Tail & Loch Skeen

Clamber above a mighty waterfall where peregrine falcons nest and wild goats roam

NEED TO KNOW

START/FINISH: Grey Mare's Tail nature reserve NTS car park (5km/3 miles northeast of DG10 9LH, the closest postcode for sat-nav purposes) – 15.5km (10 miles) northeast of Moffat (parking charges may apply)

DISTANCE: 4.5km (2¾ miles) (out-and-back)

TIME: 1½–2 hours

KEY SPECIES: Peregrine falcon, wild goat, vendace

MAP: OS Explorer 330

TRANSPORT: Moffat High Street bus stop – 15.5km (10 miles) southwest

WALK ACCESSIBILITY: Not wheelchair/pushchair accessible; dogs under close control

DIFFICULTY: Moderate

MORE INFORMATION: nts.org.uk

Perigrinne falcon

The thunderous presence of Grey Mare's Tail, Britain's fifth-highest waterfall, contrasts with the solemn stillness of Loch Skeen, Southern Scotland's highest-elevation loch. With bare angular hills all around, it's fiercely beautiful but surprisingly stark stuff. Novelist Sir Walter Scott, a long-term Borders resident, evocatively described it thus in his epic poem *Marmion*:

> *Where deep deep down and far within,*
> *Toils with the rocks the roaring linn;*
> *Then, issuing forth one foamy wave,*
> *And wheeling round the Giant's Grave,*
> *White as the snowy charger's tail,*
> *Drives down the pass of Moffatdale.*

WILD GOATS

A farm animal in Britain from Neolithic times, goats have likely been wild in Scotland's hills since either the 18th- and 19th-century Highland Clearances or the decline of goat-hair wigs around the same time. They have brown-white shaggy coats.

Too savage for human settlement, this walk's terrain appeals to some hardy fauna. Peregrine falcons nest in waterfall crags in spring; ravens, kestrels and merlins patrol the skies; feral goats graze the slopes and the vendace, Britain's rarest freshwater fish, lurks in Loch Skeen.

The first half of the walk is all up, the second all down. Parts of the ascent/descent are steep but the path is always well-defined.

ROUTE DESCRIPTION

1) A surfaced all-ability path runs from the car park across a footbridge to a **waterfall viewpoint** on the east side of the stream of Tail Burn, from where the stepped stony path to Loch Skeen ascends steeply (the west side has a path leading part-way up, to another waterfall viewpoint).

2) The path zigzags up steeply, then swings northwest to follow the course of Tail Burn in the deepening gorge below. **Grey Mare's Tail**, as becomes more apparent with your every approaching step, ranks among Britain's most impressive waterfalls: its 60m high cataract squeezed between formidable, near-vertical hillsides. The crags around the waterfall are where you're most likely to spy peregrine falcons.

3) After passing the waterfall, your path ascends more gradually along a hanging

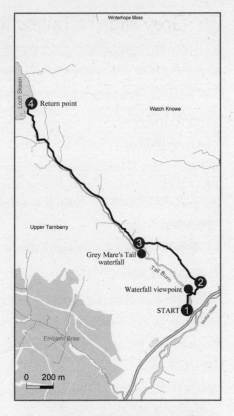

valley, drawing closer to the stream but never crossing it: watch out hereabouts for wild goats. After passing a stream confluence on the left, the still-clear path keeps hugging the eastern (right-hand) bank of the Loch Skeen outflow, reaching the loch edge 1km above the waterfall.

4) Loch Skeen (510 masl), inhabited by the elusive vendace, is a lonely locale. The higher surrounding moorland sometimes yields sightings of red grouse and mountain hares, while barren ridges rear behind. Your outward route ends here: return the same way.

271

77. The Glen Finglas Estate, Loch Achray & Loch Katrine via the Great Trossachs Path

Uncover the reasons why this region's scintillating scenery was where Scottish tourism began – and why it is a vanguard of rewilding today

NEED TO KNOW

START/FINISH: Glen Finglas Visitor Gateway car park, Lendrick Hill, FK17 8HR – 800m (½ mile) east of Brig o' Turk (parking free)/Loch Katrine car park, FK17 8HZ – 5.25km (3¼ miles) west of Brig o' Turk (parking charges may apply)

DISTANCE: 18.5km (11½ miles) (part one way, part out-and-back)

TIME: 5½–6 hours

KEY SPECIES: Red squirrel, pine marten, otter, rowan

MAP: OS Explorer OL46

TRANSPORT: War Memorial bus stop, Callander (buses to Stirling) – 9.25km (5¾ miles) east

WALK ACCESSIBILITY: Accessible to wheelchair/pushchair users; dogs allowed

DIFFICULTY: Moderate

MORE INFORMATION: lochlomond-trossachs.org, woodlandtrust.org.uk and forestryandland.gov.scot

The beguiling buffer zone between lowland and highland, clad in the woodsy charm of the former yet peppered by plenty of the latter's lofty peaks, Loch Lomond & The Trossachs NP has been a huge tourist pull for well over two centuries. Early visits by romantic bards William Wordsworth and Sir Walter Scott, and later Queen Victoria, an admirer of Scott's writing, brought Scotland's first big numbers of holidaymakers to the lyric-worthy lakeshores here. Early on, visitors were eager to experience the landscapes so evocatively described in Scott's *Lady of the Lake* poem and patronised by the queen who enjoyed the 'solitude, the romance and wild loveliness of everything here'. But for wildlife lovers, the reasons to come kept stacking up. The region became

Scotland's first national park in 2002. And its heart has now become The Great Trossachs Forest NNR and the site of one of the UK's largest native woodland regeneration projects.

The bolstering of the ancient woods through extensive planting of rowan, oak, hazel and hawthorn has created, alongside previously planted conifer, an eclectic miscellany of forest. Combined with the moors and mountains above, this appeals to many of Scotland's big fauna spots: red deer, pine marten, otter and golden eagle are all regulars, while red squirrels are so abundant you might even spy the scamps from the car park. Beavers have also recently begun to inhabit the NP. This walk begins by reconnoitring Glen Finglas' gorgeous native woods and reservoir, following up with a stint along Loch Achray before traversing forest along to captivating Loch Katrine.

September and October, when the deciduous forest and moors start smouldering in russet and gold and the bellows of rutting red deer reverberate through the glens, is just glorious.

ROUTE DESCRIPTION

1) Across the car park is **Glen Finglas Visitor Gateway**, a brilliant resource with displays on the metamorphosis of this area, formerly a vast, over-grazed sheep farm, since the Woodland Trust began managing it in 1996. Steps taken have included huge native tree replanting efforts and controlled cattle grazing, enabling smaller, rarer plants to thrive that would otherwise be smothered by bracken. While the woodlands here are vital for wildlife, the most important habitat in the Glen Finglas Estate is the wooded upland pasture, of which it has Scotland's finest example. Here, widely spaced, old-growth trees grow on pastureland, letting in ample light for understorey to develop, yet rendering the remainder of the ground impractical for agricultural improvement: fine news for the plants and creatures flourishing on unimproved ground. Cross the bridge north of the car park on the eastbound Great Trossachs Path. This long-distance footpath connects Callander (east) with Inversnaid on Loch Lomond (west). Pass through a gate and wind up

ROWAN

What would a British countryside walk book be without a special mention of rowans, those hardy survivors rooting on rugged uplands where other trees cannot? The rowan's scarlet berries are a rich autumnal food source for birds and the tree has its own distinct mythology too, particularly in the Celtic world. In Scotland, cutting down a rowan for any cause was strongly frowned upon.

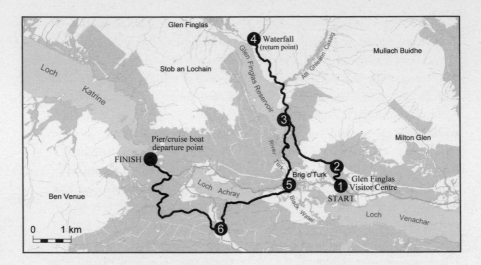

the wooded hillside west-northwest, northeast and north-northwest before the Great Trossachs Path contours east at a path junction after 700m.

2) Your route, here one of the visitor gateway's waymarked walks (the Leitrim Hill and Dam walk), now threads west and then north for 2.3km, presently leaving the forest and traversing a belt of open moorland. This grants you lovely vistas before you re-enter forest closer to **Glen Finglas Reservoir** and descend to a broader track near the reservoir's southeast corner.

3) Your onward route leads left from here. However, it is utterly worth the 5.7km out-and-back diversion right on the track along the reservoir shore, with some of the walk's finest scenery on the line. The forest falls back for

a stretch to enable you to see the views and this, the quietest part of the walk, is also a great time to watch for cruising raptors and otters and pine martens ferreting around the reservoir and streams feeding it. The **waterfall** on Allt Gleann nam Meann makes a good turn-back point.

4) It's now 4.1km, backtracking to map Point 3 and on down to Glen Finglas Road. The access road to the reservoir dam is right; you turn left for 400m, passing a group of houses on the right and reaching a right-hand path just before a stream. This curves left to follow the **River Turk** downriver. Just before the river passes under the A821 road, your path swings left for 175m, coming alongside the road then crossing straight over it at a gap in a wooden fence onto the Byre Inn's driveway.

5) Back on the Great Trossachs Path, pass the inn and curve right past Achray Farm to bear right at the track junction. Continue for 800m with Loch Achray soon on your right. Meet the broad forest track of the Three Lochs Forest Drive (accessible to public vehicles spring through autumn and otherwise the usual pedestrians/ cyclists/horse-riders). Bear right, following the forest drive along **Loch Achray** loch shore. The drive curves left (south) away from the shore in 600m: stay with it, bearing right (southwest) where another wide forest track joins from the left, to a car park. The track then curves past the car park to a T-junction in 275m where you swing right to the A821.

6) Turn briefly right along the road, then left on the bridge's far side. This path leads through tree-stippled moorland into denser conifer forest behind to veer right on the forest track in 250m. The track curves for 2.1km through patches of forest and scrubby moor, ignoring minor side-turns, to a forest track crossroads. Swing right 400m to a T-junction (Loch Achray Hotel is right here if you need refreshment) then left for 425m. A path then branches right to cross Achray Water. Afterwards, turn right on the lane – a private, non-vehicular road – and follow this 600m to the A821. Turn left. The road terminates at Loch Katrine car park 550m later. Walk through the car park to the loch's visitor centre, café, cruise boat departure point and pretty shorefront. The setting for Scott's *Lady of the Lake* poem and the subsequent Gioachino Rossini opera *La Donna del Lago*, the lake's beauty is well known, but stroll a little way and you can escape most of the crowds to enjoy the place in peace.

RETURNING TO START: Bike or car

78. Lochranza & Beinn Bhreac

Head up handsome glens for golden eagles, red deer, Scotland's purest water and the world's rarest tree

NEED TO KNOW

START/FINISH: Lochranza Hotel car park, Lochranza, KA27 8HL (parking free)

DISTANCE: 19km (11¾ miles) (part circular, part out-and-back)

TIME: 6½–7 hours

KEY SPECIES: Catacol whitebeam, golden eagle, red deer

MAP: OS Explorer 361

TRANSPORT: Ardrossan Harbour railway station – 45km (28 miles) southeast, on mainland. Walk 200m west to Ardrossan ferry terminal and take the CalMac ferry to Brodick, 23.25km (14½ miles) southeast, then car or bus to Lochranza Hotel

WALK ACCESSIBILITY: Not wheelchair/pushchair accessible; dogs allowed

DIFFICULTY: Moderate–Difficult

SPECIFIC EQUIPMENT: Compass, insect repellent

MORE INFORMATION: visitarran.co.uk

Firth of Clyde island Arran purports to offer 'Scotland in Miniature'; here is a charming seaside village, a castle ruin, a wonderfully wild coast well-frequented by dolphins and seals, while bringing you close to talismanic Scottish creatures the golden eagle and the red deer, visible year round. More claims to fame? Scotland's purest water (Loch na Davie) and the world's rarest tree (Gleann Diomhan's catacol whitebeam). Late summer days are spectacular, when mountain views stretch far, radiantly framed by heather.

Arran's mountain-bound crowds mostly stick to Goatfell, so this route stays relatively quiet and wildlife-rich.

> **CATACOL WHITEBEAM**
> One of the planet's rarest trees is a hybrid of rowan and cut-leaved whitebeam. The few known examples are all on the Isle of Arran, surviving in a ravine bounded by glens Catacol and Diomhan on this walk.

The climb from sea level to 408masl is no joke and boggy patches can be arduous. Paths are mostly distinct save for those through the birch woods near the finish, but bring a compass for poor visibility.

ROUTE DESCRIPTION

1) From **Lochranza Hotel**, start out along the waterside A841 road towards the mainly 16th-century **Lochranza Castle**, standing on a peninsula jutting into Kilbrannan Sound. Turn left on the castle access road to explore the ruin. Afterwards turn left along the A841, continuing 800m to Newton Road, a dead-end lane on the left. Here, it's worth a detour 1km or so down the road, which unravels around shoreline where grey seals often laze.

2) Returning to the A841/ Newton Road junction, turn left, proceeding along the A841 another 675m to **Lochranza Distillery**. The distillery takes its water from Scotland's cleanest source (according to Glasgow University), Loch na Davie, to which you will presently climb. After the distillery, turn right before a stone bridge on a grassy riverside path, the beginnings of the fine Gleann Easan Biorach glen.

3) It's now an ascent of almost 4.5km towards **Loch na Davie**, during which you'll gain 350m altitude. Keep close to the river throughout. Glens below rocky peaks like this are prime golden eagle territory, and you may also see grazing red deer. Steady climbs at the beginning and end are separated by a leveller, longer, boggy middle section, with impressive waterfalls between the Allt a Chrithich and Allt Dubh tributaries and just after, and huge views off left to island high point Goatfell.

4) Glimmering Loch na Davie (361masl) is on your left as you pass it, fetchingly framed ahead is Goatfell and up right rears the bare rounded summit of **Beinn Bhreac** (575masl). This walk does not climb the peak but you do soon begin swinging away from the glen, rounding Beinn Bhreac's shoulder and ascending to a *bealach* (saddle). You reach 408masl at the walk's high point, just after skirting the summit's southern flanks, then descend northwest into Gleann Diomhan. Look around: another glen, another golden eagle and red deer spotting opportunity.

5) The path running northwest along the burn's right-hand bank is obvious, and from the bealach it's a pretty 1.75km descent to an enclosure protecting the world's few **Catacol whitebeams**, plunged down a ravine here. Enter and exit the reserve through the gates.

6) Now gently descend into Glen Catacol, joining another path incoming from the left by a cairn. Keep the river just left as you bear north along an improved path before presently swinging northwest again. Open mountain country ends ahead as the river curves left (west) close to a field boundary. Your path curves in the same direction, squeezed between tree-fringed river and field edge, crosses a stile, then swings northwest 200m to the A841.

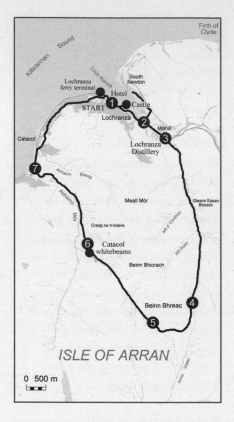

7) Turn right for 575m to a right-hand gated track turn in Catacol, a teensy hamlet. You can continue along the road to Lochranza (the safe choice) or follow this walk's route (the adventurous choice) along the old postie's path, skittering through birch woods and heath above the wooded crags flanking the road. The path is hard to follow and boggy at times but has better views and the attractive aforementioned birch woods. Pass through the gate and a small wooden gate visible ahead. Your main navigational aid is now a telegraph pole line above left, which you climb towards and follow about 300m until roughly level with Catacol's last house below. The path then drops diagonally left (north-northwest) slightly to follow a winding up-and-down way north-northeast through the birch woods. You'll pass beneath another line of

telegraph poles perpendicular to the first before swinging east after 1km to follow the original line of poles. Another 500m and this more distinct path forks: turn left (north-northeast). This path descends away from the woodland, soon swinging right (northeast) and passing left of a ruined house before making for a house driveway at a bend. Do not follow this track to the house but instead continue east to descend into Lochranza. Turn right on the A841 for 275m to Lochranza Hotel.

CAIRNGORMS & SOUTHERN HIGHLANDS

79. Rothiemurchus Forest & Loch an Eilein from Coylumbridge

Lose yourself in the Cairngorms' Caledonian pines, where rare creatures like capercaillies and wildcats reside

NEED TO KNOW

START/FINISH: Lay-by on B970 by Rothiemurchus Camping & Caravan Park entrance, Coylumbridge, PH22 1QU (parking free)

DISTANCE: 15km (9¼ miles) (circular)

TIME: 4½–5 hours

KEY SPECIES: Capercaillie, Scottish crossbill, Scottish wildcat

MAP: OS Explorer OL57

TRANSPORT: Coylumbridge Hotel bus stop (buses to Aviemore/Cairngorm Mountain) – 450m (¼ mile) west

WALK ACCESSIBILITY: Mostly accessible to wheelchair/pushchair users; dogs on short leads (Mar–Aug) and always under close control

DIFFICULTY: Easy–Moderate

SPECIFIC EQUIPMENT: Insect repellent

MORE INFORMATION: rothiemurchus.net

Who can fathom how much ancient Caledonian pine forest once carpeted Scotland? Judging by Rothiemurchus Forest, its largest remnant, at its greatest extent it must have been spellbindingly beautiful. While romantically touted as a representation of untamed Scotland before humans began tampering too much with the landscape (the surviving forest is a direct descendant of the first pine trees to populate Scotland after the last Ice Age), Rothiemurchus Forest more pertinently symbolises the compelling wildlife we must focus on cherishing today.

The chief treasure is the capercaillie, a large, bizarre-looking woodland grouse so rare it teeters on the brink of extinction, and you should take extreme care on forest walks during the birds' March to August breeding season, keeping dogs on leads and sticking to paths. Almost as sought-after by ornithologists is the Scottish crossbill, the scarlet (male) and green (female) finch that is Britain's only endemic bird. Scottish wildcats have the forest as one of their final refuges, and there are significant red squirrel and red deer numbers too.

The above creatures could be seen at any time, but stay well away from capercaillies March through August, and do not seek them out. September is radiant, when weather is often excellent, red deer rut and the moors glow ruddily through the trees. While set against a humbling rugged backdrop of immense Cairngorm peaks, this part of the NP has level terrain and paths are top-quality, so wheelchair/pushchair-users could explore many routes.

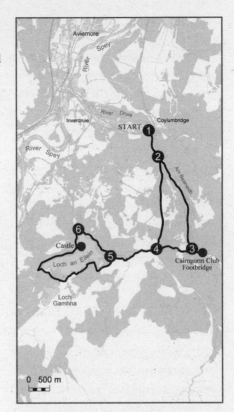

ROUTE DESCRIPTION

1) Keep your eyes peeled throughout for all the introduction-listed species. To begin, turn into Rothiemurchus Camping & Caravan Park entrance and, rather than turn left into the campsite, bear straight ahead on a solid forest track. You reach a former parking area and shortly afterwards a gate: keep on along the main track to where it splits 300m later and fork left.

2) The walk's next section is 2.5km, heading southeast and later south, with a tributary of the River Spey a constant companion on your left. This is a surprisingly silent and resplendent tract of mature pine forest. You'll cross bridges over two burns along the way to a junction with a wider, more-tramped path.

3) Bear left on the short out-and-back route to the iconic **Cairngorm Club Footbridge**, a legendary hiker's river crossing constructed in 1912 and a pretty picnicking spot, before returning to the junction and now taking the left-hand fork. Proceed for 950m across more open ground

– a mixture of thinly dispersed trees, regenerating forest and scrub – to the comely Lochan Deo. Here, mark the path crossroads in a sudden patch of denser forest parallel with the end of the lochan: the right-hand path will later be your return route (and can be now, if you don't want to see the delightful Loch an Eilein).

4) It's 1.25km from the crossroads west-southwest across the tree-dotted scrub to another path junction, again in denser woodland, which signifies the beginning of your circuit around **Loch an Eilein**.

5) This route circles the loch clockwise, and therefore goes left at this point. The loch, with its ruined **castle** on an island, pines fringing the shores and some of Britain's best mountain scenery soaring above, is ridiculously picturesque, replete with tempting picnicking spots and understandably mighty popular.

CAPERCAILLIE

Reduced within the UK to mere hundreds, capercaillies depend on large extents of native Scottish pinewood for their survival. The male birds are the really flamboyant ones with their melange of blue-grey, green, brown and black colouring, red eyepatches and distinctive calls sounding like long series of popping gurgles.

Circling it, it's almost impossible to go wrong. It's 1.75km along the south shore until you pass nearby Loch Gamhna on your left and cross a footbridge, then 600m to a path junction at the loch's western end where you pivot sharp right onto a wide path. The northwestern shore – 1.5km – is perhaps loveliest of all. The route first winds northeast to Loch an Eilein Cottage, from where the island castle is close. It then heads north to where a path runs across the northernmost loch edge from a small shingle beach, overlooked by a cottage.

6) The broad track north from here goes to a car park and information centre. But you trace the loch shore along its north edge, over a footbridge to turn right on the broad track following the eastern shore. This wanders – quite far back from the water at times – for 975m, passing a cottage and reaching the path junction at Point 5. Now retrace your outward route to the path junction at Point 4 and turn left on the walk's final leg. This is a straightforward 2.25km on a good northbound track. You'll traverse a wide area of open ground, scrub and grassland with impressive views southeast to Cairn Gorm summit (location of walk 84 in this book) in between the stretches of forest and reach Point 2. Retrace your outward route to the start.

80. The Glen Tromie Triangle & Insh Marshes from Ruthven Barracks

Get gripped with a beautiful glen-side build-up before the thriller: one of the continent's best wetland birdwatching spots

NEED TO KNOW

START/FINISH: Ruthven Barracks car park on B970 (250m east of PH21 1NR, the closest postcode for sat-nav purposes) – 1.5km (1 mile) southwest of Kingussie (parking free)

DISTANCE: 10.5km (6½ miles) (circular)

TIME: 4–4½ hours

KEY SPECIES: Whooper swan, redshank, osprey

MAP: OS Explorer OL56

TRANSPORT: Kingussie railway station – 1.25km (¾ mile) northwest

WALK ACCESSIBILITY: Not wheelchair/pushchair accessible; dogs allowed

DIFFICULTY: Moderate

SPECIFIC EQUIPMENT: Compass, insect repellent

MORE INFORMATION: visitcairngorms.com, rspb.org.uk and wildland.scot

Whooper swan

Little is known of the lonely country making up the middle of this walk in a rarely visited nook of the Cairngorms NP, but the beginning and end are of national significance. Ruined Ruthven Barracks, one of Scotland's grandest examples of 18th-century military architecture, presides over the route's start. Next to negotiate is the gloriously wild V-shape over moors to Glen Tromie and its solemn birch forests and then down the glen to the grand finale: one of Europe's most important wetland bird sites – Insh Marshes NNR. This 10km² avian playground entices diverse birdlife: ospreys and breeding waders curlews, lapwings, snipe and redshank in spring and summer, with migrants whooper swans and greylag geese in winter.

This is a great bad-weather alternative for when higher mountains are in cloud and holds year-round appeal for nature lovers. Paths are unkempt over to Glen Tromie, a stretch where compass skills are recommended, but well-defined thereafter.

ROUTE DESCRIPTION

1) Ruthven Barracks, King George II's almighty response to the 1715 Jacobite Rebellion and built in the years following to house 120-odd soldiers capable of quashing uprisings, impressively dominates the start from a hilltop and deserves exploring. Head briefly away from the barracks along the B970 road, then take a sharp left on a farm track climbing behind the car park. There are two gates on the right: take the second, briefly following a fence to the right, then turning right along the left side of a tumbledown dry-stone wall that runs initially parallel to the farm track. This track soon swings left

WHOOPER SWAN

Britain's few overwintering whooper swans spend summers in Iceland, arriving at Insh Marshes in October and staying until April. Their honking voices and yellow triangular beak patches distinguish them from those year-round UK residents, the commoner mute swans.

(south), ascending steadily. Just before a house 425m later, leave the track, passing left of the house. Cross a stile in the next fence and then the Burn of Ruthven stream and its tributary, 100m beyond the house.

2) The track afterwards is faint enough that a compass is advised now until Glen Tromie, though it becomes more distinct when bounded by heather higher up. The track climbs, heading generally southeast for the first 425m, aiming right (west) of the masts on Beinn Bhuidhe summit. You then swing south and pass to the right (west) of the summit along its flanks. About 275m later with the summit behind you, continue again ascending southeast: around 950m along the now-fading track in this direction you hit a fork.

3) Carry straight on here (leftmost of the forks) on a heathery path reaching a cairn-marked high point, then descending towards the **Woods of Glentromie** visible ahead. Make for a ladder stile in the deer fence to enter the woodland: there is a patch more moor and then the wood's fine birch trees take over. The path here is faint but marked intermittently by posts. At a fork, go left (miss this and you'll hit the deer fence again and should retrace your steps to the fork) and wind through woodland on a

rough path down to a stile onto the
driveway of Glentromie Lodge near
the glen bottom. Turn left, crossing
the River Tromie.

4) Turn left on the main glen track,
grand views of the birch woods off
left. The track meanders down,
largely following the river, for over
3km to the B970, joining the Speyside
Way for the final 250m.

5) Turn left on the road over the
river, then right through a gate into

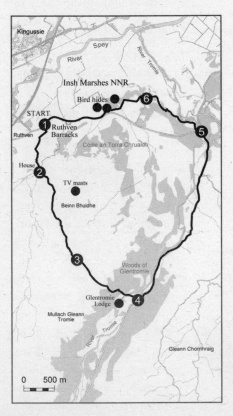

Insh Marshes NNR. The route is
now waymarked, passing through
woods then around the riverside edge
of a meadow harbouring several
orchid species. As the river on your
right twists north, you branch away
from it at a marker post through a
gate up a bank. Now wend along
an edge of woodland running
northwest-southeast, the flat fertile
fields bordering the marshes below
right. About 550m after departing
the riverbank, curve sharp left to
cross the drive serving the buildings
at Invertromie.

6) Your path soon bends up over open
ground with the woodland below
right. Head southwest across this open
ground, afterwards joining the wood
edge on your immediate right and
following the treeline along almost to a
car park. Just beforehand, curve right
around a picnic area and branch right
to the middle of three **bird hides**,
with excellent views across the marshes
to the Monadhliath Mountains. The
path brings you back up onto a track
next to the car park, now off left.
Conclude the walk by turning right
on this track, following it as it sticks
close to the B970 and switches to the
other roadside after 450m. Ruthven
Barracks looms ahead; the walk start is
just beyond.

81. Coignafearn & the Upper Findhorn

Swoop up this lonely Monadhliath Mountains valley in the company of golden eagles

NEED TO KNOW

START/FINISH: Coignafearn car park, near the end of the road up Strathdearn (5.25km/3¼ miles southwest of IV13 7YB, the closest postcode for sat-nav purposes) – 20.75km (13 miles) southwest of Tomatin (parking free)

DISTANCE: 20.75km (13 miles) (part circular, part out-and-back)

TIME: 5½–6 hours

KEY SPECIES: Golden eagle, peregrine falcon, water vole

MAP: OS Explorer 417

TRANSPORT: Clune Road End bus stop, Tomatin (buses to Inverness/Carrbridge) – 19.75km (12¼ miles) northeast

WALK ACCESSIBILITY: Accessible to wheelchair/pushchair users; dogs allowed

DIFFICULTY: Moderate

SPECIFIC EQUIPMENT: Compass, insect repellent

North of the Cairngorms is another, far less-visited range: a wild welcome, then, to the mysteriously little-known Monadhliaths. Few hikers come here, for there are few paths. In fact, the snaking River Findhorn followed by this walk is undoubtedly the best incursion into this stark spread of summits and, together with the 4x4 tracks also followed here, also offers the most straightforward exploration of the area.

And easy navigation equals more time to observe the nature

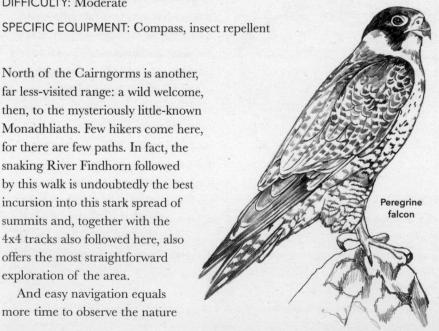

Peregrine falcon

thriving here where humans seldom tread. This is probably Scotland's best place to see golden eagles, particularly on a warm day when they soar from higher peaks and coast the thermals over the Findhorn's stunning *strath* (broad valley). Birdwatchers also know this as prime peregrine falcon and buzzard territory. The Findhorn is a major salmon river, but also a nationally important stronghold of the water vole, while the moors may bring you glimpses of red deer, wild goats and mountain hares. Come on a clement spring day, once the snow has melted, but while mountain hares still retain white winter coats.

You'll climb 375m on the walk, but the Findhorn stretch is level and even the steeper climbs feel fine on such solid tracks.

ROUTE DESCRIPTION
1) Continue up the River Findhorn along the wide strath, Strathdearn, from the car park, soon reaching the road end at **Coignafearn Old Lodge**. A good track then continues another 4km southwest along the

River Findhorn. Watch the riverside for water voles and the skies for the region's raptors as you proceed to huge Coignafearn Lodge. You now enter remote country: there is no civilisation of any kind for 14km. Another 375m after the lodge, turn left across the river on a bridge (ignoring a bridge off left just afterwards).

2) You now follow another track of surprising quality, given the remote setting, which ascends the glen containing Elrick Burn for the next 4km. The track follows the western riverbank, running south, then after the burn's course curves southeast, switches to the other bank. You will eventually arrive at a bridge over the **Crochan Beag Bun Fhraioch burn** near its convergence with Elrick Burn.

3) Over the burn, you meet a track junction; turn left. After a couple of zigzags and bearing left at another track junction, your track follows the burn and then another, Caochan na h-Eighe Duibhe. You forge northeast up onto high moor between the bare Carn Choire Odair and Carn na Caillish summits. On the shoulder of the former it reaches 740masl before picking up the Caochan Glasaichean Beag burn, initially on your right and later on the left. You're still running generally northeast here through very remote country. After being

287

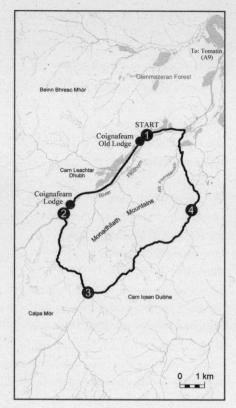

joined by another tributary, Caochan Glasaichean Beag noticeably widens on your left, and 450m later another track branches left across the burn. Continue straight and presently reach a wooden hut used by shooting parties.

4) With one final rise over Càrn Easgainn Mòr the track starts descending, winding north-northwest for 2.5km to a conifer plantation at Coignafeuinternich. Brush the left-hand (west) end of the plantation, cross the bridge over another River Fidhorn tributary and continue on the track to soon cross the **River Findhorn**. On the other side, cut across the grass to rejoin the road along which you turn left to the start.

82. The Head of Glen Esk around Loch Lee

Head up around Glen Esk's lovely heathery head for a high chance of
adders, raptors and red deer

NEED TO KNOW

START/FINISH: Car park east of Lochlee Parish Church, DD9 7YZ – 6km
(3¾ miles) northwest of Tarfside (parking free)

DISTANCE: 16km (9¾ miles) (part circular, part out-and-back)

TIME: 4½–5 hours

KEY SPECIES: Adder, palmate newt, golden eagle

MAP: OS Explorer OL54

TRANSPORT: Panmure Arms bus stop, Edzell (buses to Brechin) – 25.75km
(16 miles) southeast

WALK ACCESSIBILITY: Not wheelchair/pushchair accessible; dogs allowed

DIFFICULTY: Moderate–Difficult

SPECIFIC EQUIPMENT: Compass, insect repellent, swimwear

MORE INFORMATION: visitangus.com

Open and wood-enclosed, auburn
with bracken, yellow-green with birch
and every so often splashed scarlet by
rowan, Glen Esk, longest of the Angus
Glens, gets the Royal seal of approval:
Queen Victoria and Prince Albert
spent the night here in 1861. The
top of the glen, headed by Loch Lee,
is a splendid southeast entrance into
the Cairngorms NP, where a slew of
lesser but nevertheless glorious
summits – and, on this
walk, beautiful waterfalls –
compete for your attention.

Glen Esk is Scotland's most superb
spot for spying adders: you'll likely
encounter one sunning itself on the
way this walk wends along Loch
Lee in spring or summer, while at

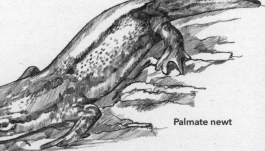

Palmate newt

similar times in the route's ditches and puddles palmate newts, Britain's smallest newt, breed. Then there are the fantastic fauna fixtures of many Scottish late springtime upland scenes to be seen: ground-nesting lapwings, waders like curlews and golden plovers on their fair-weather moorland sojourns, red deer, peregrine falcons and intermittent golden eagles. May's primroses and August's heather bestow extra magic on the backdrop.

The mainly solid tracks and paths on this circuit come with two significant caveats: a steep climb beyond the Falls of Unich and a section thereafter of indistinct boggy path where a compass is a blessing.

ROUTE DESCRIPTION

1) Being able to climb this far up a Scottish glen on a paved road is relatively unusual – the car park is already at 258masl – and, turning right out of the car park further up Glen Esk, the lane continues a little longer. Pass a church and then the right-hand track that turns to Queen's Well (Victoria and Albert drank here on their visit) and Mount Keen, Scotland's most easterly Munro summit. Next cross the river bridge, shortly after which the lane ends in a 2-way track fork by a house. Right here leads to Invermark Lodge: Victoria and Albert once stayed here

ADDER

Adders, also known as vipers, are Britain's best-known and only venomous snake species. Their bites, while very seldom causing serious injury to adults, are dangerous to children and dogs. They are distinguishable by the dark zigzag pattern down their backs.

and holidaymakers still can – several lets are available in summer. You, however, fork left, continuing to **Invermark Castle**, a lofty and mostly intact 16th-century tower house built as a defence against bandits.

2) This next section is excellent adder-spotting terrain. The broad stony tracks attract the sun's heat, making a fine summer break destination for snakes. The way continues through gently scenic woodland more reminiscent of Southern England than Highland Scotland. You pick up the Water of Lee, keeping this off left until reaching the edge of **Loch Lee** 1.25km after the castle. At this point, you're close by the hamlet of Kirkton. Continue on the path with the north shore of Loch Lee on your left for 2km, passing Kirkton's ruined lochside church as the hillsides ramparting the loch on three sides grow wilder and start to steepen.

3) At the loch's end is the left-hand track to a house at Inchgrundle. Ignore this turning – but note it, you will be returning this way – and keep straight, passing a derelict house on the right. You're now in Glen Lee and the Water of Lee remains your companion on your left. Stick with this westbound later northwest-bound track for another 1.8km. The sheer rockfaces of Craig Maskeldie (687masl) loom large, although your route has scarcely climbed at all since the start (this changes soon enough). Gaze heavenwards for golden eagles and peregrine falcons as you go.

4) After ignoring another left-hand track, you'll notice the track ahead swinging right (north), and the Water of Lee's course likewise veering sharply right to meet it. Ahead here a footbridge can be seen:

branch slight left to cross it. You now skirt anticlockwise around Craig Maskeldie's lower flanks, beginning easily enough with a decent path to pretty **Falls of Unich** on the Water of Unich (1km from the footbridge). The next leg is tougher: keep on the Water of Unich's west side as it narrows into an impressive gorge and climb steeply onto the moor to avoid the churning river below left, but do not deviate too far from the course the river cuts. A miry stretch follows in which you need to keep the river in range as a marker off left to pass the **Falls of Damff** and then come down to a footbridge crossing the Water of Unich shortly afterwards.

5) There is a faint path on the other side, albeit a very boggy one. This heads southeast to presently follow the bank of a Water of Unich

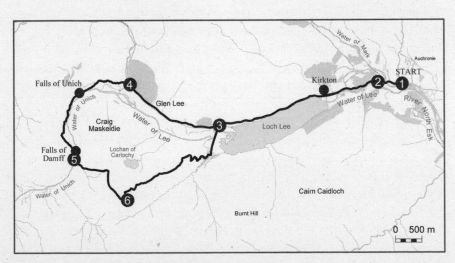

291

tributary southeast around 125m. Next, head east, the faint boggy path still visible, on a gradual ascent passing cairns along the way. The map-marked burn snakes along to your right, and you round this by reaching a col at the 650masl mark from where Loch Lee is visible below east. Here you swing south for approximately 250m, then southeast for approximately 375m to cross Cairn Lick (682masl) and finally hit a track on which you turn left.

6) Descending northeast from here down the Shank of Inchgrundle there are brilliant views to Loch Lee ahead but also, a few hundred metres along, off left (north) to the **Lochan of Carlochy**, wrapped by Craig Maskeldie's craggy sides. The track begins a series of serpentines above a spread of conifers and continues twisting through them to cross Burn of Tarsen by the buildings at Inchgrundle. Head north-northeast on the track across Loch Lee's western end to reach map Point 3 and turn right to follow your outward route back to the start.

83. Coire Gabhail (Lost Valley)

Undertake a hike-cum-scramble into the summit-surrounded secret valley, where the region's MacDonald clan once hid stolen cattle

NEED TO KNOW

START/FINISH: Three Sisters Viewpoint car park (6.5km/4 miles) east of PH49 4HX, the closest postcode for sat-nav purposes) – 8km (5 miles) east of Glencoe (parking free)

DISTANCE: 7.25km (4½ miles) (out-and-back)

TIME: 2½–3 hours

KEY SPECIES: Red deer, golden eagle, raven

MAP: OS Explorer 384

TRANSPORT: Glencoe Visitor Centre bus stop (buses to Glasgow/Fort William/Portree) – 6.5km (4 miles) west

WALK ACCESSIBILITY: Not wheelchair/pushchair accessible; dogs allowed

DIFFICULTY: Moderate–Difficult

MORE INFORMATION: discoverglencoe.scot

There is power and poignancy to Glen Coe, which harbours much of the Southern Highlands' finest mountain scenery and one of its most famously tragic tales. Here in 1692 30-odd clan MacDonald members were slaughtered by their guests, purportedly for not pledging allegiance to joint monarchs William III and Mary II, in what became known as the Glencoe Massacre. Some MacDonalds are thought to have escaped by fleeing to the Lost Valley this walk explores, a Glen Coe side-glen totally hidden from view, where the clan once supposedly secreted rustled cattle.

The valley is exquisite: the grass-and-rock walls of the flanking peaks soaring from a strikingly flat valley bottom, with the pointy panorama of three Munro peaks heading up

> ### RAVEN
> This huge crow might be more associated with the Tower of London, but in the wild these corvids like remote mountains and forests, feeding there on carrion. Its wingspan can reach 1.3m, bigger than a buzzard's.

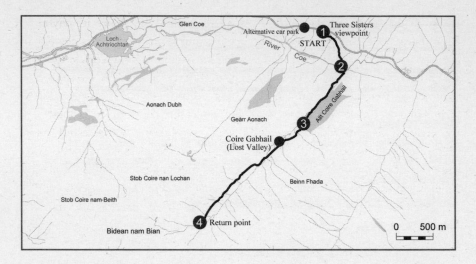

the far end. Seeing it, you'll likely concur that this is, indeed, Scotland's prettiest short hike. Terrain-wise, the mountains are show-stealers, but the birch woods on the way are just as hypnotic. Red deer regularly roam the glen, while ravens, buzzards and, less commonly, golden eagles glide overhead.

This is a tough walk for its length, entailing rough, rocky paths and a smidgeon of scrambling. Do not attempt it in icy or overly misty conditions.

ROUTE DESCRIPTION

1) Views are sublime from step one as the chiselled ridge of Aonach Eagach, a climber's paradise, thrusts up off north while the **Three Sisters**, the knobbly trio of peaks Aonach Dubh, Beinn Fhada and Geárr Aonach towards which this walk heads, loom

to the south. A clear path leads from the southeast corner of **Three Sisters Viewpoint** car park down to the old track, clearly visible from the main A82 road, that runs along the glen closer to the River Coe. If this car park is full, more parking awaits 200m down the A82, also with a connector path down to the same track. Turn left on the well-surfaced track, which curves down to a metal staircase down to the River Coe, plunged in birch woods, after 450m.

2) Cross the river footbridge, after which the path instantly gets rougher, scaling a rocky section with cables strung alongside to help. You now ascend a wildly beautiful birch-wooded gorge, squeezed between the dramatic peaks of **Beinn Fhada** (left) and **Geárr Aonach** (right). The way is never really in doubt, as you stick near the **Allt Coire Gabhail** burn throughout, and the mountain scenery, fringed by weather-buckled tree branches, is superlative. The path, however, is no countryside stroll. Mild scrambling over rocks either side of the stream is needed, while some side-drops are steep. You'll cross the stream once or twice, depending which route you choose, once via slippery stepping stones if possible, during the first km after the bridge. Be careful: burn water is often at least knee-deep. There are countless opinions on which way to negotiate trickier sections: at one point, the choice is either a more gently inclined yet exposed scramble on the right or a steeper, less-exposed scramble off left. However, hikers with little hillwalking experience but reasonable fitness can and do manage the path straightforwardly and you'll only need the odd steadying hand. Choose (with care) your own path.

3) Above the rocky slopes, it's payback time: your rewards are views down into the stunning **Lost Valley**, and with rocks positioned to form steps that aid your descent. The valley is perfect for well-deserved picnics, with several sizable boulders and ample grassy slopes pilfered cattle would presumably have been equally contented with in times past (though getting the beasts up here can't have been straightforward).

4) Take time to explore, along valley sides finely formed by Beinn Fhada and Geárr Aonach, up to the base of multi-peaked **Bidean nam Bian** massif at the end. Your outward route ends here: return the same way.

Golden eagle

84. Tomintoul to Cairn Gorm via Glen Avon

Trek through wild glens, up mountains and past Britain's only free-ranging reindeer

NEED TO KNOW

START/FINISH: Tomintoul car park, AB37 9EX/Cairngorm Mountain Railway Base Station, PH22 1RB – 5.5km (3½ miles) southeast of Glenmore (parking charges may apply)

DISTANCE: 39km (24¼ miles) (one way)

TIME: Full day

KEY SPECIES: Reindeer, lapwing, red grouse

MAP: OS Explorer OL57/OL58

TRANSPORT: Speybridge Smokehouse bus stop (buses to Aviemore) – 20km (12½ miles) northwest

WALK ACCESSIBILITY: Not wheelchair/pushchair accessible; dogs allowed but on leads on Cairn Gorm

DIFFICULTY: Difficult

SPECIFIC EQUIPMENT: Compass, insect repellent

MORE INFORMATION: tomintoulandglenlivet.com, cairngormmountain.co.uk

This epic hike starts sedately amidst farmland, which provides excellent breeding grounds for meadow birds and waders, and reconnoitres one of Scotland's great undiscovered glens, Glen Avon, famed for its grouse. It finishes with a spectacular, seldom-taken ascent of the nation's seventh-highest mountain, Cairn Gorm, inhabited by Britain's only free-ranging reindeer herd. The reindeer, alongside rare flowers like Alpine sow thistle, enjoy the mountain plateau, the only Arctic-Alpine climate zone to be found in the UK.

The walk is generally on firm, gently ascending metalled tracks but climbs 900m of elevation, the final 500m quite steeply. A compass is useful: two short sections have faint paths. Choose a spring, summer or early autumn day for the walk to maximise the daylight hours available. The best time is late summer, when glens blaze auburn with bracken and plateau-growing flowers bloom.

ROUTE DESCRIPTION

1) From Tomintoul car park entrance, turn right on Main Street through the likeable grey stone-built houses of **Tomintoul**. After one block, there is an optional 1km out-and-back detour to **Tomintoul bird hide**, where curlews, oystercatchers and lapwing relish the soggy farmland: to do so, turn left on the A939, taking the path after the last house on the left.

2) Back on the Main Street/A939 crossroads, continue following Main Street to take the third right on Delnabo Road. After 1km this lane reaches a left-hand track to a car park, also signposted 'Tomintoul Country Walk.'

3) Turn onto the track. You can also park your car here, at the entrance to the vast, beautiful Glen Avon Estate. You now enter wild country: there is

scarcely any civilisation for 37km, at this walk's finish. Pass through a gate onto the estate track, soon passing a footpath to a viewpoint on the left, re-joining the continuation of the still-tarmacked lane after 2.25km.

4) Turn left. This, the main estate road/track, follows the river south through **Strath Avon**. From this point, the road/track passes houses at Birchfield and Torbain, staying close to the River Avon until the Inchrory Estate, after 8.75km. The way is tarmacked until just before Inchrory, dividing before the lodge entrance; take the left-hand branch to curve around the property, descending to a bridge near the confluence of the River Avon and Bulig Burn.

5) Cross the bridge, staying on a stony estate track. Ignore the minor left-

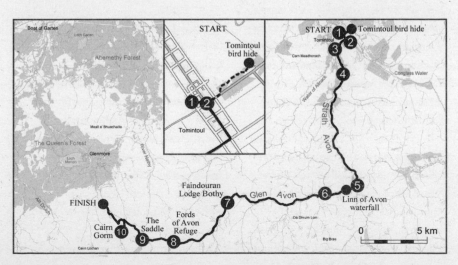

hand track climbing to the summit of Meall Gaineimh, then admire where the River Avon gushes down **Linn of Avon** waterfall on the right soon afterwards. Keeping the River Avon on the right, the track wends gently up Glen Avon, descending to another river bridge 2.75km after the last.

6) Over the bridge, the main track twists up the hillside, but your route continues along the north riverbank on a narrow, often boggy but distinct path. Rejoin the track about 900m later as it descends back to the river at a bend. Now follow the track as it runs above the north riverbank, with an increasingly dramatic group of craggy Munro summits, reaching **Faindouran Lodge bothy** after 7km.

7) Your route stays following the river's course, but the track soon deteriorates into a path. This is initially faint but improves, climbing southwest then west above the river to a major path crossroads at **Fords of Avon Refuge**, at the 700masl contour and 5.75km from Faindouran Lodge.

8) The going is now boggy as you follow the uppermost stretch of the River Avon up along its northern side to Loch Avon. A rocky path then clambers up to the north of the loch, heading west and away from the shoreline, to a path crossroads at **The Saddle** (807masl), at the southern
298

head of Garbh Allt burn.

9) One path heads down the burn from here but your path now climbs in earnest north-northwest up Cairn Gorm's eastern flanks. Good compass skills help as your path ascends over one stream to come alongside (but not cross) a second around the 1050masl contour. The summit of Cnap Coire na Spreidhe is now north ahead: here, the faint path bends northwest and then west to ascend over boggy ground towards **Ptarmigan Station**, Cairngorm Mountain Railway's upper terminus. Reindeer often favour this area for grazing. The terrain looks remote, but it is hard to go too wrong: heading northwest, you hit Ptarmigan Station and, heading west, the well-defined path from Ptarmigan Station to Cairn Gorm's summit. It's 1km from Ptarmigan Station to the top.

10) Cairn Gorm summit (1244masl) sports some of the Cairngorms' finest views. The path down passes substantial ski development, swinging sharply southwest at Ptarmigan Station, then after a while northwest, on a zigzagging descent with the Base Station now visible below.

RETURNING TO START: Car

NORTHERN HIGHLANDS & ISLANDS

85. Balranald Reserve, Aird an Rùnair & Traigh Iar

Meander along machair and silver-sand beaches, staying vigilant for corncrake calls in this bastion of birdlife

NEED TO KNOW

START/FINISH: RSPB Balranald car park, HS6 5DL – 550m (¼ mile) south of Hogha Gearraidh (parking free, entry charges may apply)

DISTANCE: 8.5km (5¼ miles) (part circular, part out-and-back)

TIME: 2½–3 hours

KEY SPECIES: Corncrake, machair, turnstone

MAP: OS Explorer 454

TRANSPORT: Uig ferry terminal (buses to Portree/Fort William) – 77.25km (48 miles) east, on Skye. Then take CalMac ferry to Lochmaddy – 25.75km (16 miles) east. Or Benbecula Airport (flights from Glasgow) – 30.5 km (19 miles) southeast.

WALK ACCESSIBILITY: Not wheelchair/pushchair accessible; dogs under close control

DIFFICULTY: Easy

SPECIFIC EQUIPMENT: Swimwear

MORE INFORMATION: rspb.org.uk

Corncrake

The timid corncrake chose well: one of only two British locations where it is still found, Balranald Reserve is a remarkable spot. Protected by the RSPB since the 1960s, this loch-spattered grassland on the Outer Hebrides' westernmost edge on North Uist is a haven for many birds, including lapwings, Arctic skuas, barnacle geese and turnstones. And it's all set against the sublime backdrop of two huge arcs of silvery beach, fringed by probably the planet's finest machair, an internationally rare habitat of grassy, flowering dunes.

May and June are magical, when corncrakes can be heard (sometimes seen) in shore-side vegetation, turnstones go shoreline foraging, oystercatchers and terns descend on the lochs and the machair flowers with birds-foot trefoil, red clover and tufted vetch.

This walk's paths, leading around hammerhead-shaped Aird an Rùnair peninsula, are not always distinct, but the going is level, never challenging and never in doubt, with large sections along sandy beach.

ROUTE DESCRIPTION

1) Follow the track from the car park west past **RSPB Balranald Visitor Centre** (where you can learn more about the birdlife here) and the croft buildings, crossing a stony track. Turn left along a path through machair around the sandy shoreline of horseshoe-shaped **Traigh nam Faoghailean beach**. Pass Balranald Hebridean Holidays campsite off left and bear slightly back from the shore to follow the track 325m beyond the campsite. Continue past a parking area and information board and shortly

> **CORNCRAKE**
> These secretive birds are related to moorhens, but live on dry land, favouring coastal grassland vegetation. The first sign of their presence will likely be the male's rasping call. They visit Balranald between April and September.

afterwards, with the end of the beach to your right, turn right.

2) Your route now traces the right-hand (east) side of **Aird an Rùnair** peninsula, westernmost point of the Western Isles (and of inhabited Great Britain). The path is often faint but marker cairns indicate the way. Stick close to the shore for 650m before the route skips across a stream, through a gate and begins curving right to reach the northwest edge of the peninsula after a marker cairn. The path fades here, but the going over rock-studded grassland is still easy enough: you are circling the peninsula anticlockwise with the coast on your right, and it is impossible to go too wrong. Watch out for Arctic skuas hereabouts, which will occasionally dive-bomb humans on their territory.

3) Progress along the northwest peninsula edge, slightly back from the shoreline, crossing a stream and following eight cairn markers, to reach a loch by the beach after

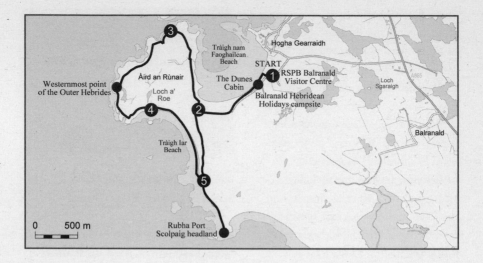

1km. Here, the only land in Great Britain further west than you, are the Monach Islands with their grey seal colony, Haskeir and seabird-rich St Kilda. Pass the loch on the seaward side, continuing around the shore and past another two marker cairns to reach a kissing gate. Immediately after, cross the outflow of **Loch a' Roe** visible off left, and a cacophony of chattering plovers, oystercatchers and terns come early summer.

4) You now reach the exceptional 1.75km-long silver-sandy arc of **Traigh Iar**. Walk as far as you wish along the beach: this walk continues to its end – **Rubha Port Scolpaig** headland – then returns part-way (675m) to where a field boundary meets the shore.

5) Leave Traigh Iar here to pick up a track just behind running north-northwest, parallel with the beach, for 850m. At a track junction, turn right on your outward route, returning with Traigh nam Faoghailean on your left to the car park.

86. Faraid Head from Balnakeil

Amble along an alluring beach to this headland harbour porpoise and puffin haunt

NEED TO KNOW

START/FINISH: Balnakeil Church car park, IV27 4PX – 800m (½ mile) north of Balnakeil (parking free)

DISTANCE: 6.5km (4 miles) (part circular, part out-and-back)

TIME: 1½–2 hours

KEY SPECIES: Harbour porpoise, minke whale, puffin

MAP: OS Explorer 446

TRANSPORT: Balnakeil Craft Village bus stop (buses to Inverness) – 800m (½ mile) south

WALK ACCESSIBILITY: Not wheelchair/pushchair accessible; no dogs Apr–May, on leads at other times

DIFFICULTY: Easy–Moderate

SPECIFIC EQUIPMENT: Swimwear

MORE INFORMATION: visitscotland.com

Adventurers' eyes, travelling this far north, might be firmly fixed on reconnoitring Cape Wrath, Britain's rugged northwestern point, but the next headland along Scotland's north coast, Faraid Head, is a gentler and more beguiling place in many ways. Here, Cape Wrath still impresses in the distance, but one of Britain's most dazzling beaches – the 2km-long white-gold arc of Balnakeil Beach that flanks one side of Faraid Head – commands most of your attention. But watch the waters closely too. This is perhaps the best place in Scotland for spying harbour porpoises, particularly between July and February, while minke whales and Risso's dolphins are also descried. Puffins nest and natter on rocks off the east side of the headland in summer and grey seals can be observed year round.

There are no significant climbs on this walk: paths are either sandy or grassy.

ROUTE DESCRIPTION

1) There are few finer start points for a walk in the British Isles. Opposite the car park stand the ruins of **Balnakeil Church**, one of Northwest Scotland's most photogenic ecclesiastical buildings. Originally founded in the 8th century AD by St Máel Ruba, it was one of the region's most important Celtic centres of Christianity. A grave in the churchyard remembers Elizabeth Parkes, aunt of Beatles frontman John Lennon: Lennon spent many family holidays in the vicinity.

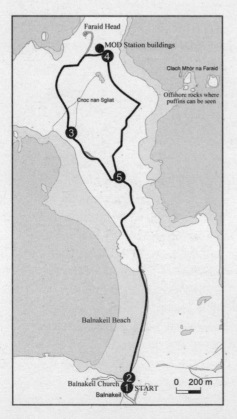

Ahead, the wide, dune-backed sands of Balnakeil Beach point the way out to Faraid Head, while off-centre rears the moody bulk of mainland Britain's remotest headland: Cape Wrath.

2) Pass through the metal gate onto **Balnakeil Beach**, crossing it to the far (northernmost) end. A promontory edged by broken rocky cliffs halfway along juts onto the beach, dividing it into two sections. Come up from the sand onto the MOD road that runs above it, via paths in the grassy dunes either east of the promontory or at the end of the second section of beach. The MOD road runs to the MOD complex at the tip of Faraid Head.

3) At the end of the second section of beach the MOD road bends away from the shore, curving north then northeast to Faraid Head MOD Station. With the MOD station fence on your immediate left, cross to the cliffs on the east side of the headland, also lined by a fence.

4) Proceed south (later southeast for about 300m and then southwest for about 700m) to reach the MOD road again via Faraid Head's eastern side. The fence is to your left but you need not stick right along its edge provided you follow its general direction. A short way along on the right is a prominent **cairn**, while presently on the left a group of large **offshore rocks** are a prime spot for watching puffins come early summer. Ahead you can already clearly see the dunes you passed on your outward route: many minor paths lead through the dunes and all bring you back to the MOD road sooner or later.

5) Turn left on the MOD road, following it through the dunes. This will return you to the car park, as will retracing your steps back along Balnakeil Beach.

MINKE WHALE
At 7-9m long, minkes are the smallest baleen (non-toothed) whale found in UK waters. Distinguish them through white markings on their front flippers and their tall, backwards-curving fin. Their vocalisations reach an astonishing 150 decibels: more ear-splitting than a jet engine at a 30m distance!

Puffin

87. Fortrose, Chanonry Point, Rosemarkie & the Fairy Glen

Be entertained by Britain's easiest-to-spot bottlenose dolphins on this
Moray Firth coastal caper

NEED TO KNOW

START/FINISH: Fortrose Cathedral car park on northwest side of cathedral, IV10 8TB (parking free, entry charges may apply)

DISTANCE: 10.5km (6½ miles) (part circular, part out-and-back)

TIME: 3–3½ hours

KEY SPECIES: Bottlenose dolphin, spotted flycatcher, dipper

MAP: OS Explorer 432

TRANSPORT: Fortrose Post Office bus stop (buses to Inverness/Rosemarkie) – 50m north

WALK ACCESSIBILITY: Not wheelchair/pushchair accessible; dogs allowed

DIFFICULTY: Moderate

MORE INFORMATION: black-isle.info and moraydolphins.co.uk

By far Scotland's mightiest firth (estuary), the Moray Firth impresses in many ways but none compare to the majestic maritime spectacle happening here when members of its 200-strong bottlenose dolphin pod are frolicking off Chanonry Point. Because of how the point protrudes into a narrow strait separating the Inner and Outer Moray Firths, passing dolphins are seen up closer than anywhere else in Britain. This walk delivers you straight to the dolphin action and, in between visits to likeable settlements Fortrose and Rosemarkie, and a 2.5km-long beach, dallies in the magical bird reserve of Fairy Glen.

May through September is the acme of dolphin activity, although the creatures are present year round. Springtime spreads of

> **DIPPER**
> Dippers are the only songbirds that can also wade, dive and swim in rivers. The plump, short-tailed, thrush-sized avian is identified by the white bib on its throat and breast.

**Bottlenose
dolphin**

bluebells and primroses in Fairy
Glen delight, while dippers scouting
for invertebrate snacks and spotted
flycatchers darting to nab insects
around Markie Burn make good
summertime entertainment.

ROUTE DESCRIPTION

1) From the main entrance
(northwest side) of **Fortrose
Cathedral**, a magnificent
13th-century red sandstone ruin,
head anticlockwise around the
cathedral fence on Cathedral Square,
following the road onto Academy
Street. Turn left on Academy Street,
which becomes Wester Greengates
after Fortrose Academy. This reaches
a small grassy parking area with
picnic tables on the right. Pass
through this area to join a path
heading onto the long, thin strip of
Fortrose Bay Campsite. Keep close
to the shore, walking through the
campsite to a 3-way signpost at a
corner of Wester Greengates.

2) Keep straight on a path alongside
a golf course. After 1.25km, you
meet the roundabout at the end of
Ness Road. Ahead is whitewashed
Chanonry Lighthouse. The views
across the Moray Firth are already
exceptional from here, reaching their
optimum at **Chanonry Point** (to get
here, either walk along the beach right
of the lighthouse or trace the path left
of the bungalow on the roundabout)
where views across to **Fort George**,
a vast 18th-century fortification across
the firth, are splendid. Chanonry Point
has a greater reputation, however, for
its bottlenose dolphins, often sighted
catching fish just metres from shore.

3) The next stretch follows the sand-
and-pebble beach into Rosemarkie.
Pass the golf course and a caravan
site on the left to come alongside
Marine Terrace (you can stay walking
along the beach). Passing almost all of
comely **Rosemarkie** village, return
onto the road at the end of Marine

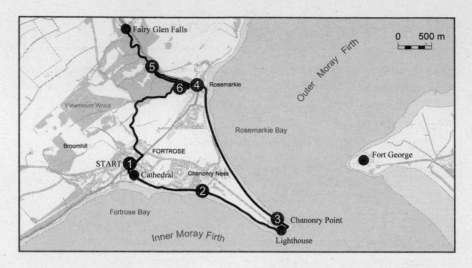

Terrace before a white house. Pass in front of the house, cross a footbridge and begin following Minkie Burn's north bank inland.

4) Pass under Kincurdie Drive, entering **Fairy Glen**. Here, the magical stream of Markie Burn is flanked by venerable oaks, beeches and rowans, and is an RSPB reserve frequented by dippers, spotted flycatchers and song thrushes. Buzzards wheel overhead too. Continue under another road bridge, 550m after which your path is joined by the south bank path at a footbridge. From here it's a 1.5km out-and-back walk, re-crossing the steam at a bridge, to **Fairy Glen Falls**, a charming double waterfall. Ensure you continue to view the second set of falls, just beyond the first, from another bridge.

5) Back at the footbridge linking the burn's north and south bank paths, follow the south bank path to the car park and come onto the A832 at the car park entrance. Turn right until you reach the last house on the left, after which your signposted path branches off to the left.

6) This, the Swallow Den Path, climbs uphill through woods, soon offering great views out to Chanonry Point off left. The path hits a lane after almost 1km; turn left. Ignoring a right-hand turn, the lane bends left down into handsome **Fortrose**. Dismiss two more minor right-hand turns and presently meet Fortrose High Street. Turn right, then after 225m left on Union Street. The first turn on the right brings you back to Cathedral Square.

88. Arisaig to Camusdarach Beach

Foot it along incomparable sandy coast searching for grey seals, otters and minke whales

NEED TO KNOW

START/FINISH: Arisaig railway station, PH39 4NJ

DISTANCE: 17.75km (11 miles) (out-and-back)

TIME: 4½–5 hours

KEY SPECIES: Pine marten, otter, machair

MAP: OS Explorer 398

TRANSPORT: Arisaig railway station at start

WALK ACCESSIBILITY: Specific route not wheelchair/pushchair accessible but paved minor roads closely follow much of route; dogs allowed

DIFFICULTY: Moderate

SPECIFIC EQUIPMENT: Swimwear

MORE INFORMATION: arisaiginfo.org.uk, arisaig.co.uk and roadtotheisles.com

Otter

The silvery sands stretching between Arisaig and Morar via Camusdarach have made it big on the silver screen – immortalised in iconic comedy-drama *Local Hero* – but the real stars of this wild waterfront show are animals. Otters, grey seals, minke whales and bottlenose dolphins are often spotted, and the surrounding wilderness of Morar is one of Scotland's best places to see pine martens.

This is the ideal walk for unleashing your inner child as you ramble along beach, rocks and dunes choosing which bits of foreshore to explore. The route's continual proximity to such remote seaboard is what maximises the chances of wildlife sightings. True, it's a slow burner, taking several kilometres to build up to the best coastal scenery, but then comes the payback: perhaps Scotland's most relentlessly ravishing tract of sandy beaches. Much of this is bounded by machair – the grassy, flowering dunes comprising one of Europe's scarcest habitats – a riot of spring- and summertime colour with campions, orchids, vetches and more.

ROUTE DESCRIPTION

1) Choose low tide for this walk: it allows you to walk on the beaches, the route's big draw, for longer. Aim to begin about an hour before low tide. From **Arisaig railway station**, the UK's westernmost mainline station, follow Station Road down to the main A830 road. Turn left, crossing the road to the pedestrian cut-through onto Clanranald Place. Follow this lane to meet the B8008 road at a bus shelter after 100m. Turn right. The road bends around to **Arisaig Land, Sea & Islands Centre**.

2) The centre, in a charming whitewashed building, offers insights into local heritage and wildlife, with a webcam set up here for observing heron activity on the nearby Morroch Peninsula (they start breeding in February; April is best for observing nestlings). Afterwards, follow the B8008 along the village's waterfront to the Arisaig Hotel. Turn left here (the lane is signposted 'Arisaig Cemetery'). Ignore the turning branching

OTTER

Coast-dwelling otters, of which Scotland has an unusually high number, are often called 'sea otters' but are the same species as inland-based otters. Coastal otters generally have a smaller range than their inland cousins due to the larger quantities of fish, their favoured food, available close to shore.

immediately left to **Arisaig Marina**, offering local wildlife-watching boat trips and ferries between April and September to the Small Isles: Eigg and Muck (daily) and Rum (weekly, and the wild location for walk 89 in this book). After 250m the lane reaches a gated track on the right.

3) Follow the track, then cut up through a patch of woodland on a path towards the tower of St Mary's Church, visible ahead, rejoining the B8008 by the cemetery south of the church. Turn left on the road for 1km to a T-junction. Turn left (the road is signposted 'Back of Keppoch'). The road swings sharp right after 250m and reaches the drive to Invercaimbe Caravan & Camping 500m further on.

4) Turn left, following the drive to the campsite, then head straight through the site to the arcing silvery sands beyond. You now pick up an unforgettable stretch of sandy and occasionally rocky coastline. Turn right (north) along the beach. The going is sandy along two beautiful bays, then rockier for a while as you pass Portnadoran Caravan Site on the right, followed by another small bay, and then round the ensuing headland. The path is faint in places. Come back onto the B8008 after the headland.

5) Turn left on the road as it twists along a grassy, seaweed-strewn shore to a cream-coloured house, bends inland to the right of a conifer plantation and at the plantation's end

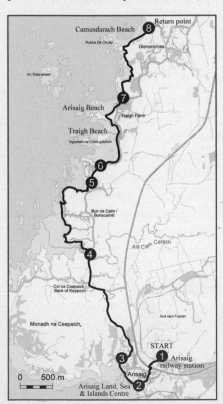

and the drive to Silversands Caravan & Campsite rejoins the sandy beach. You'll now be walking on sand or the grassy ground just behind it until Camusdarach Beach.

6) Your shoreline leg-stretch passes Traigh Golf Club, **Traigh Beach**, a car park (another potential start/finish for the walk, cutting the out-and-back distance to 4km but reducing opportunities for wildlife-watching) and Arisaig Beach. At Arisaig Beach's northern end the route returns onto the B8008 for 100m (although even here you can continue on grass and rock to the next sandy beach), bearing left at a path by a white post with the next beach along to your left.

7) Skirt a field fence to reach another beach ahead (north). Turn right along this sandy curve, almost divided by a promontory over which the main path runs in the middle. You then need to clamber away from the sand to pass through another patch of woodland. This soon opens onto the path through the dunes to **Camusdarach Beach**.

8) Regularly featuring in 'world's best beach' lists, Camusdarach's silver sands are divine. Watch for sand mason worms, glorious flowers in the machair-blanketed dunes and otters and minke whales in the sea. Your outward route ends here; return the same way.

89. Kinloch to Kilmory Bay

Adventure through an island nature reserve to spot red deer and cetaceans

NEED TO KNOW

START/FINISH: Isle of Rum ferry terminal, Kinloch, PH43 4RR

DISTANCE: 20km (12½ miles) (out-and-back)

TIME: 5–5½ hours

KEY SPECIES: Red deer, minke whale, Manx shearwater

MAP: OS Explorer 397

TRANSPORT: Mallaig railway station, 28km (17 miles) east, on mainland. Walk 150m northwest to Mallaig ferry terminal and take the CalMac ferry to start

WALK ACCESSIBILITY: Not wheelchair/pushchair accessible; dogs under close control

DIFFICULTY: Moderate–Difficult

SPECIFIC EQUIPMENT: Compass, swimwear

MORE INFORMATION: isleofrum.com, nature.scot

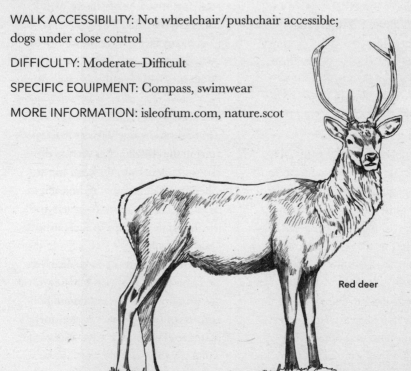

Red deer

Rugged Rum, along with fellow islands Eigg, Muck and Canna, make up the lion's share of the Small Isles, an archipelago between Skye and Mull. But small is a relative term when you boast, like Rum, some of Britain's most exciting wildlife. It's all going on here, and this walk endeavours to get you close to the animal action. The island is an NNR, protected since 1957, and has just a few dozen human inhabitants, so fauna here can thrive almost unchecked.

Top billing goes to the Rum red deer herd, which starred in *Autumnwatch* in 2012. One of the world's longest-running studies into the behaviour of a vertebrate, the Isle of Rum Red Deer Project has been studying the red deer population here since the 1950s, and this walk runs through a glen to which deer often gravitate.

Bird-wise, Loch Scresort, the trail's start point, sees summertime red-throated divers while greylag geese, curlews and oystercatchers are year-round sights. Golden eagles and merlins soar over the moors and Kilmory Bay is Rum's best spot for seeing ringed plovers and late-summer migrants like redshank and dunlins. Rum's Manx shearwaters deserve special mention. Some 40 per cent of the UK population breed here, and you may see these seabirds gathering

> ### RED DEER
> Britain's largest native land mammal, red deer can weigh in at up to 225kg. Rutting season (September–November), when males fight over territory and the herd's females, is a sight to behold. The rangers on Rum offer guided walks to see the island's rut.

offshore on this walk. Their preferred breeding site, though, is high in Rum's mountainous south. The waters encircling Rum are also cetacean-rich, with common and bottlenose dolphins, harbour porpoises and minke whales making appearances, along with otters and seals.

The walk is mostly on well-defined but sometimes very stony tracks. Waymarking is scant.

ROUTE DESCRIPTION

1) Rum is car-free. From the ferry terminal, this walk first makes the short (1.5km) out-and-back trip to the otter hide. As the main track to Kinloch leaves the terminal and swings right (west), a gravel path marked with an otter sign leads sharp left (east) through a wood, bearing left at a fork to the **otter hide** on the wood's far side. Overlooking a beach, this is somewhere to spot not only otters but also Loch Scresort's birdlife and, potentially, some of the island's cetaceans out at sea.

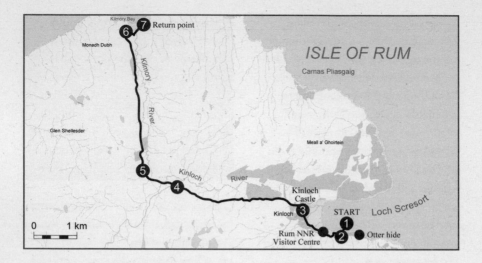

2) Back on the main track curving around Loch Sresort to Kinloch, continue past the school to a fork. Bear right. Pass **Rum NNR Visitor Centre**, then a bunkhouse and campsite. At the track junction afterwards, you head straight on (bearing slightly right, not taking the right-hand turn along the shore) on the track signposted to Kinloch Castle, which you reach after walking through an avenue of trees. **Kinloch Castle**, an ostentatious red sandstone mansion, was built as a retreat-cum-hunting estate by the Bullough family and finished in 1900.

3) Continuing along the track to another track junction, with the island café and shop just along the track ahead, your route now turns left on a track initially following Kinloch River. You now enter wild country:

there is no civilisation from this point on for 15km of walking. Ignore the minor riverside track off right after 450m to remain on the broad, stony main track, gradually ascending in a westerly direction. This soon leaves the woods, crosses open moorland, and reaches a track fork 3.25km from the junction near the café/shop.

4) Follow the right-hand track fork. This first crosses a Kinloch River tributary, then Kinloch River itself and then two tributaries of the Kilmory River before swinging north into Kilmory Glen.

5) Almost immediately a left-hand path branches towards Guirdil Bothy on Rum's west coast: keep following the main track. This heads through two plots of woodland and descends down **Kilmory Glen**, with stunning views of the Isle of Skye's jagged Cuillin Range soon opening up. This part of the island is the site of the Isle of Rum Red Deer Project, and red deer sightings are highly likely.

6) As the track nears a cottage used by researchers (avoid approaching the cottage and respect the researchers' privacy), a boulder painted with the word 'Beach' indicates the point where you turn to the right, leaving the track. Bearing right of a low rocky outcrop, pick your way down to the wide sandy curve of Kilmory Bay, which begins 150m due east from the cottage.

7) Kilmory Bay, where Kilmory River empties into the sea, is one of Britain's great meeting points of land-based and marine wildlife. As well as grazing in the glen, red deer like beach time (they eat the seaweed), while the chances of cetacean sightings are even better on this remoter coastline than they are around Kinloch. From here, return the same way back to Kinloch.

90. North Ronaldsay Circular

Scramble craggy shorelines scanning sky and sea for an astonishing array of birds

NEED TO KNOW

START/FINISH: North Ronaldsay Airport, Hollandstoun, KW17 2BE

DISTANCE: 19.25km (12 miles) (circular)

TIME: 7–7½ hours

KEY SPECIES: Scarlet rosefinch, seaweed-eating sheep, basking shark

MAP: OS Explorer 465

TRANSPORT: Kirkwall Airport (flights from Glasgow, Edinburgh, Inverness and Aberdeen) – 53km (33 miles) southwest, on mainland Orkney. Then take the thrice-daily flight to North Ronaldsay Airport to start.

WALK ACCESSIBILITY: Not wheelchair/pushchair accessible; dogs allowed (but reaching the island with a dog is difficult)

DIFFICULTY: Moderate–Difficult

MORE INFORMATION: northronaldsay.co.uk and nrbo.org.uk

The northernmost and remotest of the already far-flung Orkney Islands, wind-blasted North Ronaldsay is an island apart: geographically, culturally and ecologically.

North Ronaldsay's most distinctive feature, glimpsed from the air aboard the eight-seater plane delivering most visitors here, is the dyke constructed right around its coastline to keep island sheep not *in* within the flat green interior but *out*, on the rocky shores. North Ronaldsay sheep have thus evolved to subsist on seaweed.

More exceptional, though, are the island's avian visitors. North Ronaldsay sits at a major migratory crossroads and is one of Britain's best birdwatching spots. The varied birdlife includes greylag geese and whooper swans in winter; redshanks, curlews and Arctic terns in spring; and snowy owls and booted eagles in summer.

> **BASKING SHARK**
> The world's second-largest shark and reaching up to 12m in length, this plankton-eater has its own special name on the Orkneys: *ho-mither* (mother of the dogfish).

September – autumn migration – is the most riveting time, when birds scarcely seen elsewhere in the UK, like scarlet rosefinches and Arctic warblers, show up regularly. The North Ronaldsay Bird Observatory, which this walk runs by, is an invaluable resource on the island's birds. Basking sharks and grey seals star as non-avian fauna highlights.

Low-lying this walk may be, but easy-going it is not. Much of this route negotiates rugged, rock-bestrewn seaboard, some with no clear path. The rewards are some one-of-a-kind sights along the way.

ROUTE DESCRIPTION

1) This walk begins at the airport, as most people arrive on the island thus (ferries do serve the island but are an impractical means of approach). Walk down the airport road to the crossroads at the war memorial. Turn left, following the road to the north of the island. This divides after 1.1km; bear left.

2) This lane kinks right and then left, reaching North Ronaldsay's north shore. Where the lane turns left upon meeting the coast, your route passes through a gate onto the shore.

3) Turn right alongside the wall, part of the **sheep dyke** encircling the island, which you will follow for much of this walk. At over 19km long and up to 2m high, this numbers among the world's largest dry-stone structures. From this point on, you will intermittently spot seaweed-eating sheep grazing the kelp-covered coast. The shore path, alternately grassy and rocky, bends for 2km around Trolla Vatn lochan to arrive at your first objective, clearly visible ahead: red-and-white-striped **North Ronaldsay Lighthouse**.

4) Built in 1852, this is the UK's tallest land-based lighthouse, and also hosts a welcome refreshment stop, plus a visitor centre. A short out-and-back path leads here from the shore at a whitewashed lighthouse outbuilding. Afterwards, continue your progress along the shoreline.

5) After 800m you reach the long-disused but photogenic **Old Beacon**, raised in the 1780s and Britain's oldest still-standing lighthouse. The beacon is surrounded by old kelp-burning pits (islanders eked out a living through kelp-harvesting in the 18th century) and dry-stone-walled enclosures called crues, formerly used for vegetable growing. Keep along the shore, rounding Dennis Head.

6) Pass south of Dennis Loch to reach an old pier. Next, navigate a rocky section of shore around Snash Ness to the long, tan curve of sandy beach along **Linklet Bay**. Follow the sand, then the grassy ground beyond, around Linklet Bay to reach a lane at Hooking, alongside Hooking Loch.

7) Keep seaward of the buildings here, picking up another sandy stretch of beach, followed by more rocks around Bride's Ness headland. Proceed past Bride's Loch by a lane end, continuing 1km along rough shore to the Point of Burrian. Here stands the **Broch of Burrian**, the remnants of an Iron Age settlement. Grey seals frequently lounge on nearby rocks.

8) Rounding the Point of Burrian, the island's southernmost tip, carry on and skirt sandy South Bay. At the beach's end, you meet the road to North Ronaldsay's ferry terminal, at which point a short out-and-back detour branches off to **North Ronaldsay Bird Observatory**. The observatory sports a café alongside its wealth of resources about island birdlife. At the pier, you pass through a gate to continue your walk outside the sheep dyke wall.

9) Your route now threads along the top of some low cliffs and reefs, soon swinging northeast and passing Loch Gretchen. Look right 250m from the dry-stone wall intersecting with the coast immediately thereafter to spot **Stan Stane**, an impressive 4m-high

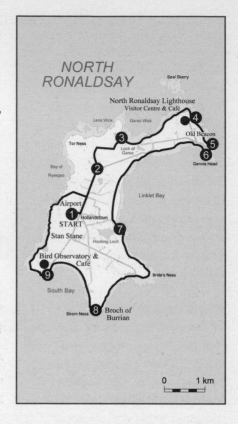

standing stone. Following the coast along, the airfield appears to your right. Pass two rocky inlets, Gairsna Geo and Doo Geo. After the latter, you reach a rare wall-less section of coast at a stile. Continue to a second stile, then head diagonally away from the shoreline to a gate onto a road. The road reaches a crossroads, intersecting with your outward route. Turn right, then right at the war memorial crossroads to return to the airport.

91. Esha Ness from Tangwick

Marvel at a weather-cleaved coast hosting otters, seals, seabirds and polecats

NEED TO KNOW

START/FINISH: Tangwick Haa Museum car park, Tangwick ZE2 9RS (parking free)

DISTANCE: 14km (8¾ miles) (circular)

TIME: 4½–5 hours

KEY SPECIES: Otter, red-throated diver, polecat

MAP: OS Explorer 469

Polecat

TRANSPORT: Aberdeen railway station – 416km (259 miles) south, on mainland. Walk 325m east to ferry terminal. Take Northlink ferry to Lerwick – 59.5km (37 miles) southeast. Or Sumburgh Airport (flights from Edinburgh/Glasgow) – 96.25km (59¾ miles) southeast

WALK ACCESSIBILITY: Not wheelchair/pushchair accessible; dogs allowed

DIFFICULTY: Moderate–Difficult

MORE INFORMATION: shetlandamenity.org

The Shetland archipelago was under Norse control until 1472, and on top of these islands' far-flung feel, their Old Norse place names, which stuck, render them still more otherworldly. One that keeps cropping up is 'ness', a distinctive landmark visible from sea. Esha Ness translates as 'ness of the flaking stone' and exploring this elemental peninsula in Shetland's Northmavine region today, the moniker seems apt. 'Broken, wave-battered stone,' would be spot on.

Nowhere else is Shetland's coastline more spectacularly riven and few places, in Shetland or elsewhere in Britain, attract such varied wildlife.

Otters and grey seals surround the cliffs, porpoises patrol the waters, seabirds, including puffins, throng Calder's Geo and one of the best chances to spot red-throated divers, the UK's smallest diver, awaits as it performs avian acrobatics in the lochs. As you cross the moors, you may also spy polecats, among Britain's rarest mammals. April through August sees the puffins convening, while October is best for seeing the red-throated divers and seals pupping. In truth, you could write a book on the wildlife here alone: just ask *Springwatch* presenter Simon King, who lived on Shetland for a year.

This walk tracks some rough, wild coast but is easier going than you might expect, quite level and with the ground underfoot manageable.

ROUTE DESCRIPTION

1) Tangwick Haa Museum, a 17th-century laird's house, is an informative beginning or end to your coastal adventure, offering historical insights into life on Northmavine. Take the track right of the museum to the far side of a bay, The Houb. Your path now twists along low grassy cliffs, sporting views out to **Dore Holm** island with its huge rock arch. Watch for otters hereabouts. The coast below you is already a geological fantasyland of rock arches and caves, though most are viewable only from sea. Proceed past one headland and after skirting the east (passing a memorial cross) and south sides of the second, swing north, approaching **Stenness Beach**. Pass a beachside ruin, climbing to the end of the B9078 road at a gate/stile.

2) Now cut back through another kissing gate diagonally left, resuming the route along the coast again. A 2km section follows to 1929-built **Eshaness Lighthouse**, passing a bay-side sheepfold, swinging north at the offshore rocks of The Bruddans and running left of Gerdie Loch. Cliffs rise up dramatically en route.

3) At the lighthouse, skirt the cliffs with care to view the deep, vertiginous inlet of **Calder's Geo**, a tempestuous place with a cave chamber on the north side that is possibly Britain's largest. Seabirds, including fulmars and puffins, love these cliffs, and it's a thrilling introduction to a geologically stunning coastal stretch. Squeeze between the cliff and **Loch of Framgord**, continuing around the geo's northern side to walk along clifftops to the **Lochs of Dridgeo**. There are fine views of chunky **Moo Stack** here. Scan the rocky shores for seals, offshore for porpoises and along the freshwater lochs this walk passes for red-throated divers.

POLECAT

The polecat is approximately the size of (and a feral version of) a ferret. A largely nocturnal creature, it has dark-brown-and-buff fur. Once almost persecuted into extinction, it now fares better, especially on Scotland's islands.

4) About 400m and one stile after the second Loch of Dridgeo, an out-and-back path branches right to **Holes of Scraada**, an almighty cliff-flanked depression where the sea cuts underneath the ground on which you are standing to sweep along what appears to be an inland beach. Beyond, the path reaches **Loch of Houlland**, on a promontory of which sits **Eshaness Broch**, a ruined Iron Age round tower. Return to the coastal path, whereupon your route sallies north, via more geos, stacks and wondrously wave-sculpted coast. Cross several field boundaries on stiles as the cliffs get progressively lower again and pass Loch of Stow off right.

5) Upon reaching Esha Ness' northern coast, off left is **Da Grind o da Navir**, a testimony to the sea's violent power. Waves have thrust rocks 15m above sea level to form a raised beach, trapping a lochan behind it. Bear right onto the peninsula's north shore through a gap in a dry-stone wall and presently across the shingle beach north of Croo Loch. After this, a clearer path curves around Hill of Ure to an inlet, Geo of Ure, negotiating a couple more field boundaries via a gate and stiles. Skirt the following headland, with the east side ushering you into Dale of Ure bay. South of a small promontory in the bay, pick up a field boundary and your path west

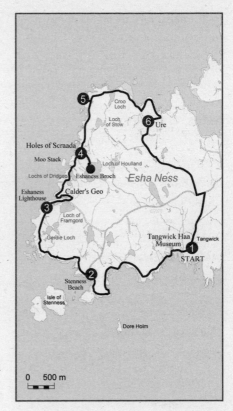

across the moor towards the farm buildings and road end at Ure.

6) Follow the road as it bends right then left past houses and then between two lochs to meet the B9078 after 2km. Turn left, then take the first right, signposted 'Tangwick'. If, as is likely, you drove down this lane to begin the walk, you'll know it passes several houses and arrives at Tangwick Haa Museum after 1km.

92. Beinn Alligin from Torridon

Bag two Munro peaks, some overwhelming mountainscapes and wildlife sightings from ptarmigans to pine martens

NEED TO KNOW

START/FINISH: Car park opposite Torridon Stores & Café, Torridon, IV22 2EZ (parking free)

DISTANCE: 19.25km (12 miles) (part circular, part out-and-back)

TIME: 10–10½ hours

KEY SPECIES: Otter, mountain hare, red deer, grey seal

MAP: OS Explorer 433

TRANSPORT: Strathcarron railway station – 42.75km (26½ miles) southeast

WALK ACCESSIBILITY: Not wheelchair/pushchair accessible; dogs allowed

DIFFICULTY: Difficult

SPECIFIC EQUIPMENT: Compass, insect repellent

MORE INFORMATION: nts.org.uk

Many give the Torridon Range the prestigious tag of the finest mountain scenery in Britain, rivalled only by Skye's Cuillins (location of walk 95 in this book). This hike, through resplendent NTS-owned wilderness, is a wildlife-watchers version of the traverse of the range's most outstanding summit, Beinn Alligin: capturing the thrill of the resident animals as well as the ascent.

The route therefore tarries along sea loch shores where otter, grey and common seal sightings are likely, climbs through woods where there are pine martens and tramps foothills where red deer graze and mountain hares bound. Golden eagles and ptarmigan are descried on high peaks; red-throated divers in upland lochans. It's hard to top a sharply lit early autumnal day here, when the

GREY SEAL

The best chance of a glimpse of grey seals, the world's rarest seals, in Torridon is during pupping season (November/December). The pups are born with distinctive white coats.

roars of red deer rutting ricochet through the mountains.

This is a tough route, entailing a climb from sea level to almost 1000masl via some craggy mountain paths, plus a section of cross-moor walking with precious little path. Do not attempt this in icy or overly misty conditions. For your efforts, you'll stand atop two mighty summits and come close to one of Scotland's most impressive concentrations of wildlife.

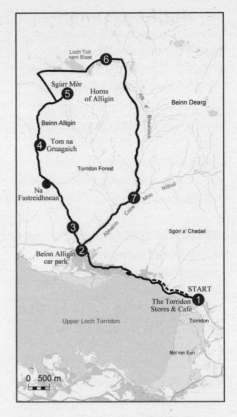

ROUTE DESCRIPTION

1) Follow the coast road out of the village, **Upper Loch Torridon** on your left. You soon reach a pier, by which a footpath sign points up right signposted 'Bay of MacGregor'. Take this grassy path, running prettily along the line of the telegraph poles above parallel to the road. The path's extra elevation can help you observe sealife action below: otters, grey and common seals can be seen. Descend back onto the road after 1km by a lay-by. Turn right, continuing to a road fork where you bear right. The road now twists steeply up before levelling and gently descending to woodland-ensconced Beinn Alligin car park after 2km (you can start/finish the walk here too, saving 7km but missing out on the shoreside wildlife).

2) Take the second path on the right, directly opposite the car park

on the far side of wooded Abhainn Coire Mhic Nobuil stream. You now enter remote country: there is no civilisation of any kind for the next 12km. The path almost immediately exits the wood, clambering northwest over moor to scale a deer fence after 600m. Red deer relish these lower mountain slopes.

3) Things now get wilder and more spectacular as you continue up the moor, Upper Loch Torridon panoramas opening up below. Enter the Coire nan Laogh, tracing the stream northwest on the western side. The bulky shoulder of Na Fasreidhnean rises up left (southwest). At the 800masl contour, cross two stream heads just above where they fork, eventually emerging on a leveller plateau with the first of multi-summited Beinn Alligin's Munro peaks **Tom na Gruagaich** (922masl) off right (east).

4) The next 1.5km to high point Sgúrr Mor is one of Europe's best ridge walks. From the Tom na Gruagaich end, with its curving descent and ascent to Sgúrr Mor, it is showcased at its best. The ridge is broad enough not to induce vertigo, although drops off right are sheer. At one point you must drop 0.75m over a small rockface; later, just before Sgúrr Mor, the ridge is cleaved by Eag Dubh gully: pass this to the left. **Sgúrr Mor** (986masl) even outdoes Tom na Gruagaich for views. Majestically serrated peaks stretch in all directions, myriad lochans glimmering tinfoil-like below. Directly east are the **Horns of Alligin**, with their challenging scrambling route back down to the Abhainn Coire Mhic Nobuil glen. Keep a look out up here for ptarmigans, game birds that turn snow-white in winter, and soaring golden eagles in the sky above.

5) This walk takes an easier way down. Return to the lowest point of the ridge to where the descent northwest over the grassy slopes is easiest. Keep a stream head well to the left. The contours start un-bunching around 600masl, where you swing right (east), keeping Sgúrr Mor's steeper slopes close on the right. Pass south of Loch Toll nam Biast, where you might spy red-throated divers, but then swing northeast to pass left of the smaller lochans beyond.

6) After the lochans, you follow the left side of Allt a Bhealaich stream as it runs east 500m then bends south. After 500m it crosses the first of three tributaries in quick succession. With Sgúrr Mor's steeper slopes on your right and the main course of Allt a Bhealaich initially about 125m to your left, pick up a path that becomes more distinct and runs down south for almost 3km to join Abhainn Coire Mhic Nobuil.

7) Turn right, the stream on your right, for a lovely, straightforward descent 2km down the glen to the Beinn Alligin car park. Turn left and now follow your outward route 3.5km back to Torridon, although you can vary it by following the coast road, maximising chances of sealife sightings.

93. Inchnadamph to Kylesku Bridge via Eas a' Chual Aluinn

Take on this trek through the Assynt wilderness and your reward could be a rendezvous with red deer, eagles or seals

NEED TO KNOW

START/FINISH: Inchnadamph Rock Trail car park, near The Inchnadamph Hotel, IV27 4HN (parking free)/Kylesku Bridge North car park, IV27 4TL – 1.25km (¾ mile) northwest of Kylesku (parking free)

DISTANCE: 29.25km (18¼ miles) (one way)

TIME: Full day

KEY SPECIES: Golden eagle, white-tailed sea eagle, grey seal, eider duck

MAP: OS Explorer 442

TRANSPORT: Inchnadamph Hotel bus stop (buses to Ullapool/Lochinver) at start

WALK ACCESSIBILITY: Not wheelchair/pushchair accessible; dogs allowed

DIFFICULTY: Difficult

SPECIFIC EQUIPMENT: Compass, insect repellent

MORE INFORMATION: discoverassynt.co.uk

Locals in the sparsely populated Inchnadamph region may tell of the legend concerning the area's main loch: Loch Assynt. A chieftain, so the story goes, promised the hand of his beautiful daughter Eimhir to the devil in return for help with the building of his stronghold, Ardvreck Castle, which still stands on the loch shore. When the castle was raised in days, the devil came to claim his prize but, rather than marry him,

EIDER DUCK

The UK's fastest-flying and heaviest duck, the attractive eider is a maritime bird through and through, feeding on molluscs. The sight of myriad pairs of them, skimming above the water near Kylesku in their springtime mating season, is magical.

Eimhir flung herself into the loch and was never seen again. The chieftain was beside himself with grief: when

Inchnadamph's weather closes in, this is the chieftain mourning. The surrounding pockmarked rocky landscape of Assynt is the devil's work: enraged at being cheated of Eimhir, he summoned huge boulders to bombard the chieftain's territory into oblivion. Far-fetched stuff, perhaps, but a colourful tale was, until late-19th-century geological studies, the only way to explain away the bizarre topography of broken ridges, big rockfaces and stony emptiness that this hike traverses.

Running through some of the British mainland's remotest scenery and visiting its highest waterfall, Eas a' Chual Aluinn, this route offers strong chances of special wildlife sightings. Red deer roam lower-elevation moors while lochs towards the walk's end get notably good golden eagle and white-tailed sea eagle sightings. Kylesku Bridge is one of the Northwest Highlands' finest places for seal-spotting, and seafaring birds like razorbills, cormorants and eider ducks also venture inland down Loch a' Chàirn Bhàin to take advantage of Kylesku's sheltered coastal waters.

September is the best month for a visit: stags rut in the glens, sealife is more in evidence with fewer humans around and tourist facilities are still open. Prepare properly and get an early start for this challenging full-day hike, where navigation skills are essential and one section is pathless: help is far away if you get into difficulty. Avoid this hike in icy and misty conditions.

ROUTE DESCRIPTION

1) Strike out north along the A837 road, Loch Assynt glimmering off left. Cross the river, then turn right on the metalled track with the green footpath sign to Gleann Dubh. Continue alongside the river-hugging track for 925m. You pass Inchnadamph Explorer's Lodge and several other houses, head through a gate and later pass a left-hand house drive before reaching your left-hand onward track.

2) This clearly defined route ascends northeast with Allt Poll an Droighinn initially on your right and the summit of Cnoc an Droighinn off left. After 1.9km it swings north, away from the stream, climbing to a path fork just before a tiny lochan.

3) Take the left fork, running left of the lochan. You soon pass a small loch off left and then skirt another off right before reaching the edge of larger Loch Fleodach Coire 800m after the fork. It's soggy going edging the western loch shore's bog before the path becomes distinct again, snaking up from the northwest loch corner north, northwest above Loch Bealach na h-Uidhe and finally north onto

Bealach na h-Uidhe saddle, with Glas Bheinn summit to the west.

4) Views from here north down to Loch Beag and Loch Glencoul boast a raw, remote beauty in good visibility, when this is a great place for wild observation. You could catch red deer unawares on the greener land below. The descent path is initially clear, zigzagging but overall bearing northeast for 2km to reach a distinctive double-pronged loch, which it skirts the north side of. Another left-hand path bears off at the loch to the top of Eas a' Chual Aluinn, but your route skirts the loch shore southeast, then reaches a path junction.

5) Keep left here, descending quite steeply southeast before swinging northwest and crossing a burn. The path now fades for some time, so descend northeast to the Abhainn an Loch Bhig river, keeping to the rough ground on its left-hand (southwestern) bank until it bends west, at which point you cross it. With all this navigation, don't forget to look up to majestic **Eas a' Chual Aluinn** cascading down the cliff off left (west) in a 200m drop. Keeping the river around 150m to your left to avoid the boggy ground, now proceed north-northwest to the southern end of Loch Beag, coming closer to the river near the loch.

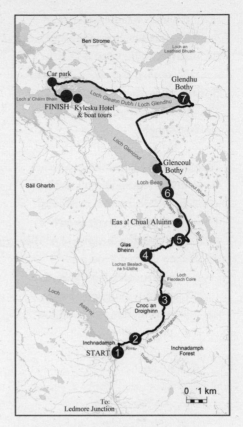

6) Pick up a rough path tracing Loch Beag's east shore. After 1km, the route improves after you come to a jetty, veering away north from the loch before curving northwest to **Glencoul Bothy**. Skirt along the loch, crossing Glencoul River on the footbridge. Briefly turn right along the far bank before swinging sharp left to ascend the rough track northwest over the Aird da Loch peninsula. After the ground you have covered, this is a tiring climb, and the path faint at times. Look to swing northeast

327

in 2.4km and descend towards the southern shore of Loch Gleann Dubh, the path becoming clearer as you near the eastern end with **Glendhu Bothy** visible ahead. Cross Abhainn a' Ghlinne Dubh on a footbridge to reach the bothy.

7) Afterwards, follow the good track along Loch Gleann Dubh's north shore for 7.25km to the A894 road. This tranquil, easy-going stretch is perfect for spotting the diverse wildlife: this is a sea loch and you could easily see seals, along with golden and white-tailed sea eagles. For the last 1.6km, shoreside forest around the houses at Kylestrome makes a refreshing terrain change. There is a car park for arranging your return to the walk start just before the road. But this walk continues slightly further, turning left along the road (the scenery is delightful and the road quiet) for 1.3km to end at Kylesku Bridge North car park. The bridge and surroundings are excellent for grey seal sightings, and for seeing springtime flocks of eider ducks. Nearby at Kylesku pier is a hotel and wildlife-watching boat trips, should you wish to extend your time here.

RETURNING TO START: Car or bike

94. Carsaig Arches

Venture where white-tailed sea eagles dare along the Isle of Mull's
spectacularly wild and serrated coastline

NEED TO KNOW

START/FINISH: Carsaig Pier car park, PA70 6HD – 6km (3¾ miles) south of
Pennyghael (parking free)

DISTANCE: 13km (8 miles) (out-and-back)

TIME: 5½–6 hours

KEY SPECIES: White-tailed sea eagle, golden eagle, grey seal

MAP: OS Explorer 375

TRANSPORT: Oban railway station – 53.5km (33¼ miles) northeast, on
mainland. Walk 100m southwest to Oban ferry terminal, take CalMac ferry
to Craignure – 37.25km (23¼ miles) northeast

WALK ACCESSIBILITY: Not wheelchair/pushchair accessible; dogs allowed

DIFFICULTY: Difficult

MORE INFORMATION: isle-of-mull.net

**White-tailed
sea eagle**

The second-biggest island of the Inner
Hebrides and the UK's fourth-largest
island, the Isle of Mull has carved
out a name for itself as a wildlife
haven and walking heaven, and has
featured on *Springwatch* and *Autumnwatch*
numerous times. Yet rugged shores
deter all but the hardiest humans from
this adventure out along the untamed
south coast of the island's Ross of Mull
peninsula. Do not be one of those to
hold back. The challenging traipse
along the boulder-scattered coast to the
Carsaig Arches, twin rock arches jutting

out cinematically below jaw-droppingly jagged cliffs, rewards you richly in scenery and in wildlife alike.

Mull has become a bastion of the white-tailed sea eagle, with many pairs now nesting here. *Springwatch* has traced the re-introduction of these birds to the island by conservationists for many years. You could also spy golden eagles. The start point is a superb seal-watching location, red deer and feral goats are likely to eye you up along the way and the arches themselves ricochet with the cries of seabirds.

Terrain-wise, this is one of this book's toughest walks because of the rough, occasionally indistinct path scrambling along the shore. The above creatures can be seen year round, but choose a dry day (thereby minimising slips) and a low tide for the hike.

ROUTE DESCRIPTION

1) The steep, singletrack lane down to photogenic **Carsaig Pier** is an

adventure in itself. From the pier, a lovely spot for watching grey seals, walk back along the approach road to a track on the left marked 'No Through Road'. Follow this track, running along the top of the shore, bearing left at a fork and slipping through a gap between a wall and gate onto the beach. You now enter remote country: there is no civilisation of any kind for the next 12.5km of walking. The path continues along the beach top to another gate, before which you should divert left onto the shore to cross two burns at their easiest fording points.

2) Rejoin the path above the shore, which is boggy, with occasional planks aiding your passage. Presently pass through a kissing gate set and onto the rough, rocky shore-hugging path beneath the cliffs. Many of the forthcoming minor branch-off paths along here are merely goat tracks, with some leading to sheer drops. If in doubt, make your way along the shore, where the going is arduous but never dangerous.

3) After 1.75km along the shore, your route reaches **Nun's Cave**, supposedly once used as shelter by nuns fleeing the abbey on the nearby Isle of Iona during the Reformation. On the left of the cave as you enter are carvings – crosses – that could

WHITE-TAILED SEA EAGLE

Britain's largest bird of prey (their wingspan reaches over 2m) became extinct during the 20th century, but a reintroduction programme has brought UK numbers to around 150 breeding pairs. Their diet is predominantly fish, along with some birds, rabbits and hares and, in wintertime, carrion.

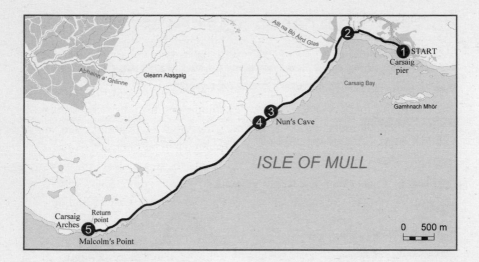

date from the 6th century AD. The most regular users of the cave these days are feral goats, plus the odd hiker seeking refuge from the weather.

4) Your path now continues in much the same vein: waterfall-splashed cliffs to your right and wild sea to your left. Incredible views over to fellow Inner Hebridean islands Jura and Islay open up, and golden and white-tailed sea eagles may well be spotted. From the cave, it's 3.5km along the shore to Carsaig Arches. Just beforehand, round craggy **Malcolm's Point**.

5) It's now one final scramble over the rocks to the viewpoint for the first of the **Carsaig Arches** visible across a water-filled inlet. This first arch is deep, moody and murky and appears to open directly onto the sea. A precarious path leads up the cliff,

riven in basalt columns, to descend to the second arch, which cannot be seen from the viewpoint. Only attempt this path if you are an experienced hillwalker with a head for heights and know one slip down the precipitous rock face could be fatal. The second arch is smaller but higher and perhaps more spectacular as the stand-alone formation surrounding it resembles a castle, crowned by a towering pinnacle of rock. The area around the arches is great for observing seabirds like guillemots. Your outward route ends at the viewpoint: return the same way.

95. Glen Sligachan to Sgùrr na Strì

Go with the golden eagles and red deer up this mountain-flanked glen to a peak often touted as Britain's finest viewpoint

NEED TO KNOW

START/FINISH: Car park east of River Sligachan on A87 across from Sligachan Hotel, IV47 8SW (parking free)

DISTANCE: 25km (15½ miles) (out-and-back)

TIME: 7½–8 hours

KEY SPECIES: Golden eagle, greenshank, red deer

MAP: OS Explorer 411

TRANSPORT: Sligachan Hotel bus stop (buses to Uig/Portree/Broadford/Fort William) – 275m west

WALK ACCESSIBILITY: Not wheelchair/pushchair accessible; dogs allowed

DIFFICULTY: Difficult

SPECIFIC EQUIPMENT: Compass, insect repellent

MORE INFORMATION: isleofskye.com

Greenshank

This untamed trail through the Isle of Skye's singular Glen Sligachan is for those who love mountains but care less for climbing. The glen is the glorious divide between the Red and Black Cuillins ranges, the latter being Scotland's most handsome mountain chain and its toughest to traverse. Impressive high-altitude vistas are on either side as you progress upriver to your objective – comparatively diminutive summit Sgùrr na Strì, barely a third of the height of some giant peaks hereabouts. But who needs stature when you've got gobsmacking 360-degree views, reckoned by many hillwalking connoisseurs to be Britain's best? And the panorama – out to an island-flecked ocean and up Loch Coruisk to the Black Cuillins crowding around in immense igneous spires – needs to be seen, rather than just read about.

The isolated terrain, a SPA, is a swooping and stomping ground for several birds and animals. This is one of Britain's best places to see golden eagles: several pairs nest in the surrounding crags. Red deer are regularly seen in the glen too, as well as birds like the greenshank, a scarce wader. Attempt this on any day with decent visibility and it will be a treasure.

This is among the book's tougher walks, with boggy sections, sometimes-faint paths and a (non-vertiginous) scramble needed to ascend Sgùrr na Strì. That said, most of it is on distinct paths and fairly level, except that final climb.

ROUTE DESCRIPTION

1) Take the track down from the car park across the entrance drive to Sligachan Bunkhouse towards photogenic triple-arched **Sligachan Old Bridge**, built by Thomas Telford. Beyond, **Sligachan** hamlet is essentially a hotel and mountain rescue station. Before the bridge, turn left on the temporarily wide, well-surfaced path to the **Collie and Mackenzie Statue**, remembering two early Cuillin

> ### GREENSHANK
> As few as 700 of these dark-grey-backed, green-legged waders are thought to breed in Britain, including 50 pairs in the Glen Sligachan area.

mountain explorers. You now enter wild country: there is no civilisation from this point on (24km). Bear left of the statue, your path passing alongside a fence and Allt Daraich burn. Ignore a gate 200m later to bear away from Allt Daraich up Glen Sligachan.

2) Mountain vistas get steadily more spectacular as your path trundles across several smaller burns and the wider **Allt na Measarroch** burn after 3km. First, it's the Red Cuillins off left, then after Allt na Measarroch mighty views up to the Black Cuillins, including high point Sgùrr Alasdair (992masl) and the Inaccessible Pinnacle (Sgùrr Dearg), hardest of Scotland's Munro peaks to scale. But don't forget to look groundwards for moorland plant wonders like the insect-catching common butterwort.

3) Shortly after passing Lochan Dubha and its tributary, originating on the slopes of **Marsco** (736masl) off left, and around 6.5km after the statue, you reach a cairn at a path fork. Bear right, with craggy **Blà Bheinn** (929masl) watching on off left and **Sgùrr Hain** (418masl), the peak sitting in front of your end objective, ahead. The path climbs, reaching a large cairn at a path fork. The right-hand path goes down to **Loch Coruisk**, already visible, but you take the left fork.

4) Compass skills are advised, especially in poor visibility, as you now contour around **Sgùrr Hain** on a rough but generally visible path that stays below the ridgeline, heading first south, then southwest, then south and south-southeast, for 2.25km to the foot of **Sgùrr na Strì** (494masl). There is no clear path on the final short push to the summit: head either up the burn and then right or over the rocks to the burn's right.

5) Enjoy the sensational views from the top, while watching for red deer on the lower ground and golden eagles above. Your outward route ends here: return the same way.

NORTHERN IRELAND

96. Cuilcagh Boardwalk

*Climb into Northern Ireland's most ecologically precious habitat –
blanket bog*

NEED TO KNOW

START/FINISH: Cuilcagh Mountain Park car park, BT92 1ER – 3.75km
(2¼ miles) southwest of Wheathill (parking charges may apply; pre-booking
advised)

DISTANCE: 11km (6¾ miles)
(out-and-back)

Common lizard

TIME: 2½–3 hours

KEY SPECIES: Golden plover, common
lizard, blanket bog

MAP: OSNI Discoverer 26

TRANSPORT: Blacklion bus stop (buses to Sligo/Enniskillen) – 8.75km (5½
miles) northwest

WALK ACCESSIBILITY: Not wheelchair/pushchair accessible; no dogs

DIFFICULTY: Easy–Moderate

MORE INFORMATION: cuilcaghlakelands.org and theboardwalk.ie

The popular Cuilcagh Boardwalk, also
known as the 'Stairway to Heaven',
is your ticket into a treasured yet
threatened moorland terrain: upland
blanket bog. The Cuilcagh Mountains
harbour one of Europe's largest
unspoilt tracts of this landscape,
and the elevated boardwalk on the
mountain slopes lets you venture
into the middle of them without
damaging the ecosystem. The
blanket bog bristles with sphagnum
moss, crowberry and dwarf willow,
while Ireland's only native reptile,
the common lizard, basks on the
rocks. Merlins and buzzards patrol
the lonesome skies, skylarks perform
their dulcet trills and the rare golden
plover nests in bog vegetation. The
area is designated as the UK's first
internationally recognised Geopark:
Cuilcagh Lakelands Geopark. This
also encompasses Marble Arch Caves,
Northern Ireland's biggest cave
system, a short stroll or drive from the
walk start point. April (lizard courtship

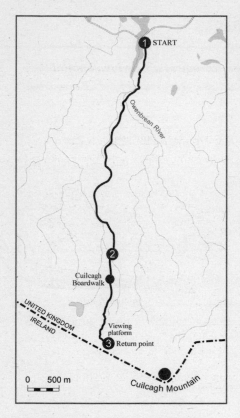

START

Owenbrean River

2

Cuilcagh
Boardwalk

UNITED KINGDOM
IRELAND

Viewing
platform

3 Return point

0   500 m

Cuilcagh Mountain

start point) a stony farm track leads south. Follow this distinct track for 4km, passing into the stark, fascinating upland blanket bog landscape, which makes a home for flowers like butterwort and sundew, which excrete sticky fluid that traps insects. Also of interest along here are the vestiges of Ireland's rural heritage. You'll pass abandoned cottages, dry-stone walls and 'lazy beds', bumps delineating former potato cultivation.

2) The track becomes a stepped boardwalk clambering the shoulder of Cuilcagh Mountain through boulder-strewn terrain. Watch for common lizards indulging in some boulder-top sunbathing!

3) The boardwalk reaches a **viewing platform** below Cuilcagh summit. The immense views can stretch from the Sperrin Mountains in the nation's northeast to the Dartry Mountains (northwest). This vantage point might, with luck, yield views of breeding golden plovers. Your outward route ends here: return the same way.

season) or May (when golden plovers begin breeding) are great times to visit.

It's a metalled track or boardwalk throughout underfoot. The walk makes one significant climb up Cuilcagh's mountain slopes, but not to the very top.

ROUTE DESCRIPTION

1) From Cuilcagh Mountain Park car park (if there is no space here or if you prefer to park further away for free, park at Killykeeghan Nature Reserve car park, 1.4km northwest, turning left along Marlbank Road to reach the

COMMON LIZARDS

Averaging 13cm in length, Ireland's only indigenous reptiles are additionally special for giving birth to live young (most reptiles lay eggs). Watch for them on bogs, uplands, grasslands and certain coastal sites.

97. Craignamaddy Circuit

Delight in some of Northern Ireland's comeliest upland walking, where easy-to-navigate tracks and lanes make for opportune bird observation

NEED TO KNOW

START/FINISH: Barnes car park, BT79 8EN – 7.75km (4¾ miles) east of Plumbridge (parking free)

DISTANCE: 20.25km (12½ miles) (circular)

TIME: 6–6½ hours

KEY SPECIES: Red grouse, skylark, golden eagle

MAP: OSNI Discoverer 13

TRANSPORT: Plumbridge Post Office bus stop (buses to Omagh) – 7.75km (4¾ miles) west

WALK ACCESSIBILITY: Accessible to wheelchair/pushchair users; dogs on leads where livestock are present

DIFFICULTY: Moderate

MORE INFORMATION: discovernorthernireland.com

The Sperrin Mountains are not Northern Ireland's highest mountain range, but they are the biggest by extent, fanning for a serene 65km along the borders of County Tyrone and County Derry. They form one of the country's largest wildlife playgrounds and one of its eight AONBs. It's all wonderful off-the-beaten-track walking terrain, but the backdrop to the Craignamaddy Circuit blends the mottled mauve-browns of the moor, the gold-green hues of farmland and the grey-blue shades of serpentine river together to near perfection.

Salmon are plentiful in rivers like the Glenelly, where herons fish and otters are also sometimes descried. Yet it is the upland birdwatching that really stands out. One of the nation's key red grouse populations and breeding golden plovers (the latter May through August only) hide out in the heather here. The moor is the hunting ground of sparrowhawks and peregrine falcons and the skylark's dulcet strains are audible over open farmland and moor alike. Golden eagles have been reintroduced in close-by Donegal and there have now been several sightings of these magnificent birds in this part of the Sperrins.

Countryside colours become most intense in midsummer, and this exposed walk is more enjoyable when wild weather is far away. Despite bisecting some rugged landscapes, this route stays on solid lanes and tracks throughout, giving you, dear nature lover, all the more time to focus on the fauna, the flora and the views.

ROUTE DESCRIPTION

1) Across the lane from the car park are the beginnings of two lanes: do not take the one directly opposite the car park entrance but the second a few metres further on, signposted 'Magherabrack Road' and also 'Craignamaddy Circuit & Vinegar Hill'. Continue gradually uphill past a farmyard to a T-junction, then turn right. Keep on the lane for 650m as it negotiates the brow of the hill, glorious moorland rearing off left and forest sweeping through the valley below right. When you reach a metalled track, turn left.

2) The next 3.8km could be the walk's finest as you progress along the quiet moorland track, contouring **Mullaghbolig**'s hilly slopes. Look out for skylarks, especially between March and November, curlews in late spring and

> **SKYLARK**
> Inconspicuous on the ground, it is these plain, brown, crested birds' beautiful song flights that will likely draw your attention to them: males rise up vertically, flutter in one position in the air, then parachute down to ground, trilling the entire time they are airborne. The passerines, which moved Romantic poets Shelley and Wordsworth to odes, are currently common birds, but have suffered dramatic recent declines.

the introduction-listed raptors year-round. You'll curve south and then southwest to pass through another farm and meet the valley road along the Owenkillew River. Turn left for 1.5km, passing houses at Scotch Town, crossing straight over the lane crossroads and presently arriving at another junction with a lane heading left and a gravel track bearing prettily right uphill between fields.

Skylark

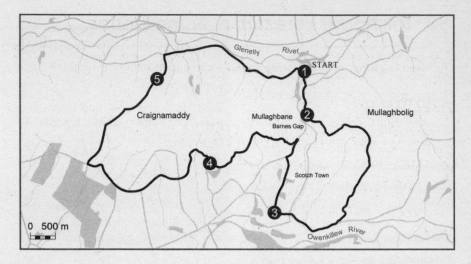

3) Proceed on the track for 1.25km, at the end bearing left on a metalled lane to rejoin Magherabrack Road and turn right. It's 475m, with two exquisite curves of moorland ahead, to a left-hand track bending immediately left for a while before steadying a course northwest through the fields below **Mullaghbane** hill. After passing a patch of woodland the route swings left (southwest), passing a motorbike track circuit. Then ignore a right-hand and then a left-hand turn as you meander to meet the tarmac again at Meenadoo Road, 950m after the motorbike circuit.

4) Keep ahead, following this sinuous lane for 3.6km to the junction with Trinamadan Road. Now turn right for a lonely 2.4km northeast, tracing the waymarked gravel track steadily up over the titular **Craignamaddy** hill (382masl) and passing the bracken-blanketed summit off right. This is another fine stretch for bird-spotting.

5) Next, bear right at a Y-junction and continue along a tarmacked lane to hit the main Glenelly Valley road (still, in this rural area, a somnolent narrow lane). Swing right here for the circuit's finale. The lane brushes close to **Glenelly River** at first – watch for otters – and then ignores several small turnings to farms and houses as it threads back to the start car park.

98. Tollymore Forest Park & the Drinns

Become engulfed in enchanting forest awash with arboreal wonder

NEED TO KNOW

START/FINISH: Tollymore Forest Park car park, BT33 0PR – 800m (½ mile) southwest of Bryansford (parking charges may apply)

DISTANCE: 14km (8¾ miles) (circular)

TIME: 3½–4 hours

KEY SPECIES: Yew, fallow deer, Mandarin duck

MAP: OSNI Discoverer 29

TRANSPORT: Cup & Saucer bus stop (buses to Newcastle) – 2.5km (1½ miles) east

WALK ACCESSIBILITY: Not wheelchair/pushchair accessible; dogs allowed

DIFFICULTY: Moderate

MORE INFORMATION: nidirect.gov.uk

Northern Ireland's best-known forest, surprisingly, still remains relatively under-the-radar in terms of the country's go-to destinations. This is despite providing the wood that decorated the *Titanic* interior, the opening scene of famed fantasy TV series *Game of Thrones* and tract upon tract of superlative trees. Tollymore weaves its magic by mixing forest that has been managed to astound and delight since the 1700s with wilder spreads of conifer and moor. It is threaded by two rivers, too. The forest falls within the Mourne Mountains AONB that swoops up handsomely behind and is an ASSI in its own right.

This walk thrills with a forest best-of: you'll tread resplendent ornamental riversides before ascending to the forest edge where moors and the Mournes' raw power await. You'll be treated to majestic trees from beeches to cedars to maples and a collection of yews among Europe's most important. A 150-strong fallow deer herd also graze here and the park has produced numerous Northern Ireland nature headlines: hosting the first great spotted woodpeckers to have bred in Ireland in centuries and Ireland's only established Mandarin duck population. Otters, kingfishers, badgers and foxes may be seen too.

The forest is usually tramped as a poor-weather alternative to hillwalking the Mournes because of its tree cover and well-surfaced tracks. But best is a clear, crisp day in autumn, where the bold broadleaf russets, inky conifer greens and churning white river water contrast and compete.

ROUTE DESCRIPTION

1) From the southwest corner of the larger car park by church-like 18th-century **Clanbrassil Barn**, actually erected to house estate horses, take the tarmacked path to the other smaller car park, a broad lawn ahead. From this car park's southwest corner, take the **Azalea Walk** to pass under ornamental **Horn Bridge**. This tarmacked path runs down beside a stream, joins another path and reaches the salmon-rich **Shimna River**.

2) Turn right, following the winsome riverside path for 1.75km. The river sports several bridges, a set of

> ### YEW
> Britain's yews are among the world's oldest living things, worshipped since at least Celtic times with their locations later assimilated into Christian religious sites. The tree is entirely poisonous, except for its red fruit flesh. Some birds and badgers eat the fruit without digesting the unpalatable seeds.

stepping-stones and the **Hermitage**, a charming folly, along this stretch. The bridge you are searching for is stone-built **Parnell's Bridge** (a sign helpfully identifies it as such!). Do not cross the bridge but continue along the riverside path to the next bridge, **Boundary Bridge**. Cross the river, following the **Mourne Way** to a 4-way track crossroads after about 250m. Here the Mourne Way bears right: cross the larger track, proceeding along a Shimna River tributary.

3) Your path now climbs through forest towards the southern boundary with the Mourne Mountains. Arc left away from the tributary after 350m, reach a track crossroads 750m further on and here swing sharp right, almost back upon yourself initially, to the forest edge. Views off right up into the Mournes, including to Luke's Mountain, dazzle intermittently.

4) Continue along the forest top before a zigzagging descent, ignoring one left-hand turn, to reach a wider forest track after 1.25km. Turn right, immediately crossing **Spinkwee River** via Hore's Bridge. You are back on the Mourne Way here. Climb again, your track meeting another bearing right after 425m. Take this track up onto The Drinns, soon hitting the forest edge again: moorland and views up to Slievenabrock summit rear

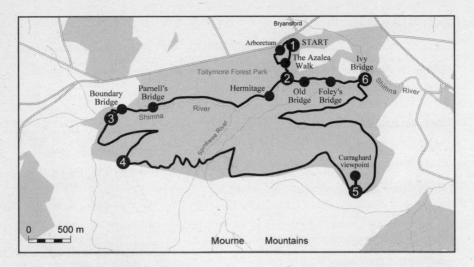

Bryansford

Arboretum — START

The Azalea Walk

Ivy Bridge

Tollymore Forest Park

Hermitage

Parnell's Bridge

Old Bridge

Foley's Bridge

Shimna River

Boundary Bridge

River

Shimna

Spinkwee River

Curraghard viewpoint

0   500 m

Mourne   Mountains

beyond. A gate leads onto the moor here if you wish to explore it further. Your track continues within the forest park bounds, albeit through wide patches of open ground. Ignore a left-hand track after 1km, curving right to reach the turn-off up to **Curraghard Viewpoint** (225masl) 1.75km after the moorland gate.

5) It's a short left-hand out-and-back path to the viewpoint, then a sweeping 2km descent through conifer forest, curving gradually around left before a sharp right-hand turn and another 1.4km descent to come down beside the Shimna River at **Ivy Bridge**.

6) Cross the bridge then turn left along another lovely tract of riverside path. You pass **Foley's Bridge** then **Old Bridge**, perfectly framing

a short but beautiful waterfall behind it, reaching your outward route 200m afterwards. Head away from the river, up under Horn Bridge and along the Azalea Walk to a path junction near the smaller car park. Here, vary your return route dramatically by passing through one of Ireland's oldest, loveliest **arboretums**, where highlights include grand specimens of maple, cedar, yew and cork oak, by turning left, then right again at a junction to bear right around to the larger car park.

Mandarin duck

343

99. Slemish

Follow St Patrick's footsteps up this legendary hill for wondrous views, birdwatching and instant countryside bliss

NEED TO KNOW

START/FINISH: Slemish car park, BT42 4PF – 7.75km (4¾ miles) southeast of Broughshane (parking free)

DISTANCE: 1.5km (1 mile) (out-and-back)

TIME: 1 hour

KEY SPECIES: Buzzard, meadow pipit, Irish hare

MAP: OSNI Discoverer 9

TRANSPORT: Aughacully Road bus stop (buses to Ballymena/Carnlough) – 5.25km (3¼ miles) north

WALK ACCESSIBILITY: Not wheelchair/pushchair accessible; dogs allowed

DIFFICULTY: Moderate–Difficult

MORE INFORMATION: discovernorthernireland.com

Buzzard

Rugged rocky summit Slemish, an extinct volcano, swoops surreally out of the innocuous farmland and bog below. But this County Antrim locale does not hold a sacred place in Irish hearts for its shape. It was on these slopes (presumably the lower, grassier ones) that St Patrick, enslaved into working for a local chieftain as a livestock herder in the 5th century AD, purportedly found God. Today it's an understandably popular pilgrimage and, at 1.5km out-and-back, one of Northern Ireland's swiftest methods of catapulting yourself into wild countryside. As well as the fantastic panoramas across patchwork fields and undulating moor, it is a favoured haunt for birdwatchers. Buzzards and ravens are big presences in the skies here, while the meadow pipit, Britain's most abundant upland songbird, and the wheatear are also seen. Also keep vigil for the Irish hare, a genetically distinct subspecies of mountain hare.

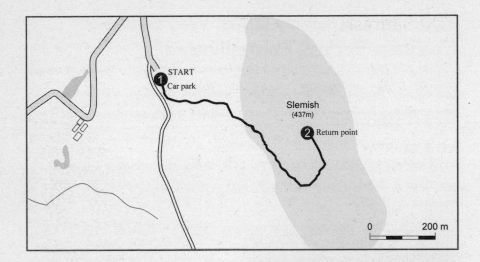

Any time with good visibility from March through October should maximise your hilltop vistas and wildlife-watching. It's straightforward to describe the short route up, but don't underestimate it: it's significantly hard to do and, depending on the way you scale its steep slopes, entails some scrambling.

ROUTE DESCRIPTION

1) From the car park head south, passing the toilets on your left and through the gate. Then swing left (southeast) away from the road and gently up over the moor on a grassy track to the base of the hill. It's then up to you which way you climb (and, sometimes, scramble) up: marked on the map is the route that runs initially to the right (southeast) to then veer northeast up the hill, approaching the top finally from the south.

BUZZARD

Slemish's immediate environs – exposed moor, fields and slight tree cover – create great conditions for buzzards: countryside stalwarts UK-wide and Europe's commonest raptor. Still, coming from towns and cities where the birds are rarely seen, they present some spectacle, with wingspans reaching 128cm and a call often likened to a mewling cat.

2) Slemish (437masl) is perhaps County Antrim's best viewpoint: you'll see all the way across to the Scottish coast on a good day. Spend some time up here view-gazing, birdwatching and just being. Your outward route ends here: return the same way.

100. The Causeway Coast Way between Carrick-a-Rede & Portballintrae

Get all your coastal thrills – seabirds, cetaceans, geological wonders and gorgeous beaches – on Northern Ireland's must-do hike

NEED TO KNOW

START/FINISH: Carrick-a-Rede NT car park, BT54 6LS – 900m (½ mile) northeast of Ballintoy (parking charges may apply)/Portballintrae Hotel Corner bus stop, BT57 8RS

DISTANCE: 26km (16¼ miles) (part one way, part out-and-back)

TIME: Full day

KEY SPECIES: Harbour porpoise, basking shark, bottlenose dolphin

MAP: OSNI Causeway Coast and Rathlin Island Activity Map

TRANSPORT: Carrick-a-Rede Rope Bridge bus stop – 500m (¼ mile) southwest

WALK ACCESSIBILITY: Not wheelchair/pushchair accessible; dogs allowed

DIFFICULTY: Moderate–Difficult

SPECIFIC EQUIPMENT: Swimwear

MORE INFORMATION: causewaycoastway.com and nationaltrust.org.uk

The 40,000-odd basalt columns interlocking in a spread of natural crazy paving along Northern Ireland's north coast is, depending on which story you prefer, the consequence of volcanic activity during the Palaeocene geological epoch about 60 million years back or the beginnings of a causeway to Scotland built by Irish giant Fionn mac Cumhaill in order to accept the challenge of a fight from Scottish colossus Benandonner.

Either way, County Antrim's Giant's Causeway draws dramatic focus to the Causeway Coast surrounding it: an elemental, rockily riven seaboard between Ballycastle and Portstewart, linked up by long-distance path the Causeway Coast Way. Ruined castles and fetching fishing harbours prettify the picture and to heighten the spectacle, the trail has been designed theatrically. Where other coastal paths would retreat inland at the obstacles geology has plonked in their way, this route embraces them: a vertiginous rope bridge teetering above the turgid Atlantic, check, a route right through a rock arch, check. This walk really does takes you to the Unesco-listed coastline's best bits.

Because of its relentless proximity to rugged shores, the route brushes close to lots of seafaring fauna too. The coast often yields sightings of harbour porpoises, basking sharks, bottlenose dolphins and common and grey seals. Kittiwakes, razorbills and fulmars chatter in Carrick-a Rede's cliffs while White Park Bay has rabbits and rare orchids in its dunes and the odd otter on a fishing trip.

May and June are excellent for basking sharks and seabirds. Also ensure you are passing certain walk points (map-marked 'avoid this section at high tide') at lower tides. With so much going on, allow a full day for this hike. The way is well-signposted and on good paths but remains a strenuous tramp.

ROUTE DESCRIPTION

1) While your route heads northwest along the coast, don't miss the 2.75km out-and-back coastal jaunt eastwards to **Carrick-a-Rede** first. The name of this craggy island, connected by the famous **Carrick-a-Rede Rope Bridge**, translates as 'rock in the road' in Irish Gaelic: the 'road' being

HARBOUR PORPOISE

The UK's smallest (1.5-2m long) and commonest cetaceans nevertheless make outstanding wildlife sightings, as they are shyer than dolphins. This walk presents one of Northern Ireland's best chances to see the species. Look for their dark-grey backs and pale bellies.

the Atlantic salmon run. It became a major fishing site from the 17th century; fishermen constructed the first bridge across in 1755. You have to pay to cross one of the world's few bridges across the Atlantic (the bridge has been renewed since 1755), a hair-raising experience delivering you to Carrick-a-Rede, where you can explore the old fishermen's cottage and seabird-watch. Back at the start car park, proceed northwest and to the left of **Larrybane Quarry** to swing west along the clifftops for 550m. Where the headland northeast of Ballintoy Harbour thrusts north, continue straight along field edges to the white church on Harbour Road. Turn right for the helter-skelter descent into **Ballintoy Harbour**, a pretty fishing harbour you may recognise from fantasy TV series *Game of Thrones*, where it is masqueraded as the Iron Islands.

2) The path winds on along a great section for spotting sealife, passing a holiday cottage after the car park and then running through fields below verdant cliffs, as battered skerries and rock stacks lie scattered just offshore. You'll round a low headland at the cliff base before the sandy arc of **White Park Bay Beach**. The dunes here have a resident rabbit population plus nine orchid varieties to spot and otters have been seen here as well as harbour porpoises and dolphins. Fulmars also hog the cliffs come spring. Walk along the beach for 2.25km: the path wriggles its way around the rocks at the end of the beach to reach idyllic fishing harbour number two: **Portbraddan**.

3) Follow the shore around the first headland after Portbraddan, pass through a rock arch, cross a stream mouth and divert to the grassy clifftops at the next bay. A little later, follow these cliffs inland for a distance to find the route doubling almost back on itself to descend to lower grassy ground and Dunseverick Harbour ahead. At the car park here, join the approach road briefly. Then a grassy right-hand turn at a ladder stile tumbles down shoreside again. Twist through another belt of grassland and fields to cross over Dunseverick River. An out-and-back path then ventures out to see **Dunseverick Falls** crashing beautifully into the ocean. The onward route winds around field edges to a dazzling spread of gorse from where views across to broken **Dunseverick Castle** are fantastic, but you'll need to swing inland alongside Causeway Road to the car park to reach it on a sinuous out-and-back path. The castle site has been a stronghold so long that even St Patrick, in the 5th century AD, supposedly stopped by.

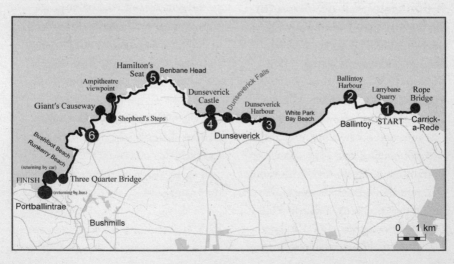

4) Now, it's time for the hike's longest off-road stretch (9km – until Giant's Causeway). From Dunseverick Castle car park the path rises along big clifftops, passing isolated Port Moon Bothy below on the cliff base and negotiating headlands Contham Head, Bengore Head and then **Benbane Head**, mainland Northern Ireland's northernmost point. Vistas are most impressive looking east-northeast to Rathlin Island mid-distance and Scotland's Mull of Kintyre beyond on a clear day: at their best from **Hamilton's Seat** on Benbane Head.

5) Another 3km along the clifftops brings you into Giant's Causeway Unesco World Heritage Site zone and to the top of **Shepherd's Steps**. Here, swing right to descend the cliff to the **Giant's Causeway** itself. Start with the out-and-back to the **Ampitheatre Viewpoint** (exactly what you'd expect: great views of an amphitheatre-like curve of cliff-face) before continuing with the cliffbase path to the bonanza of basalt columns you doubtless want to see. Higher up are the taller, more jumbled columns and shore-side, the perfectly interconnecting ones. The site is breathtaking, if crowded: a shock after the quiet walk just beforehand. It's worth the trip up to the flashy clifftop **Giant's Causeway NT Visitor Centre**: a paid-for attraction with interactive experiences, audio guides and answers for every question you'll have about the geological marvel.

6) The walk's last leg sees you head around the Causeway Hotel, resuming the coast path route. You pass a picnic area, edge the inlet enfolding Portcoon Jetty, round one more bulky headland and skirt the end of Runkerry Road to come down beside **Bushfoot Beach**. This long sandy strand merges into **Runkerry Beach**, beyond which is Portballitrae. The main path trundles through tussocky dunes beside the Giant's Causeway and Bushmills Railway: take this or walk along the beach. At the beach's far end Three Quarter Bridge brings you over Bush River. Swing right for 425m to Portballintrae's Salmon Rock Beach car park, the finish if you're returning to the start by car. For the bus users' finish line, trace Beach Road 575m around Portballintrae harbour. Just left along Ballaghmore Road is the bus stop.

RETURNING TO START: Bus 252 (Antrim Coaster) (May–Sep)/402/172, car or bike

Abbreviations & Terms

Abhainn – Stream in Scottish Gaelic

Afon – River in Wales

Allt – Stream in Scottish Gaelic

AONB – Area of Outstanding Natural Beauty

ASSI – Area of Special Scientific Interest in Northern Ireland; similar to an SSSI but also including manmade structures

Bealach – Saddle between peaks in Scottish Gaelic

Beck – Stream in Northern England

Burn – Stream in Scotland

Cairn – A mound of stones acting as a navigational aid in remote country; also, in the ancient sense, a stone-built prehistoric memorial or marker where people and/or their artefacts were often buried

Col – Similar to a saddle (the lowest point between two summits) but generally understood to be in a high-elevation area, where the summits are not necessarily flanking it either side

Combe – Narrow wooded valley in Southwest England

Cwm/Corrie/Coire – Cirque (an amphitheatre-shaped valley head formed due to glacial erosion) in Wales/Scotland/Scottish Gaelic

Dark Sky Reserve – An area of land delineated for its especially clear views of the night sky, with little or no light pollution

Down – Chalk upland in Southern England

FE – Forestry England

Foss – Waterfall in Northern England

Geopark – A protected area of land with internationally significant geology

Leat – Manmade water conduit

Llyn/Loch/Lough – Lake in Wales/ Scotland/Ireland

LNR – Local Nature Reserve

Lochan – Tarn in Scotland

Masl – Metres above sea level

MOD – Ministry of Defence

Munro – Summit in Scotland above 3000 feet (914.4m)

Nant – Stream in Wales

NCI – National Coastguard Institute

NNR – National Nature Reserve

NP – National Park

NSA – National Scenic Area (in Scotland)

NT – National Trust

NTS – National Trust for Scotland

NWT – Norfolk Wildlife Trust

Porth – Cove or inlet in Cornwall

Ramsar – Signifying the Ramsar Convention on Wetlands of International Importance Especially as a Waterfowl Habitat, which lists over 2000 wetland sites of major importance to wildlife. The UK has the most sites on the list

Red List – A list of birds in the UK that are rare, severely threatened or rapidly declining, periodically reviewed and updated. An Amber List details birds with some cause for concern over their wellbeing; Green List birds are those with little or no concern over their survival

RSPB – Royal Society for the Protection of Birds

SAC – Special Area of Conservation, which can protect any natural habitat or feature

Sgurr – Mountain peak in Gaelic

Skerries – Jagged, normally low-lying reef-like rocks just off-shore

SPA – Special Protection Area, each one of which protects one or more bird species

SSSI – Site of Special Scientific Interest

Strath – A river valley in Scotland wider than that of a glen

Super-NNR – NNRs that are either large in size (combining several separated former nature reserves) or in ambition (with wider conservation and sustainability goals)

Tarn – Mountain lake

UNESCO – United Nations Educational, Scientific and Cultural Organisation

Wold – Open or uncultivated upland, particularly in Lincolnshire and Yorkshire

Key Information

COUNTRYSIDE CODE

This should be adhered to at all times when travelling through countryside in the UK, and particularly relates to anyone traversing countryside off public roads. It sets out responsibilities both to visitors and to landowners. The code applies to England and Wales; Northern Ireland has its own Countryside Code and Scotland has the Scottish Outdoor Access Code, both covering countryside users' obligations. View the codes at gov.uk.

LAND OWNERSHIP/ MANAGEMENT/CONSERVATION

The land through which these walks pass is often owned/managed/ conserved by various bodies. Some of the more common ones encountered include **Forestry and Land Scotland** (forestryandland.gov.scot), **Forestry England** (forestryengland. uk), **Ministry of Defence** (gov.uk), **National Trust** (nationaltrust.org. uk), **National Trust Scotland** (nts. org.uk), **Natural Resources Wales** (naturalresources.wales), **RSPB** (rspb.org.uk), **Unesco** (unesco.org), **Woodland Trust** (woodlandtrust.org. uk) and various regional wildlife trusts.

Walks also pass through land owned/managed/conserved by national parks, AONBs, NNRs, SSSIs, SACs and ASSIs (in Northern Ireland). Privately owned land is also passed through via public footpaths, permissive paths and tracks. In all cases, walkers should abide by the relevant conditions and codes. The walks in this book have been selected for the outstanding flora and fauna they feature and show no preference to any land-owning/managing/ conserving body.

HOW TO TREAT WILDLIFE ON THESE WALKS

Wildlife encountered should always be treated with respect, never harmed or compromised in any way and left in the condition it was found, in order to safeguard it for generations to come. Please pay particular attention to:

- Observing all local signage relating to wildlife. The local signage will post the most relevant and recent advice to heed.
- Sticking to footpaths at all times when passing through sensitive wildlife environments, and not entering land marked out as environmentally sensitive. This is especially important during the breeding/growing seasons of rare

or threatened fauna (such as the capercaillie, Walk 79), flora (such as bastard toadflax, Walk 8) or terrain type (such as upland blanket bog, Walk 96).

- Refraining from getting too close to any creature – you are on their territory, not they on yours.
- Refraining from provoking, scaring, surprising or in any way adversely affecting any creature where possible.
- Refraining from feeding any creature – you will never be best placed to judge what a particular creature may or may not like to eat or drink, and feeding a creature may be dangerous both for it and you.
- Refraining from picking or taking cuttings from all flora.
- Being responsible for your dog and preventing your dog from hurting or disturbing wildlife (see more under Walk Accessibility: Dogs).
- Reporting anything unusual that you see to the relevant authority – things worthy of report could include sighting a creature that appears injured or distressed, or anyone that you see that appears to be behaving irresponsibly. (The relevant authorities are usually listed in the individual walk's 'Need to Know' section.)

EQUIPMENT

The individual walks list any specific equipment necessary. Also, consider taking:

- Appropriate footwear (essential)
- Appropriate clothing (essential)
- Day rucksack containing sufficient food and water for the walk's duration (essential)
- Waterproof/wet weather gear (essential)
- Fully charged phone for emergencies (essential)
- Hard-copy OS Explorer map(s) covering walk area (advised)
- Digital version of walk map as back-up (advised)
- Waterproof map cover (advised)
- Cash for emergencies (advised)
- Camera (advised)
- Binoculars for wildlife-watching (advised)
- Suncream (advised)

For walks in wilder parts of the country, also notify someone of the route you intend to take in case of an emergency.

FEES

Most of these walks can be enjoyed for free. Places incurring a charge are mentioned in the individual walk's 'Need to Know' section or in the route description. There are two sorts of charges on the walks in this book. The first is for parking, applicable to many walk start/finish points. The second is for an entrance fee to a reserve or attraction included on the walk route. Most of the places mentioned where a fee is payable to experience them are optional (the detailed route can pass around them free of charge). In a few cases, the places where fees are payable to experience them are obligatory on the detailed route (you will need to devise your own alternative route if you do not wish to pay to enter).

MAPS

The maps given in this book should be used as general route overviews only. In addition to this book's walk maps and route descriptions, we strongly recommend bringing a hard copy of the orange OS Explorer map(s) relevant to your walk.

ONE WAY WALKS

Several walks in this book are described as one way (A to B). All of these have a 'Returning to Start' section at the end, which details feasible ways of returning to the walk start:

- **Returning by car:** Come with two cars, first parking one at the walk finish, then travelling altogether in the other car to the walk start. Alternatively, order a taxi to pick you up at the endpoint to return

you to the start (you should order one with plenty of advance notice – at least one day in remoter areas of the country – and ensure you leave plenty of time to arrive at the finish at the pre-agreed time).

- **Returning by bike:** Come with a bike, depositing the bike at the finish before driving to the walk start (one of your party then cycles the bike back to the car afterwards).
- **Returning by bus:** Many walks end at or close to bus stops with buses back to the walk start. Check bus schedules carefully beforehand to ensure you arrive at the finish before the day's final bus.

OPENING HOURS

Some walks in this book pass through reserves or other areas that are only open between certain hours or on certain days. Check beforehand if your walk has any specific opening hours via the More Information detailed in the individual walk's 'Need to Know' section.

REFRESHMENTS

Specific places to eat and drink along the route are only mentioned if they are particularly iconic or act as useful directional aids. Otherwise, refreshments are available in the towns, villages and locations along the walk route

MORE INFORMATION

Online resources where you can learn more about your chosen walk are detailed in the individual walk's 'Need to Know' section, and these usually provide further information on any parking charges, admission fees or opening hours relevant to the walk. General resources include:

- Gov.uk (resources on topics including Countryside and Highway Codes, Ministry of Defence-managed land and firing range times, nature reserves and sites managed by Natural England – the government's advisor for the natural environment in England)
- Nationaltrail.co.uk and scotlandsgreattrails.com (providing information on many long-distance trails in England/Wales and Scotland)
- Ordnancesurvey.co.uk (the most comprehensive mapping of England, Wales and Scotland in 1:25000 and 1:50000 scale)
- Spatialni.gov.uk (the most comprehensive mapping of Northern Ireland)

ROAD WALKING

Some walks in this book pass along public roads (country lanes, B-roads and occasionally A-roads or trunk roads). For all the time that you are walking along a road, please adhere to the Highway Code (gov.uk), applying to England, Wales and Scotland, and the Highway Code for Northern Ireland (nidirect.gov.uk), applying to Northern Ireland.

PUBLIC TRANSPORT TO THE WALK START

We urge you to take public transport to these walks if possible. Distances from the nearest useful public transport stop (with two or more daily weekday connections) to the walk start are given in metres/kilometres and in miles.

WALK ACCESSIBILITY: WHEELCHAIR AND PUSHCHAIR USERS

Wildlife often gravitates to areas far from where humans can make accessible pathways, and the chief purpose of this book is to showcase the best walks for enjoying wildlife. However, much effort has been channelled into ensuring a percentage of these walks are accessible: either fully or at least to the extent whereby a wildlife-watching route can be planned following a similar course. Some walks are fully accessible; others, which are accessible in part, have wheelchair- and pushchair-friendly alternative routes added where possible.

WALK ACCESSIBILITY: DOGS

Specific restrictions on bringing dogs on the walk are detailed in the individual walk's 'Need to Know' section. You and your four-legged friend can enjoy many of these walks. However, wherever wildlife is or stands a chance of being encountered, you should keep your dog under control as it could harm the wildlife – especially in designated protected areas. If in doubt, do not bring your animal with you.

WALK DIFFICULTY RATINGS

Walks are rated as Easy, Easy–Moderate, Moderate, Moderate–Difficult and Difficult. Novice walkers will have no problem on easy walks, where paths are clear, gradients unchallenging and distances typically under 10km (6¼ miles). Any reasonably experienced walker should be fine on a moderate walk, where there are often some challenging gradients, rough paths and distances typically between 10 and 20km (6¼ and 12½ miles). Difficult walks are for those with solid all-day hiking experience: gradients could regularly be challenging, paths often rough with navigation skills sometimes required and distances often more than 20km (12 miles).

WEATHER

This is the UK, where weather is capricious. A sunny start could change to rain, when wet-weather gear will be necessary; dramatic decreases in temperature, when warm clothing will be important; and poor visibility, when compass and map-reading skills will be required. The reverse scenarios are possible too. For maximum enjoyment of the walk, particularly on longer walks, it is responsible to prepare for all potential weather.